HIPAA
A Practical Guide to the Privacy and Security of Health Data

June M. Sullivan

Practical Guide Series

HIPAA

A Practical Guide to the Privacy and Security of Health Data

June M. Sullivan

AMERICAN BAR ASSOCIATION
Defending Liberty
Pursuing Justice

AMERICAN BAR ASSOCIATION
HEALTH LAW SECTION

Cover design by Cathy Zaccarine.

The materials contained herein represent the opinions and views of the authors and/or the editors, and should not be construed to be the views or opinions of the law firms or companies with whom such persons are in partnership with, associated with, or employed by, nor of the American Bar Association or the Health Law Section, unless adopted pursuant to the bylaws of the Association.

Nothing contained in this book is to be considered as the rendering of legal advice, either generally or in connection with any specific issue or case. Nor do these materials purport to explain or interpret any specific bond or policy, or any provisions thereof, issued by any particular insurance company, or to render insurance or other professional advice. Readers are responsible for obtaining advice from their own lawyer or other professional. This book and any forms and agreements herein are intended for educational and informational purposes only.

Printed in the United States of America.

08 07 06 05 04 5 4 3 2 1

Library of Congress Cataloging-in-Publication Data

Sullivan, June M.
HIPAA : a practical guide to the privacy and security of health data / by June M. Sullivan
p. cm.
Includes bibliographical references and index.
ISBN 1-59031-396-8
1. Medical records–Law and legislation–United States. 2. Medical records–Access control–United States. 3. Privacy, Right of–United States. 4. Actions and defenses–United States. 5. United States. Health Insurance Portability and Accountability Act of 1996. I. Title.

KF3827.R4S85 2004
344.7304'1–dc21

2004019038

Discounts are available for books ordered in bulk. Special consideration is given to state bars, CLE programs, and other bar-related organizations. Inquire at Book Publishing, ABA Publishing, American Bar Association, 321 North Clark Street, Chicago, Illinois 60610.

www.ababooks.org

Contents

Foreword ix
Acknowledgments xi
Introduction xiii

Chapter 1
Overview of HIPAA **1**

Summary of the HIPAA Privacy Rule 2
Purpose 2
Who Needs to Comply? 3
What Information Does HIPAA Protect? 5
General Rules for Disclosure 6
What Are the Duties and Obligations of the Covered Entities? 7
Notice 7
Safeguards 8
Training 8
Privacy Officer 8
Accounting for Disclosures 9
Conclusion 9
Notes 10

Chapter 2
Authorizations under HIPAA **13**

Consent versus Authorization 13
Consent 13
Authorization 14
Core Elements of Authorizations 14
Identity of the Party Authorizing the PHI Disclosure 14
Identity of the Party Receiving the PHI Disclosure 16
The Identity of the Person(s) Who Provide the Disclosure of PHI 16
Description of Information for Disclosure of PHI 17
The Purpose for Disclosure of the PHI 18

An Expiration Date or an Expiration Event of the Authorization 18
Date of the Individual's Signature on the Authorization 18
Required Statements in Authorizations 19
Individual's Right to Revoke the Authorization 19
Treatment Not Conditioned on Signing Authorization 19
Redisclosure of PHI 20
Other Requirements for Authorizations 20
Plain Language 20
Copy to the Individual 20
Other Considerations for Authorizations 21
Copy of an Authorization Is as Valid as Original 21
Authorizations Prepared by Third Parties 21
No Required Format 21
Cover Letter Accompanying the Authorization 21
Exempt from Minimum Necessary Requirement 22
State Law Requirements 22
HIPAA Preempts State Laws 22
Elements of Authorizations under State Law 24
Psychiatric Records under State Law 24
Notes 24

Chapter 3
Disclosures without Authorizations **27**

Treatment, Payment, or Health Care Operations 27
Treatment 28
Payment 29
Health Care Operations 30
Business Associate Agreement 30
Reasonable Assurances Agreement 35
Threat to Health or Safety and Compliance with Legal Duties 35
Averting a Serious Threat to Health or Safety 35
Law Enforcement 36
Public Health Activities 38
Victims of Abuse, Neglect, or Domestic Violence 38
Lawful Oversight Activities 39
Judicial and Administrative Proceedings 40
Informational and Promotional Disclosures 42
Facility Directories 42
Friends and Relatives 43

Marketing 44
Fundraising 45
Research 45
Workers' Compensation 46
Notes 46

Chapter 4
Administrative Requirements for Covered Entities 51

Notice 51
Required Elements of Notice of Privacy Practices 52
Header 52
Uses and Disclosures 52
Separate Statements for Specific Uses or Disclosures 53
Rights of the Individual 53
Duties of the Covered Entity 55
Complaints 56
Contact Information 56
Effective Date 56
Optional Elements of Notice of Privacy Practices 56
Revisions to the Notice of Privacy Practices 56
Availability of the Notice of Privacy Practices 57
Joint Notice of Privacy Practices by Separate Covered Entities 58
Documentation of Notice 58
Safeguards 58
Policies and Procedures 62
Training 63
Privacy Official 64
Accounting 64
Exceptions 64
Contents of the Accounting 65
Accounting of Disclosures for Research 66
Time to Respond to Request for Accounting 66
Fees 66
Documentation of the Accounting 67
Other Areas of Concern 67
Public Health Department 67
Unknown Date of Service 68
Business Associates 69
Notes 70

Chapter 5

Penalties and Enforcement **75**
Enforcement 75
Requirements for Filing a Complaint to OCR 76
Compliance Reviews and Investigations 77
Resolution by the Office for Civil Rights 77
Civil Penalties 78
Monetary Fines 78
Procedural Limitations 78
Fines Apply to the Covered Entity 79
Criminal Penalties 79
Knowingly Obtaining or Disclosing 79
False Pretenses 79
Intent to Sell or Use for Personal Gain or Harm 79
Business Associates and Others 80
Case Law 80
In re PPA Litigation; New Jersey 80
Campos v. Payne; New York 81
Lemieux v. Tandem Health Care of Florida, Inc.; Florida 82
National Abortion Federation v. Ashcroft 82
HIPAA Opens the Door to Litigation 83
Office for Civil Rights Regional Addresses 84
Notes 87

Decision Trees

Do I Need a HIPAA Authorization? 89
Is My Business a Covered Entity? 90
Who Is a Business Associate? 91

Appendices

A: Background Information 93
B: Authorization for Release of Protected Health Information 107
C: Business Associate Agreement 109
D: Reasonable Assurances Agreement 115
E: Notice of Privacy Practices 119
F: Health Insurance Portability and Accountability Act 127

Table of Cases 243
Index 245
About the Author 253

Foreword

The Health Law Section of the ABA is pleased to publish *HIPAA for Litigators,* the first in a series of practical guides aimed at providing focused, economical resources for the health lawyer.

As noted in the Acknowledgments that follows, many people volunteered their time to provide support for this ambitious book, and all of them deserve the Section's appreciation. In particular, the Section expresses special thanks to the following individuals for their leadership and support of this project during its preparation: Bonnie S. Brier, Immediate Past Chair of the Health Law Section, and Bruce J. Shih, Immediate Past Chair of the Publications Committee. The Section also expresses its special thanks to Shannon Hartsfield, chair of the eHealth Privacy & Security Interest Group, who, along with several volunteers from this Interest Group, provided outstanding editorial assistance.

Finally, but most important, we thank author June Sullivan who wrote this inaugural book for the series. Her willingness to share her expertise and insights with her colleagues exemplifies the best of the Section.

The Section is proud to offer this work, which it knows will contribute to the development of this emerging area of the law.

J.A. (Tony) Patterson, Jr.
Chair (2004–2005)

Michael E. Clark
Publications Chair
Health Law Section
American Bar Association

Acknowledgments

This author expresses her heartfelt thanks for the valuable assistance she received from colleagues and skillful editors in the preparation of this book. This author is indebted to Bruce Shih at the Health Law Section of the American Bar Association for his insight in endorsing the idea for this manuscript. A special "thank you" goes to Michael E. Clark of Hamel, Bowers & Clark, LLP, for his support and encouragement for this project and for giving so generously of his time and effort in reading, correcting, clarifying, and constructively criticizing the manuscript. This author especially recognizes and expresses her gratitude to Shannon B. Hartsfield of Holland & Knight, LLP, for her diligent efforts and meticulous attention to detail in coordinating the editors, advising the author, and editing the manuscript.

This author also conveys her appreciation to Jackie Myles Crain of the National Health Law Team at Holland & Knight, LLP; Catherine M. Walberg, vice president and general counsel at KaMMCO (Kansas Medical Mutual Insurance Company); and Ann Bowden-Hollis of Butler, Snow, O'Mara, Stevens & Cannada, PLLC, for making the time commitment to edit, correct, and revise this book and for striving for excellence in their painstaking work. Through the efforts of the above mentioned dedicated professionals, this author was able to correct errors, clarify ambiguous statements, and eliminate irrelevant material. This book is a product of the corroboration and contribution by these devoted and enthusiastic attorneys and this author is grateful for their assistance.

This author also expresses her thanks to the American Medical Association for its permission to reprint copyrighted materials.

Last, but not least, this author acknowledges the support and encouragement of her husband, John, and sons, Cory and Evan. Their unwavering love, understanding, and tolerance of frozen dinners propelled this project forward until its completion. This author is thankfully blessed with their patience, caring, and compassion. The drafting of this manuscript would have been much more difficult without their thoughtfulness and caring. Moreover, it would not have been successfully completed.

Acknowledgments

Introduction

This book will set forth the practical aspects of the Health Insurance Portability and Accountability Act of 1996, more commonly known as HIPAA. HIPAA affects every aspect of health care, including treatment, payment, and management of a health care group. HIPAA also has a tremendous effect on other professions, especially the practice of law. In particular, HIPAA directs how attorneys and other professionals obtain, control, and release medical records and other health-related documents. HIPAA provides strict guidelines for protection of the confidentiality of health information. This book will describe practical ways to obtain, maintain, and manage medical information under HIPAA.

HIPAA contains multiple sections. Title I protects workers' health insurance when the employees change or lose their jobs. Title II permits the U.S. Department of Health and Human Services to create standards for electronic health care transactions of health care providers, health plans, and employers, including the security and privacy of health information. This book focuses on the privacy issues of Title II. A brief explanation of Title I is provided in Appendix A.

In creating standards for the electronic transfer of health information, Congress recognized that safeguards were needed to control the exchange of highly personal and confidential medical information. The standards are meant to improve the efficiency and effectiveness of the nation's health care system by encouraging the widespread use of electronic data interchange in health care.[1]

Title II is expected to reduce the costs and administrative burdens of health care by standardizing the electronic transmission of certain administrative and financial transactions that had been carried out manually on paper in the past. In an attempt to restrain health care costs, the government discovered that a high percentage of every health care dollar was spent on administrative overhead including processing for enrollment, payment, eligibility, authorizations, filing a claim, supporting a claim, coordinating payments between more than one insurance company, and notifying the provider about payment.[2]

In order to resolve these issues and to reduce the amount of paperwork, Congress enacted the Administrative Simplification portion of HIPAA. The health care industry estimates that full implementation of the simplification provisions of HIPAA could save up to $9 billion per year from administrative overhead alone, without a reduction in the amount or quality of health care services.[3]

Congress had specific concerns about the security and confidentiality of health information that required electronic processing, particularly the protection of transmission of sensitive information contained in a person's medical record such as personal information, diagnosis, prognosis, and treatment.[4] In enacting HIPAA, Congress recognized the fact that administrative simplification could not be successful if it did not also protect the privacy and confidentiality of personal health information. The provision of high-quality health care requires the exchange of personal, often sensitive information between an individual and a skilled practitioner. Vital to that interaction is the patient's ability to trust that the information shared is protected and kept confidential. Yet there are concerns by many patients that their information is not protected. Among the factors adding to this concern are the growth of the number of organizations involved in the provision of care and the processing of claims, the growing use of electronic information technology, increased efforts to market health care and other products to consumers, and the increasing ability to collect highly sensitive information about a person's current and future health status as a result of advances in scientific research.[5]

HIPAA sets a floor of ground rules for health care providers, health plans, and health care clearinghouses to follow, in order to protect patients and encourage them to seek needed care. The regulation seeks to balance the needs of the individual with the needs of the society. It creates a framework of protection that is strengthened by enforcement by both the federal and state government as health information systems continue to evolve.[6] The shift from paper to electronic health information records increases the need for legal protections related to the right to privacy in health information.

More importantly, electronic health data continue to become available nationally. As more information becomes available in electronic form, it can reach far beyond the immediate community where the patient resides. Prior to HIPAA, neither private action nor state laws provided an adequately comprehensive and rigorous legal structure to sufficiently allay public concerns, protect the right to privacy, and correct the market failures caused by the absence of privacy protections.

Therefore, a national policy with consistent rules was necessary to encourage the health care industry to increase the proper use of electronic information while also protecting the very real needs of patients to safeguard their privacy.[7]

NOTES

1. Centers for Medicare & Medicaid Services, Health Insurance Portability and Accountability Act of 1996, *available at* http://www.cms.hhs.gov/hipaa (last modified Oct. 16, 2002); accessed Nov. 15, 2003.
2. Centers for Medicare & Medicaid Services, Health Insurance Portability and Accountability Act of 1996 (HIPAA), *available at* http://www.cms.hhs.gov/hipaa/hipaa2/general/background/kkimpl.asp.
3. *Id.*
4. *Id.*
5. Centers for Medicare & Medicaid Services, Health Insurance Portability and Accountability Act of 1996 (HIPAA), Final Privacy Rule Preamble, *available at* http://www.cms.hhs.gov/hipaa/hipaa2/regulations/privacy/finalrule; accessed Nov. 15, 2003.
6. *Id.*
7. *Id.*

CHAPTER 1

Overview of HIPAA

This book focuses on the privacy issues of Title II of the Health Insurance Portability and Accountability Act of 1996 (HIPAA). A brief explanation of Title I is provided in Appendix A, which may be passed over for those of you who have no interest in the portability aspect of HIPAA. Title II of HIPAA requires the Department of Health and Human Services to establish national standards for electronic health care transactions and national identifiers for providers, health plans, and employers. It also addresses the security and privacy of health data. The standards are meant to improve the efficiency and effectiveness of the nation's health care system by encouraging the widespread use of electronic data interchange in health care.[1]

The intent of Title II is to reduce the costs and administrative burdens of health care by standardizing the electronic transmission of certain administrative and financial transactions that had been carried out manually on paper in the past. In its quest to restrain health care costs, the government determined that a high percentage of every health care dollar spent was on administrative overhead including processing for enrollment, payment, eligibility, authorizations, filing a claim, supporting a claim, coordinating payments between more than one insurance company, and notifying the provider about payment.[2]

In order to resolve these issues, Congress enacted the "Administrative Simplification" portion of HIPAA. The health care industry estimates that full implementation of the simplification provisions of HIPAA could save up to $9 billion per year from administrative overhead alone, without a reduction in the amount or quality of health care services.[3]

SUMMARY OF THE HIPAA PRIVACY RULE

Purpose

The HIPAA Privacy Rule has three major purposes:

1. To protect and enhance the rights of consumers by providing them access to their health information and controlling the inappropriate use of that information;
2. To improve the quality of health care in the United States by restoring trust in the health care system among consumers, health care professionals, and the multitude of organizations and individuals committed to the delivery of care; and
3. To improve the efficiency and effectiveness of health care delivery by creating a national framework for health privacy protection that builds on efforts by states, health systems, and individual organizations and individuals.[4]

As previously discussed, HIPAA has several components. The Privacy Rule is only one aspect of HIPAA. The major goal of the HIPAA Privacy Rule is to protect individuals' health information while simultaneously allowing health information to be transmitted to those intended in order to provide and promote high quality health care and protect the health and well being of the public. The purpose of the HIPAA Privacy Rule is to strike a balance between using an individual's health information to advance economically prudent health care while protecting the privacy of an individual seeking medical care and treatment.[5]

HIPAA does not preempt state laws that are more stringent in protecting health information.[6] HIPAA is a "floor" for protecting the privacy of health information. HIPAA preempts state laws that are both contrary to HIPAA and less protective. Currently existing or future state laws related to the privacy of health information that are *more stringent* than HIPAA remain in effect, even if they are contrary to HIPAA. A state law is more stringent when it provides greater privacy protection for the individual who is the subject of the information or greater access to the individual's own health information. HIPAA does not preempt state laws that govern public health investigations or the reporting of disease or injury, child abuse, birth, or death. State laws that require health plans to report or grant access to information for the purpose of audits, evaluation, or licensure remain in effect, even if they are less protective of individuals' privacy.[7]

Who Needs to Comply?

HIPAA applies to "covered entities." A covered entity is a health plan, health care clearinghouse, or health care provider that transmits health information in electronic form in connection with health care transactions.[8]

A *health plan* is an individual or group plan that provides, or pays the cost of, medical care. A health plan includes the following, alone or in combination:

- A **group health plan,** defined as an employee benefit plan including insured and self-insured plans, to the extent that the plan provides medical care including items and services paid for as medical care, to employees or their dependents directly or through insurance, reimbursement, or otherwise that (1) has fifty or more participants or (2) is administered by an entity other than the employer that established and maintains the plan
- A **health insurance issuer,** defined as an insurance company, insurance service, or insurance organization (including an HMO) that is licensed to engage in the business of insurance in a state and is subject to state law that regulates insurance; it does not include a group health plan
- An **HMO** (health maintenance organization)
- Part A or Part B of the **Medicare** program
- The **Medicaid** program
- An **issuer of a Medicare supplemental** policy
- An **issuer of a long-term care policy,** excluding a nursing home fixed-indemnity policy
- An **employee welfare benefit plan** or any other arrangement that is established or maintained for the purpose of offering or providing health benefits to the employees of two or more employers
- The **health care program for active military personnel**
- The **veterans health care program** under 38 U.S.C. Chapter 17
- The Civilian Health and Medical Program of the Uniformed Services (**CHAMPUS**), as defined in 10 U.S.C. § 1072(4)
- The **Indian Health Service** program under the Indian Health Care Improvement Act
- The **Federal Employees Health Benefits Program**
- An approved **state child health plan**

- The **Medicare + Choice program**
- A **high risk pool** that is a mechanism established under state law to provide health insurance coverage or comparable coverage to eligible individuals
- Any other **individual or group plan,** or combination of individual or group plans, that provides or pays for the cost of medical care[9]

A *health care clearinghouse* is a public or private entity, including a billing service, repricing company, community health management information system, or community health information system, and "value-added" networks and switches, that does either of the following functions:

- Processes or facilitates the processing of health information received from another entity in a nonstandard format or containing nonstandard data content into standard data elements or a standard transaction
- Receives a standard transaction from another entity and processes or facilitates the processing of health information into nonstandard format or nonstandard data content for the receiving entity[10]

A *health care provider* is a provider of services, a provider of medical or health services, or any other person or organization who furnishes, bills, or is paid for health care in the normal course of business.[11] *Health care* includes care, services, and supplies related to the health of an individual.[12] Under HIPAA, the term *health care provider* includes persons such as dentists, doctors, therapists, nurses, naturopaths, and acupuncturists as well as entities such as clinics, hospitals, and institutions.

It is important to keep in mind that HIPAA does not apply to all health care providers. It applies only to those health care providers, as defined above, that (1) transmit health information electronically in connection with one of the financial or administrative transactions under HIPAA (such as health claims, status of enrollment and eligibility, and authorizations for referral) *and* (2) transmit the health information in a standard electronic format (the national format required under the Administrative Simplification Compliance Act).[13] Therefore, by definition, a health care provider that uses only paper formats and does not submit insurance claims electronically is not subject to HIPAA.

What Information Does HIPAA Protect?

The privacy rule encompasses *protected health information* (PHI) in any form that is created or received by a covered entity. Protected health information is individually identifiable information that is recorded orally or in written form by a covered entity or received by a covered entity that relates to the past, present, or future physical or mental health of an individual, health care services, or payment for health care. This includes traditional medical records as well as health care providers' personal notes and billing information. It is important to remember that the information must be *individually identifiable.* In other words, it can be used to identify the individual. Health information that is "de-identified" is not subject to scrutiny under HIPAA. Information is de-identified by removing specific information that would allow the individual to be known to the reader. The specific information that must be removed includes names; geographic subdivisions smaller than a state (including addresses and full zip codes); all dates except years; telephone and fax numbers; e-mail addresses; Social Security numbers; medical record numbers; health plan beneficiary numbers; account numbers; license numbers; vehicle identifiers; device identifiers; Internet addresses; biometric identifiers such as finger and voice prints; photographs of the individual's full face; and any other unique identifying number, characteristic, and code.[14] Medical information that does not contain the data mentioned is not considered to be individually identifiable, and therefore is not protected health information.

Also, the information must be "created or received" by a covered entity. For instance, information that a patient discloses to his or her doctor is covered, but any information that is created or received by anyone other than a covered entity is not protected under HIPAA.[15] An example of health information that is not covered under HIPAA is health information that a person discloses when he or she donates blood. The staff at the blood donation center are not covered entities because, although they may be health care providers (e.g., nurses, medical technologists), they do not provide health care to the donor nor do they transmit health care information electronically in connection with payment related to the donation of blood. Another example is where a patient discloses his or her own health information to family and friends. HIPAA does not prevent the family and friends from disclosing the health information to others.

General Rules for Disclosure

Under the privacy rule, PHI is *disclosed* when it is released, transferred, or otherwise revealed to persons *outside* the covered entity that holds the PHI.[16] HIPAA prohibits covered entities from disclosing PHI without a patient's authorization.[17] However, HIPAA also provides for several ways in which a covered entity may disclose PHI without the person's authorization. Under some circumstances, a covered entity may disclose PHI without a patient's authorization in order to carry out treatment, payment, or health care operations.[18] *Treatment* is the provision, coordination, or management of health care and related services, including consultations, referrals, and coordination of health care with another health care provider.[19] *Payment* includes the activities involved in obtaining health insurance premiums, coverage, benefits, eligibility, billing, collection, preauthorization, appropriateness of care, justification of charges, and reimbursement, among others.[20] *Health care operations* are those activities that a covered entity engages in to conduct quality assessment and improvement; review the competence or qualifications of health care professionals; underwriting or premium rating; conduct or arrange for medical review, legal services, and auditing; engage in business planning and development; and manage business and general administrative activities.[21]

The government sought to effectively protect the privacy right of individuals; however, it had the foresight to realize that certain circumstances warranted disclosure. The government recognized the need to balance privacy rights with concerns for safety of the public and the individual. Along those lines, HIPAA allows covered entities to disclose PHI where there is a serious threat to health or safety of either the patient or the public.[22] The disclosure must be necessary to prevent or lessen a serious and imminent threat to the health or safety of a person or the public, and the disclosure must be made to someone who is reasonably able to prevent or lessen the threat, including the person who may be the target of that threat.[23]

Other permitted disclosures include facility directories,[24] next of kin,[25] marketing purposes,[26] fundraising,[27] health oversight activities,[28] judicial and administrative proceedings,[29] law enforcement,[30] public health activities,[31] those required by law,[32] research,[33] victims of abuse, neglect, or domestic violence,[34] and workers' compensation.[35] Certain specific required parameters under each of these types of disclosures must be met prior to disclosure of PHI. The HIPAA rule itself should be reviewed prior to making a disclosure under any of the categories mentioned. Some of these categories will be discussed in detail in the following chapters.

What Are the Duties and Obligations of the Covered Entities?

In order to comply with HIPAA, covered entities must adhere to a number of administrative requirements. The requirements are briefly addressed in this section. This section does not comprehensively analyze each and every requirement. The reader should consult other resources for such information. The purpose for briefly describing the administrative requirements is merely to paint a picture of the tasks that a covered entity must fulfill under HIPAA. When jumping through hoops to obtain medical information during litigation, the reader should bear in mind the overwhelming duties that HIPAA imposes on covered entities and the subsequent frustration of the covered entities to comply with the requirements of HIPAA.

Notice

HIPAA requires that a covered entity supply a written notice of the entity's privacy practices to individuals.[36] It is a document that is given to the individual at the first patient encounter after the HIPAA implementation deadline. Since the implementation of HIPAA, it is likely that the reader has gone to a health care provider who presented a "Notice of Privacy Practices" listing the activities the health care provider will do and will not do with the reader's PHI. The notice of privacy practices must be written in plain language and must include, among other things,

- The individual's rights regarding his or her PHI and how the individual may implement those rights
- The legal duties of the covered entity
- A description of the types of permitted uses and disclosures of PHI, including those disclosures that are allowed or required without the individual's written authorization or consent
- A description of the types of disclosures prohibited under HIPAA; if a more stringent state law supersedes HIPAA, the description must include the more stringent law
- Separate statements for certain uses and disclosures of PHI, such as appointment reminders, treatment alternatives, and services that may be of interest to the individual

- How an individual can file complaints with the covered entity and the Secretary of Health and Human Services
- The name and telephone number of a person or office to contact for further information
- The date on which the notice is in effect[37]

HIPAA also provides when and how the covered entity may revise its privacy policy and procedures. The covered entity must give notice to the individuals before any new policy can be implemented. The covered entity must expressly reserve its rights to change the terms of its privacy notice; otherwise the covered entity is bound by the privacy practices in the notice of privacy practices that was in effect at the time that the PHI was created or received. It must also specify that the changes apply to previously created or received PHI; otherwise any change will apply only to information created or received after the effective date of the revised notice.[38]

Safeguards

HIPAA requires that the covered entity put in place appropriate administrative, technical, and physical safeguards to protect the privacy of PHI. The covered entity must reasonably protect health information from any use or disclosure that would violate the provisions of HIPAA. The covered entity must limit uses and disclosures made "incidental" to a permitted use or disclosure.[39]

Training

A covered entity must train all members of its workforce on the policies and procedures regarding PHI as needed for the staff members to carry out their functions for the covered entity. The staff must be trained no later than the compliance date set for the covered entity *and* within a reasonable period of time after a new change becomes effective. A new staff member must be trained within a reasonable time after joining the covered entity. All training must be documented.[40]

Privacy Officer

A covered entity must designate a privacy officer to be responsible for the development and implementation of the policies and procedures of the covered entity. The covered entity must also designate a contact person to be responsible for receiving complaints (complaint officer). The complaint officer must be able to provide further information about the elements contained in the notice of privacy practices.[41]

There is nothing in the rule that prohibits the same person from being designated as both the privacy officer and the complaint officer.

Accounting for Disclosures

One of the major issues a covered entity faces when disclosing PHI is accounting for the disclosures. Individuals have the right to receive an accounting of disclosures of their PHI made by the covered entity six years prior to the date that the individual requests the accounting, including disclosures to or by business associates.[42] Keep in mind that the right to an accounting pertains only to *disclosures,* the sharing of PHI outside of the covered entity. The covered entity does not need to account for *uses,* the sharing of PHI within the covered entity. Accountings are not required for release of PHI to carry out treatment, payment, and health care operations; to individuals; pursuant to authorizations; in facility directories; for national security purposes; to correctional institutions and law enforcement officials; or incidental to a use and disclosure permitted or required.[43] For example, the individual does not have a right to receive a listing of all health care providers' employees that have access to his or her PHI.

The accounting must include the date of each disclosure; the name and, if known, the address of the entity or person who received the information; a description of the information disclosed; and a statement of the purpose of the disclosure.[44] The covered entity must act on the individual's request for an accounting no later than sixty days after it receives a request. If the covered entity cannot provide the requested accounting within the time required under HIPAA, it may extend the time for thirty days provided that it gives the individual a written statement of the reasons for the delay and the date that it will provide the accounting. The covered entity has only one opportunity for an extension of time to act on a request for an accounting. The individual may receive one accounting per year free of charge. Otherwise, the covered entity may impose a reasonable, cost-based fee for each subsequent request.[45]

CONCLUSION

The purpose of Title I of HIPAA is to allow the individual to continue his or her health care insurance coverage without succumbing to preclusion by a preexisting condition. To that end, electronic transfer of health information via computer, fax, and other electronic means is needed in order to promote and continue insurance coverage. Additionally, electronic transfer of health information is needed to simplify and reduce administrative health care costs, in turn reducing the overall costs of health care.

Generally, electronic transfer of information is inherently not secure enough to maintain the confidentiality of health information. Title II of HIPAA provides safeguards to protect the privacy of health information and promote administrative simplification. There are greater duties and responsibilities for covered entities to protect health information. HIPAA provides individuals with greater rights over their medical information, including the right to amend, have an accounting, and authorize disclosures.

HIPAA is the first federal law that protects the privacy of health information. Prior to HIPAA, the states had a patchwork of laws that varied throughout the nation. For example, a person living in Hawaii had very different protections from someone living in Utah. A person moving from one state to another could not depend on the laws of the former state to protect his or her health information. It was difficult for individuals to understand the different laws that varied from state to state. HIPAA provides a more uniform and consistent means for protection of health information. However, HIPAA does not preempt state laws that are more stringent in protecting health information or those that give individuals greater right to access of their health information.

NOTES

1. Centers for Medicare & Medicaid Services, Health Insurance Portability and Accountability Act of 1996 (HIPAA), *available at* http://www.cms.hhs.gov/hipaa; last modified Oct, 16, 2002; accessed Nov. 15, 2003.

2. Centers for Medicare & Medicaid Services, Health Insurance Portability and Accountability Act of 1996 (HIPAA), *available at* http://www.cms.hhs.gov/hipaa/hipaa2/general/background/kkimpl.asp.

3. *Id.*

4. *Id.*

5. U.S. Dept. of Health and Human Services, OCR Privacy Brief, Summary of the HIPAA Privacy Rule, revised May 2003, *available at* http://www.hhs.gov/ocr/privacysummary.pdf.

6. Health Insurance Portability and Accountability Act of 1996, 45 C.F.R. §§ 160.201, 160.202, 160.203, 160.204, and 160.205 (2003).

7. *Id.*

8. *See id.* § 160.102 and Centers for Medicare & Medicaid Services, Health Insurance Portability and Accountability Act of 1996 (HIPAA), Final Privacy

Rule Preamble, *available at* http://www.cms.hhs.gov/hipaa/hipaa2/regulations/privacy/finalrule [hereinafter Final Privacy Rule Preamble].

9. HIPAA, 45 C.F.R. § 160.103, and Final Privacy Rule Preamble, *supra* note 8.

10. *Id.*

11. *Id.*

12. *Id.*

13. HIPAA, 45 C.F.R. §§ 164.104 and 164.500, and Final Privacy Rule Preamble, *supra* note 8.

14. HIPAA, 45 C.F.R. §164.514(b)(2)(i).

15. *See id.* §§ 160.103, 164.501, and 164.514(a) and (e).

16. *See id.* § 164.501.

17. *See id.* § 164.502.

18. *Id.*

19. HIPAA, 45 C.F.R. § 164.501.

20. *Id.*

21. *Id.*

22. *See id.* § 164.512(j).

23. *Id.*

24. HIPAA, 45 C.F.R. § 164.510(a).

25. *See id.* §§ 164.510(b) and 164.522.

26. *See id.* §§ 164.501 and 164.508(a)(3).

27. *See id.* §§ 164.501, 164.514(f), and 164.522.

28. *See id.* § 164.512(d).

29. *See id.* § 164.512(e).

30. HIPAA, 45 C.F.R. § 164.512(f).

31. *See id.* §§ 164.512(b) and 164.514(e).

32. *See id.* § 164.512(a).

33. *See id.* §§ 164.512(i) and 164.514(e).

34. *See id.* § 164.512(c).

35. *See id.* § 164.512(l).

36. HIPAA, 45 C.F.R. §§ 164.500 and 164.520.

37. *See id.* § 164.520.

38. *Id.*

39. *See id.* § 164.530(c).

40. *See id.* § 164.530(b).

41. *See id.* § 164.530(a).

42. HIPAA, 45 C.F.R. § 164.528.

43. *Id.*

44. *Id.*

45. *Id.*

CHAPTER 2

Authorizations under HIPAA

The most effective method to obtain medical information is to provide a properly signed HIPAA compliant authorization form to the covered entity. HIPAA, the Health Insurance Portability and Accountability Act of 1996, mandates that the medical authorization form for the release of protected health information (PHI) contain certain information. Beyond the specific HIPAA requirements, the authorization must also contain any information that the particular state mandates. All covered entities must be mindful of the HIPAA requirements as well as the individual state requirements to obtain PHI.

CONSENT VERSUS AUTHORIZATION

There are two types of permission that allow a covered entity to use or disclose PHI: consent and authorization.

Consent

HIPAA allows, but does not require, a general *consent* for use or disclosure of PHI for treatment, payment, and health care operations.[1] However, the consent of an individual does not allow the covered entity to use or disclose PHI when an authorization is required or when another condition must be met for such use or disclosure. The covered entity may design the consent form as it sees fit. HIPAA does not define *consent* for the purposes of this provision nor does it mandate the substance of the consent form. An individual who refuses to sign the consent form may not realize that HIPAA does not require the covered entity to obtain the consent and subsequently, the refusal to sign a consent is of no consequence to the covered entity. The PHI may be used by the covered entity for treatment, payment, and health care operations even without the consent of the individual.

Authorization

There are uses and disclosures for which an *authorization* is expressly required under HIPAA. Basically, the rule requires an authorization for the release of any PHI that does not fit into one of the following exceptions: treatment, payment, or health care operations;[2] directories at facilities;[3] family and friends;[4] marketing;[5] fundraising;[6] averting a serious threat to health or safety;[7] health oversight activities;[8] judicial and administrative proceedings;[9] law enforcement;[10] public health activities;[11] required by law;[12] research;[13] victims of abuse, neglect, or domestic violence;[14] and workers' compensation.[15] Chapter 3 gives a more detailed analysis of these exceptions.

CORE ELEMENTS OF AUTHORIZATIONS

HIPAA allows the disclosure of PHI pursuant to a valid authorization.[16] However, the authorization cannot be a generic, blanket authorization. It must comply with the requirements under HIPAA.[17] A blanket authorization that was valid prior to HIPAA is generally no longer recognized by a covered entity. There are certain core elements that all HIPAA compliant authorizations must contain. Of course, state laws may have additional requirements for authorizations. Nothing in HIPAA prohibits a state from mandating that an authorization contain more stringent requirements for release of PHI to a third party. A valid HIPAA compliant authorization is a document that contains the following core elements.

Identity of the Party Authorizing the PHI Disclosure

HIPAA requires that the authorization contain the signature and identity of the individual whose PHI is being requested.[18] The HIPAA Privacy Rule does not require that a document be notarized or witnessed. If the individual has a person appointed to represent the individual for health care decisions, that personal representative may sign in place of the individual. If the authorization is signed by a personal representative of the individual, a description of the representative's authority to act for the individual must also be provided in the authorization.[19] HIPAA does not address *how* a covered entity should identify a personal representative. Therefore, the covered entity should continue to verify and identify personal representatives in the same way as it had done in the past.[20] However, the covered entity must obtain any documentation, statements, or representations, whether oral or written, from the person requesting the PHI when such a documentation, statement, or representation is a condition of disclosure.[21]

The personal representative cannot be someone who has a general power of attorney or a specific power of attorney for other particular reasons, such as a power of attorney to close on real estate. "Except with respect to decedents, a covered entity must treat a personal representative as the individual *only* when that person has authority under law to act on the individual's behalf on matters related to health care."[22] Most importantly, the covered entity does not need to consider the personal representative as the individual if it believes, based on professional judgment and reasonable belief, that doing so would not be in the best interest of the individual because the personal representative is the source of domestic violence, abuse, or neglect toward the individual or because considering the personal representative as the individual would place the individual in danger.[23]

HIPAA generally allows a parent to have access to the medical records about his or her child, as the minor child's personal representative, when such access is consistent with state or other law.[24] There are three situations in which the parent would not be the minor's personal representative under the Privacy Rule:

> (1) when the minor is the one who consents to care and the consent of the parent is not required under State or other applicable law; (2) when the minor obtains care at the direction of a court or a person appointed by the court; and (3) when, and to the extent that, the parent agrees that the minor and the health care provider may have a confidential relationship. However, even in these exceptional situations, the parent may have access to the medical records of the minor related to this treatment when State or other applicable law requires or permits such parental access. Parental access would be denied when State or other law prohibits such access. If State or other applicable law is silent on a parent's right of access in these cases, the licensed health care provider may exercise his or her professional judgment to the extent allowed by law to grant or deny parental access to the minor's medical information.
>
> Finally, as is the case with respect to all personal representatives under the Privacy Rule, a provider may choose not to treat a parent as a personal representative when the provider reasonably believes, in his

or her professional judgment, that the child has been or may be subjected to domestic violence, abuse or neglect, or that treating the parent as the child's personal representative could endanger the child.[25]

Identity of the Party Receiving the PHI Disclosure

Under HIPAA, the individual has a right to know who will be receiving the individual's PHI. The authorization must specifically list the party to whom the PHI will be disclosed by the covered entity. In lieu of a particular person, the authorization may identify a specific *group* of recipients.[26] For instance, in a legal action for personal injury, a disclosure to the "Law Firm of Smith and Associates or its representatives" is valid even though the authorization does not provide a specific attorney or employee of the firm who will actually receive the PHI.

The Identity of the Person(s) Who Provide the Disclosure of PHI

The authorization must contain the name or other specific identification of the person, persons, or class of person authorized to make the disclosure.[27] The individual may use one authorization form to authorize uses and disclosures by classes or categories of persons or entities, without naming the particular persons or entities.[28] For example, it is satisfactory if an authorization form authorizes disclosures by "any health plan, physician, health care professional, hospital, clinic, laboratory, pharmacy, medical facility, or other health care provider that has provided payment, treatment or services to me or on my behalf" or if an authorization form authorizes disclosures by "all medical sources."[29] "A separate authorization specifically naming each health care provider from whom protected health information may be sought is not required."[30]

Generally, the authorization provides the name of the covered entity that controls the PHI. The authorization may, but is not required to, provide specific names of each health care provider that will disclose the PHI. For instance, a proper identification of the health care provider is "Dr. John Sullivan," "Stein and Swartz, P.C.," "Holyoke Hospital," "Birch Hill Medical Associates," or "Acme Health Plan."

An individual may have PHI at more than one location if the individual is treating with several health care providers simultaneously. Providing the name of the person authorized to release the PHI puts the individual on notice as to which of the health care providers will disclose the PHI. For instance, an individual may have X-rays taken at different radiological and imaging services, but disclosure may be authorized to only one of the entities.

Description of Information for Disclosure of PHI

The authorization must provide a description of the PHI to be used or disclosed.[31] The description of the information to be used or disclosed must identify the information in a specific and meaningful fashion.[32] The information must be described in such a way as to make known to the individual what information is being disclosed. However, the information does not need to be specifically named.

An authorization is valid if it authorizes the covered entity to use or disclose an "entire medical record" or "complete patient file." However, an authorization to use or disclose "all protected health information" is not specific enough, since protected health information encompasses a wider range of information than that which is generally included in the medical record, and individuals are less likely to understand the breadth of information that may be defined as "protected health information."[33]

HIPAA does not prohibit the use, disclosure, or request of an entire medical record:

> A covered entity may use, disclose or request an entire medical record . . . if the covered entity has documented in its policies and procedures that the entire medical record is the amount reasonably necessary for certain identified purposes. For uses, the policies and procedures would identify those persons or classes of person in the workforce that need to see the entire medical record and the conditions, if any, that are appropriate for such access. Policies and procedures for routine disclosures and requests and the criteria used for non-routine disclosures and requests would identify the circumstances under which disclosing or requesting the entire medical record is reasonably necessary for particular purposes.

The Privacy Rule does not require that a justification be provided with respect to each distinct medical record. No justification is needed in those instances where the minimum necessary standard does not apply. An example of those instances includes disclosures to or requests by a health care provider for treatment purposes or disclosures to the individual who is the subject of the protected health information.[34]

The Purpose for Disclosure of the PHI

The authorization must contain a description of each purpose for the use or disclosure.[35] The purpose should have enough detail so as to give notice to the individual of the reason for the disclosure. For example, "for discovery purposes during litigation in the case of *Smith v. Jones*" and "for medical statistical and regulatory purposes related to the research of estrogen receptors" are acceptable descriptions.

An individual may sign an authorization for release of his or her PHI to himself or herself. In such instance, the statement "at the request of the individual" is a sufficient description of the purpose when an individual initiates the authorization and does not or chooses not to provide a statement of the purpose.[36]

An Expiration Date or an Expiration Event of the Authorization

HIPAA requires that an authorization contain either an expiration date or an expiration event that relates to the individual or the purpose of the use or disclosure.[37] For example, an authorization may expire "one year from the date the authorization is signed," "upon termination of the litigation, up through and including any time for appeal," "upon the minor's age of majority," or "upon termination of enrollment in the health plan."[38] Unless the individual revokes the authorization in writing before the expiration date or event, the authorization remains valid until its expiration date or event.[39] HIPAA permits the authorization to remain valid even when the expiration date on the authorization exceeds a time period established by state law.[40] However, a more restrictive state law may control how long the authorization is effective.[41]

Date of the Individual's Signature on the Authorization

The authorization must contain not only the signature of the individual but also the date that the individual signed the authorization.[42] A covered entity may disclose PHI specified in an authorization even if the information was created after the authorization was signed by the individual, if the authorization encompasses the category of information that was later created and the authorization has not expired or been revoked by the individual.[43] "Unless otherwise expressly limited by the authorization, a covered entity may use or disclose the protected health information identified in the authorization regardless of when the information was created."[44]

REQUIRED STATEMENTS IN AUTHORIZATIONS

In addition to the core elements of an authorization, HIPAA requires that the authorization contain certain statements in order to put the individual on notice of specific conditions.

Individual's Right to Revoke the Authorization

The authorization must contain a statement that notifies the individual of his or her right to revoke the authorization.[45] HIPAA allows an individual to revoke an authorization at any time *provided that* a covered entity did not rely on the authorization to make a use or disclosure of the individual's PHI. The revocation must be in writing and becomes effective when the covered entity *receives* it.[46] The revocation is not valid if it was obtained as a condition of acquiring insurance coverage and other law provides the insurer with the right to contest a claim under the policy or the policy itself.[47]

The process for revocation must be set forth clearly on the authorization itself, or, if the covered entity creates the authorization and its notice of privacy practices contains a clear description of the revocation process, the authorization can refer to the notice of privacy practices.[48] If a third party creates or submits the authorization form, the form should not imply that the revocation is effective when the third party receives it. Even with third-party authorizations, the revocation is not effective until a *covered entity* that had previously been authorized to make the disclosure receives it.[49]

Treatment Not Conditioned on Signing Authorization

The authorization must expressly contain statements that notify the individual that the covered entity may not condition the provision of treatment, payment, enrollment in a health plan, or eligibility for benefits on the individual's failure to provide an authorization for release of PHI.[50] If applicable, the authorization must also list the following exceptions, or the consequences to the exceptions:

- A provider may condition the provision of research-related treatment[51] or the individual's enrollment in a research study on the individual's execution of an authorization for the use of pre-existing health information.[52]

- A health plan may condition enrollment in the health plan or eligibility for benefits on provision of an authorization requested by the health plan prior to an individual's enrollment in the health plan if the authorization sought is for the health plan's eligibility or enrollment determinations relating to the individual or for its underwriting or risk rating determinations and the authorization is not for a use or disclosure of psychotherapy notes.[53]

Redisclosure of PHI

The authorization must explain that once the PHI is disclosed to the recipient, it may no longer be protected under the HIPAA Privacy Rule and there is a potential for redisclosure by the recipient to another entity.[54] HIPAA applies only to covered entities. The individual must be on notice that if a covered entity discloses PHI to a noncovered entity via a valid authorization, the noncovered entity is not prohibited by federal law from disclosing the health information to others.

OTHER REQUIREMENTS FOR AUTHORIZATIONS

Plain Language

The authorization must be written in plain language.[55] Plain language is generally considered to be eighth-grade reading level. There should be no complicated concepts, difficult phrases or words, or legal or medical terminology that may confuse the individual. The authorization should be readily understandable by an individual who completed grade school. HIPAA does not require the authorization to be in any foreign language.

Copy to the Individual

If the covered entity requests an authorization from an individual, the covered entity must provide the individual with a copy of the signed authorization.[56] The individual has a right to have a copy of the authorization.

OTHER CONSIDERATIONS FOR AUTHORIZATIONS

Copy of an Authorization Is as Valid as Original

HIPAA permits a covered entity to use or disclose protected health information pursuant to a copy of a valid and signed authorization, including a copy that is received by fax or electronically transmitted.[57]

Authorizations Prepared by Third Parties

Under HIPAA, a covered entity is permitted to use or disclose protected health information pursuant to any authorization that meets the Privacy Rule's requirements at 45 C.F.R. § 164.508.[58] As previously stated, HIPAA requires that an authorization contain certain core elements and statements, but it does not specify who may draft an authorization; therefore, it may be drafted by any entity. A valid authorization created by another covered entity or a third party, such as an attorney, a state bar association, an insurance company, or researcher, may be used by the covered entity to disclose PHI.[59]

No Required Format

HIPAA does not specify or dictate any particular format for an authorization.[60] The authorization may contain any sequence of the core elements and required statements as long as the authorization includes the necessary provisions. Also, the authorization does not need to be notarized or witnessed.[61]

Cover Letter Accompanying the Authorization

A transmittal or cover letter cannot be used to expand the scope of the authorization to include PHI not described in the authorization.[62] However, a transmittal or a cover letter can be used to narrow or provide specifics about a request for protected health information as described in an authorization.[63] For example, if an individual authorized the disclosure of "all medical records" to an attorney, the attorney could by cover letter narrow the request to the medical records for the last two years. The cover letter could also specify a particular employee or address for the "class of persons" designated in the authorization to receive the information. But a recipient could not by cover letter extend the time of expiration of an authorization or increase the scope of information set forth in the authorization.

Exempt from Minimum Necessary Requirement

Generally, when using, disclosing, or responding to a request for PHI, a covered entity must make reasonable efforts to limit the PHI to the minimum necessary to accomplish the intended purpose of the use, disclosure, or request for PHI.[64] However, uses and disclosures that are authorized by the individual are exempt from the minimum necessary requirements.[65] For example, if a covered health care provider receives an individual's authorization to disclose medical information to an attorney for litigation purposes, the provider is permitted to disclose the information requested on the authorization without making any minimum necessary determination. Bear in mind that the authorization must meet the requirements of 45 C.F.R. § 164.508 as stated above.

STATE LAW REQUIREMENTS

HIPAA is a federal law that may or may not supersede state laws that provide for the authorization of disclosure of medical information. HIPAA preempts state laws that are contrary to HIPAA and less protective of PHI, providing a "floor" for the minimum requirements for protection of confidentiality and privacy of PHI.[66] HIPAA allows existing or future state laws that are more stringent than the federal rule at protecting PHI to remain in effect, even when the state law is contrary to HIPAA.[67]

HIPAA Preempts State Laws

Generally, HIPAA preempts state laws.[68] This general rule applies *unless* there is a condition that falls under one of the following exceptions:

1. Where the secretary of the U.S. Department of Health and Human Services (HHS) determines that the state law is necessary
    a. To prevent fraud and abuse related to the provision of health care[69]
    b. To ensure appropriate state regulation of insurance and health plans[70]
    c. For state reporting on health care delivery costs[71]

   d. For purposes of a compelling need related to public health, safety, or welfare, and the intrusion into privacy is warranted when balanced against the need[72]
2. Where the purpose of the state law is to regulate the manufacture, registration, distribution, dispensing, or other control of any controlled substances[73]
3. Where state law relates to the privacy of PHI and it is more stringent than HIPAA[74]
4. Where state law provides for the reporting of disease, injury, child abuse, birth, or death or for the conduct of public health surveillance, investigation, or intervention[75]
5. Where state law requires a health plan to report or provide access to information for the purpose of management audits, financial audits, program monitoring and evaluation, or the licensure or certification of facilities or individuals[76]

In these circumstances listed above, a covered entity is not required to comply with a contrary provision of the HIPAA Privacy Rule. Additionally, a person, state, or other entity may request that HHS analyze a provision of state law to determine whether a state law provision which is apparently contrary to HIPAA may meet additional criteria that will prevent preemption by HIPAA.[77] In response to a request, preemption of a contrary state law will not occur if the designated HHS official determines that one of the following criteria apply: The state law (1) is necessary to prevent fraud and abuse related to the provision of or payment for health care; (2) is necessary to ensure appropriate state regulation of insurance and health plans to the extent expressly authorized by statute or regulation; (3) is necessary for state reporting on health care delivery or costs; (4) is necessary for purposes of serving a compelling public health, safety, or welfare need, and, if a Privacy Rule provision is at issue, the Secretary determines that the intrusion into privacy is warranted when balanced against the need to be served; or (5) has as its principal purpose the regulation of the manufacture, registration, distribution, dispensing, or other control of any controlled substances (as defined in 21 U.S.C. § 802), or that is deemed a controlled substance by state law.[78]

It is important to recognize that only state laws that are contrary to the federal requirements are eligible for an exemption determination.[79] For these purposes under HIPAA, *contrary* means that it would be impossible for a covered entity to comply with both the state and federal requirements, or that the provision of state law is an obstacle to accomplishing the full purposes and objectives of the Administrative Simplification provisions of HIPAA.[80]

Elements of Authorizations under State Law

As previously stated, HIPAA provides a floor by which health information is protected from unauthorized disclosures. Where a state law provision relates to the privacy of PHI and is more stringent than HIPAA, the state law prevails.[81] Thus, where a state requires additional safeguards and clauses in the authorization for release of PHI, the authorization must contain the state law requirements in addition to the HIPAA requirements for authorizations. For instance, where a state law mandates that an individual recipient of the PHI be recorded in the authorization, it is not acceptable to list a general class of recipients, as HIPAA would allow.

Psychiatric Records under State Law

Many states treat mental health records more stringently than health information involving physical conditions. In light of the more stringent requirements by some states, it may be necessary for an authorization for release of PHI containing mental health information to contain additional safeguards and privacy protection guarantees. HIPAA does not preempt the more stringent state laws for mental health PHI. Where state law has additional provisions for the release of psychiatric or mental health records, the covered entity must ensure that the authorization for release of mental health PHI complies with state laws as well as with the HIPAA Privacy Rule.

For an example of an authorization for release of PHI, refer to Appendix B.

NOTES

1. Health Insurance Portability and Accountability Act of 1996, 45 C.F.R. § 164.506 (2003).
2. *See id.* § 164.506.
3. *See id.* § 164.510(a).
4. *See id.* § 164.510(b).
5. *See id.* §§ 164.501 and 164.508(a)(3).
6. *See id.* §§ 164.501, 164.514(f), and 164.522.
7. HIPAA, 45 C.F.R. § 164.512(j).

8. *See id.* § 164.512(d).
9. *See id.* § 164.512(e).
10. *See id.* § 164.512(f).
11. *See id.* §§ 164.512(b) and 164.514(e).
12. *See id.* § 164.512(a).
13. HIPAA, 45 C.F.R. §§ 164.512(i) and 164.514(e).
14. *See id.* § 164.512(c).
15. *See id.* § 164.512(l).
16. *See id.* § 164.502(a)(1)(iv): "A covered entity may not use or disclose protected health information, except . . . pursuant to and in compliance with an authorization that complies with § 164.508."
17. *Id.*
18. *See id.* 45 C.F.R. § 164.508(c)(1)(vi).
19. HIPAA, 45 C.F.R. § 164.508(c)(1)(vi).
20. U.S. Department of Health and Human Services (HHS), Privacy of Health Information/HIPAA, Authorizations, *available at* http://answers.hhs.gov; accessed Dec. 6, 2003 [hereinafter HHS, HIPAA Authorizations].
21. HIPAA, 45 C.F.R. § 164.514(h).
22. HHS, HIPAA Authorizations, *supra* note 20.
23. *Id.*
24. *Id.*
25. *Id.*
26. HIPAA, 45 C.F.R. § 164.508(c)(1)(iii).
27. *See id.* § 164.508(c)(1)(ii).
28. HHS, HIPAA Authorizations, *supra* note 20.
29. *Id.*
30. *Id.*
31. HIPAA, 45 C.F.R. § 164.508(c)(1)(i).
32. *Id.*
33. HHS, HIPAA Authorizations, *supra* note 20.
34. *Id.*
35. HIPAA, 45 C.F.R. § 164.508(c)(1)(iv).
36. *Id.*
37. *See id.* § 164.508(c)(1)(v).
38. HHS, HIPAA Authorizations, *supra* note 20.
39. *Id.*
40. *Id.*
41. *Id.*
42. HIPAA, 45 C.F.R. § 164.508(c)(1)(vi).
43. HHS, HIPAA Authorizations, *supra* note 20.
44. *Id.*
45. HIPAA, 45 C.F.R. § 164.508(c)(2)(i).
46. HHS, HIPAA Authorizations, *supra* note 20.
47. *Id.*

48. *Id.*
49. *Id.*
50. HIPAA, 45 C.F.R. § 164.508(c)(2)(ii).
51. *See id.* § 164.508(b)(4)(i).
52. HHS, HIPAA Authorizations, *supra* note 20.
53. HIPAA, 45 C.F.R. § 164.508(c)(2)(ii).
54. *See id.* § 164.508(c)(2)(iii).
55. *See id.* § 164.508(c)(3).
56. *See id.* § 164.508(c)(4).
57. HHS, HIPAA Authorizations, *supra* note 20.
58. *Id.*
59. *Id.*
60. *Id.*
61. *Id.*
62. *Id.*
63. HHS, HIPAA Authorizations, *supra* note 20.
64. HIPAA, 45 C.F.R. § 164.502(b).
65. *Id.*
66. *See id.* § 160.203.
67. *Id.*
68. *Id.*
69. *See id.* § 160.203(a)(1)(i).
70. HIPAA, 45 C.F.R. § 160.203(a)(1)(ii).
71. *See id.* § 160.203(a)(1)(iii).
72. *See id.* § 160.203(a)(1)(iv).
73. *See id.* § 160.203(a)(2).
74. *Sec id.* § 160.203(b).
75. *See id.* § 160.203(c).
76. HIPAA, 45 C.F.R. § 160.203(d).
77. *See id.* § 160.204.
78. *See id.* § 160.203(a).
79. *See id.* § 160.203.
80. *See id.* § 160.202.
81. *See id.* § 160.203(b).

CHAPTER 3

Disclosures without Authorizations

The main goal of the Health Insurance Portability and Accountability Act of 1996 (HIPAA) Privacy Rule is to protect health information from being disclosed at the wrong time to the wrong person or for the wrong reason. In light of that purpose, HIPAA provides strict and narrow means by which a third party is able to view or obtain protected health information (PHI). The federal rule contains safeguards to which a covered entity must adhere in order to disclose PHI. The most straightforward method for obtaining an individual's medical record is simply to have the individual sign a HIPAA compliant authorization, as discussed in Chapter 2. However, the government recognized that there are times when it is not possible or practical to obtain an authorization. Therefore, HIPAA provides exceptions to the rule for various circumstances in which it is not feasible to obtain an authorization for release of PHI.

TREATMENT, PAYMENT, OR HEALTH CARE OPERATIONS

The rule allows the health care provider to disclose PHI for its own treatment, payment or health care operations.[1] The health care provider may disclose PHI or treatment activities of another health care provider.[2] The health care provider may disclose PHI to another covered entity or a health care provider for the payment activities of the entity that receives the information.[3] The rule also allows disclosure to another covered entity or health care provider for treatment, payment, or operation activities of the entity that receives the information if that entity had a relationship with the individual who is the subject of the PHI being requested, the information pertains to such relationship, *and* the disclosure is for the purpose of (1) conducting quality assessment activities related to improving health or reducing health care costs,

(2) case management and care coordination, (3) contacting health care providers and patients with information about treatment alternatives or reviewing the competence of health care professionals, health plan performance, conducting training programs, accreditation, certification, licensing, or credentialing activities.[4] The covered entity may also disclose PHI for the purpose of detecting health care fraud and abuse.[5] Additionally, if the covered entity participates in an organized health care arrangement, it may disclose PHI to another covered entity that also participates in the same organized health care arrangement.[6]

Treatment

Treatment is the provision, coordination, or management of health care and related services, including consultations, referrals, and coordination of health care between different health care providers.[7] Section 164.506 of HIPAA allows health care providers to discuss the individual's health condition, diagnosis, prognosis, and treatment without violating confidentiality. The health care providers involved in the individual's care are free to discuss the relevant information without fear of repercussions under HIPAA. Consulting with another health care provider about a patient is within the HIPAA Privacy Rule's definition of "treatment" and, therefore, is permissible. In addition, a health care provider (or other covered entity) is expressly permitted to disclose PHI about an individual to a health care provider for that provider's treatment of the individual. See 45 C.F.R. § 164.506.[8] For example, a radiologist may discuss the results of a mammogram with the individual's obstetrician/gynecologist without the individual's explicit authorization in order to manage the diagnosis, prognosis, and care of that patient. In the same respect, a physician does not need a patient's written authorization to send a copy of the patient's medical record to a specialist or other health care provider who will treat the patient.

As a practical matter, a pharmacist may use professional judgment and experience with common practice to make reasonable inferences of the patient's best interest in allowing a person other than the patient to pick up a prescription.[9] For example, the fact that a relative or friend arrives at a pharmacy and asks to pick up a specific prescription for an individual effectively verifies that he or she is involved in the individual's care, and the HIPAA Privacy Rule allows the pharmacist to give the filled prescription to the relative or friend. The individual does not need to provide the pharmacist with the names of such persons in advance.[10]

Payment

The covered entity may disclose PHI for payment.[11] Payment includes the activities involved in obtaining health insurance premiums, coverage, benefits, eligibility, billing, collection, preauthorization, appropriateness of care, justification of charges, and reimbursement, among others.[12] The Privacy Rule permits a covered entity, or a business associate acting on behalf of a covered entity (e.g., a collection agency), to disclose PHI as necessary to obtain payment for health care, and does not limit to whom such a disclosure may be made. Therefore, a covered entity, or its business associate, may contact persons other than the individual as necessary to obtain payment for health care services.[13] However, the Privacy Rule requires a covered entity, or its business associate, to reasonably limit the amount of information disclosed for such purposes to the minimum necessary, as well as to abide by any reasonable requests for confidential communications and any agreed-to restrictions on the use or disclosure of PHI.[14] For examples: HIPAA permits the disclosure of PHI in order to bill for services provided by a physician, but only the minimum necessary amount of PHI may be disclosed; HIPAA allows a provider to disclose PHI to a health plan for the plan's Health Plan Employer Data and Information Set purposes, so long as the period for which information is needed overlaps with the period in which the individual is or was enrolled in the health plan.[15]

The Privacy Rule permits covered entities to continue to use the services of debt collection agencies. Debt collection is recognized as a payment activity within the "payment" definition.[16] Through a business associate arrangement, the covered entity may engage a debt collection agency to perform this function on its behalf. Disclosures to collection agencies are governed by other provisions of the Privacy Rule, such as the business associate and minimum necessary requirements.[17] Additionally, the U.S. Department of Health and Human Services (HHS) stated that it is not aware of any conflict between the Privacy Rule and the Fair Debt Collection Practices Act.[18] Where a use or disclosure of PHI is necessary for the covered entity to fulfill a legal duty, the Privacy Rule would permit such use or disclosure as required by law.[19]

The Privacy Rule's definition of "payment" includes disclosures to consumer reporting agencies.[20] These disclosures, however, are limited to the following PHI about the individual: name and address, date of birth, Social Security number, payment history, and account number. In addition, disclosure of the name and address of the health care provider or health plan making the report is allowed. The covered entity may perform this payment activity directly, or may carry out this function through a third party, such as a collection agency, under a business associate arrangement. The Privacy Rule permits uses and disclosures by the covered entity or its business associate as may be required by the Fair Credit Reporting Act (FCRA) or other law. Therefore, HHS does not believe there is a conflict between the Privacy Rule and legal duties imposed on data furnishers by FCRA.[21]

Health Care Operations

The Privacy Rule permits a covered health care provider to disclose PHI for "health care operations" purposes, subject to certain requirements.[22] Health care operations are those activities a covered entity engages in to conduct quality assessment and improvement; review the competence or qualifications of health care professionals; underwrite or rate premiums; conduct or arrange for medical review, legal services, and auditing; plan and develop business; conduct business management; and perform general administrative activities.[23]

Disclosures by a covered health care provider to a professional liability insurer or a similar entity for the purpose of obtaining or maintaining medical liability coverage or for the purpose of obtaining benefits from such insurance, including the reporting of adverse events, fall within "business management and general administrative activities" under the definition of "health care operations." Therefore, a covered health care provider may disclose individually identifiable health information to a professional liability insurer to the same extent as the provider is able to disclose such information for other health care operations purposes.[24] For example, when a patient brings a legal action against his or her health care provider, 45 C.F.R. §§ 164.506 and 164.502(a)(1)(ii) allow disclosure of the patient's PHI to the attorney representing the health care provider, without an authorization from the patient. However, the attorney representing the physician must have a business associate agreement in place prior to the disclosure of PHI.[25]

Business Associate Agreement

A business associate is a person who, on behalf of a covered entity, performs or assists in the performance of a function or activity involving the use or disclosure of PHI for claims processing, administration, data analysis, processing or administration, utilization review, quality assurance, billing, benefit management, practice management, and repricing; or provides legal, actuarial, accounting, consulting, data aggregation, management, administrative, accreditation, or financial services to or for such covered entity, or to or for an organized health care arrangement in which the covered entity participates, where the provision of the service involves the disclosure of PHI from a covered entity or from another business associate.[26] Those persons who are members of the workforce of the covered entity are not considered business associates.[27] See Appendix C for an example of a business associate agreement.

A business associate contract is not required with persons or organizations whose functions, activities, or services do not involve the use or disclosure of PHI, and where any access to PHI by such persons would be incidental, if at all.[28] For instance, janitorial services that clean the offices or facilities of a covered entity are not business associates because the work they perform does not involve the use or disclosure of PHI, and any disclosure of PHI to janitorial personnel that occurs in the performance of their duties (such as may occur while emptying trash cans) is limited in nature, occurs as a by-product of their janitorial duties, and cannot reasonably be prevented.[29] Such disclosures are incidental and permitted by the HIPAA Privacy Rule.[30]

If a service is hired to do work for a covered entity where disclosure of PHI is not limited in nature (such as routine handling of records or shredding of documents containing PHI), it likely would be a business associate.[31] However, when such work is performed under the direct control of the covered entity (e.g., on the covered entity's premises), the Privacy Rule permits the covered entity to treat the service as part of its workforce, and the covered entity need not enter into a business associate contract with the service.[32]

In the same respect, plumbers, electricians, and photocopier repair technicians do not require access to PHI to perform their services, so they do not meet the definition of a "business associate."[33] Under the HIPAA Privacy Rule, "business associates" are contractors or other non-workforce members hired to do the work of, or for, a covered entity that involves the use or disclosure of PHI.[34] Any disclosure of PHI to such technicians that occurs in the performance of their duties (such as may occur walking through or working in file rooms) is limited in nature, occurs as a by-product of their duties, and cannot reasonably be prevented. Such disclosures are incidental and permitted by the Privacy Rule.[35]

Additionally, the Privacy Rule does not require a covered entity to enter into business associate contracts with organizations, such as the United States Postal Service, certain private couriers, and their electronic equivalents, that act merely as conduits for PHI.[36] A conduit transports information but does not access it other than on a variable or occasional basis as necessary for the performance of the transportation service or as required by law. Since no disclosure is intended by the covered entity, and the probability of exposure of any particular PHI to a conduit is very small, a conduit is not a business associate of the covered entity.[37]

However, the HIPAA Privacy Rule explicitly defines organizations that accredit covered entities as "business associates."[38] Similar to other business associates, accreditation organizations provide a service to the covered entity that requires sharing of PHI. The business associate provisions may be satisfied by standard or model contract forms that require little or no modification for each covered entity. As an alternative to the business associate contract, covered entities may disclose a limited data set of PHI, not including direct identifiers, to an accreditation organization, subject to a data use agreement.[39] If only a limited data set of PHI is disclosed, the satisfactory assurances required of the business associate are satisfied by the data use agreement.[40]

A covered entity may permit a business associate to create, receive, maintain, or transmit PHI on the covered entity's behalf only if the covered entity obtains satisfactory assurances that the business associate will appropriately safeguard the information.[41] There must be a contract between the covered entity and the business associate that provides that the business associate will (1) implement administrative, physical, and technical safeguards that reasonably and appropriately protect the confidentiality, integrity, and availability of the PHI that it creates, receives, maintains, or transmits on behalf of the covered entity; (2) ensure that any agent, including a subcontractor to whom it provides PHI, agrees to implement reasonable and appropriate safeguards to protect the PHI; (3) report to the covered entity any security incident of which it becomes aware; and (4) authorize the termination of the contract by the covered entity, if the covered entity determines that the business associate violated a material term of the contract.[42]

Implementation of Safeguards

The business associate must safeguard the PHI on behalf of the covered entity.[43] There must be certain physical limitations that allow only proper personnel to have access to the PHI. For example, written PHI should be kept in locked storage units. The business associate must also provide technical safeguards. For example, specific pass codes and firewalls should be in place to prevent unauthorized access to electronic PHI.

However, where the HIPAA Privacy Rule permits a covered entity to share PHI with another covered entity, the covered entity is permitted to make the disclosure directly to a business associate acting on behalf of that other covered entity.[44]

Agents of Business Associates Must Implement Safeguards

The business associate must receive reasonable assurances from its agents that the agents will implement safeguards to protect the privacy of the PHI.[45] These reasonable assurances should contain information that the business associate can depend on in the event of a breach. HIPAA does not provide the content of the reasonable assurances nor does it mandate that the reasonable assurances be in writing. However, a written agreement to protect PHI that specifically describes the procedures that the agent took is more reliable than an oral agreement between the business associate and its agent. It is important to remember that the business associate does work on behalf of the covered entity. A breach of confidentiality of PHI creates an obligation on the part of the covered entity to obtain information from the business associate as to those measures that the business associate took to prevent the breach. A written document for reasonable assurances between the business associate and its agent allows a straightforward approach to providing the covered entity with the information it needs to respond to an inquiry about a breach.

Report Any Security Incident to the Covered Entity

In addition to taking appropriate steps to remedy or mitigate a security incident, the business associate has a duty to report the incident to the covered entity. Section 164.304 defines a "security incident" as "the attempted or successful unauthorized access, use, disclosure, modification, or destruction of information or interference with system operations in an information system." Section 164.314(a)(2)(i)(C) requires that the contract between the covered entity and business associate obligate the business associate to "report to the covered entity any security incident of which it becomes aware."[46]

However, HIPAA allows a flexible approach to the reporting requirement.[47] HIPAA provides that

1. Covered entities may use any security measures that allow the covered entity to reasonably and appropriately implement the

standards and implementation specifications as specified in 45 C.F.R. § 164.306(b).

2. In deciding which security measures to use, a covered entity must take into account the following factors:
    a. The size, complexity, and capabilities of the covered entity
    b. The covered entity's technical infrastructure, hardware, and software security capabilities
    c. The costs of security measures
    d. The probability and criticality of potential risks to electronic PHI[48]

The cost of reporting every attempted unauthorized access may greatly exceed the anticipated benefit and would be contrary to HIPAA.[49] Therefore, not every attempted access through a firewall needs to be reported by the business associate as a security incident. HIPAA allows for some reasonableness in policies, standards, guidelines, and contract terms. The key is to apply reasonable processes based upon the risks or threats involved. A covered entity may need to have different reporting requirements depending upon the service provided. For example, there should be very strict reporting requirements for the company providing in-home hospice care to the covered entity's HIV patients and less stringent ones for the company performing the covered entity's patient satisfaction surveys.

Termination of the Contract by the Covered Entity

HIPAA mandates that the covered entity terminate the business associate agreement if the covered entity determines that the business associate violated a material term of the contract.[50]

The Department of Health and Human Services stated that the HIPAA Privacy Rule does not "pass through" its requirements to business associates or otherwise cause business associates to comply with the terms of the HIPAA Privacy Rule. The assurances that covered entities must obtain prior to disclosing PHI to business associates create a set of contractual obligations far narrower than the provisions of the rule, to protect information generally and to help the covered entity comply with its obligations under the rule.[51] The Department of Health and Human Services advises that business associates are not subject to the requirements of the Privacy Rule, and HHS cannot impose civil monetary penalties on a business associate for breach of its business associate contract with the covered entity, unless the business associate is itself a covered entity.[52] For example, covered entities do not need to ask their business associates to appoint a privacy officer or develop policies and procedures for use and disclosure of PHI.[53]

Reasonable Assurances Agreement

The contract between the covered entity and the business associate may permit the business associate to use the PHI in its capacity for the proper management and administration of the business associate or to carry out the legal responsibilities of the business associate, provided that (1) the disclosure is required by law or (2) the business associate obtains *reasonable assurances* from the person to whom the information is disclosed that the PHI will be held confidentially and used or further disclosed only as required by law or for the purpose for which it was disclosed, and the person notifies the business associate of any breaches in the confidentiality of the PHI of which it is aware.[54]

The business associate must ensure that any agent, including a subcontractor, to whom it provides PHI received from, created by, or received by the business associate on behalf of the covered entity agrees to the same restrictions and conditions that apply to the business associate.[55] In other words, the business associate has a duty to guard the PHI (as discussed above) and make certain that any agent is aware of and abides by the same restrictions and conditions as the business associate.

Although HIPAA does not require a written document in which the agent explicitly gives reasonable assurances that the PHI will be held confidentially, it is prudent practice for a business associate to obtain a written agreement from each applicable agent that the agent will adhere to the same restrictions and conditions that apply to the business associate. The written reasonable assurances agreement is useful in making information available to the covered entity or investigative entity that is required to provide an accounting of disclosures in accordance with Sections 164.528 and 164.504(e)(2)(i)(D). A sample of a reasonable assurances agreement is available in Appendix D.

THREAT TO HEALTH OR SAFETY AND COMPLIANCE WITH LEGAL DUTIES

Averting a Serious Threat to Health or Safety

As long as the use or disclosure is consistent with applicable laws and standards of ethical conduct, a covered entity may use or disclose PHI if the covered entity, in good faith, believes that the use or disclosure is necessary to prevent or lessen a serious and imminent threat to the health or safety of a person or the public. The disclosure must be made to a person reasonably able to prevent or lessen the threat, including someone who is a target of the threat, *or* the disclosure must be necessary for law enforcement authorities to identify or apprehend an individual.[56] For example, if a school bus driver, who is a patient, has a positive drug test result prior to driving his or her route, the physician may disclose PHI to the registry of motor vehicles or the police in order to prevent the patient from endangering the students who ride in the driver's vehicle.

If a disclosure is made to law enforcement authorities to identify or apprehend an individual, it must be made because of a statement by an individual admitting participation in a violent crime that the covered entity reasonably believes may have caused serious physical harm to the victim. However, the covered entity (e.g., physician) may not learn of the statement during the course of treatment to change the propensity of the individual to commit the criminal conduct that is the basis for the disclosure, or during counseling or therapy, or through a request by the individual to initiate or to be referred for the treatment, counseling, or therapy as previously described. For example, the physician may disclose a victim's treatment for a gunshot wound to the police. However, the physician cannot disclose a perpetrator's admission of domestic violence if the individual's purpose in seeking treatment from the physician is to obtain counseling to deter his or her acts of domestic violence.

The covered entity may use or disclose PHI when, appearing from all of the circumstances, the covered entity has a good faith belief that the individual escaped from a correctional institution or from lawful custody. A covered entity is presumed to have acted with a good faith belief if the belief is based on the covered entity's actual knowledge or in reliance on credible representation by a person with apparent knowledge or authority.[57] For example, if an individual wearing correctional facility clothing seeks treatment for a knife wound, the physician may disclose PHI to law enforcement officials in order to aid in the arrest of the individual.

Law Enforcement

A covered entity may disclose PHI for a law enforcement purpose only if certain conditions are met.[58] First, the disclosure must be made to a law enforcement official. Second, the disclosure must be required by law.[59] Such disclosures include disclosures of physical injuries (e.g., gunshot wounds); disclosures in response to a court order, warrant, subpoena, or summons; disclosures in compliance with an administrative request provided that (1) the material sought is relevant and material to a legitimate law enforcement inquiry, (2) the request is specific and limited in scope to the purpose for which the information is sought, and (3) de-identified information cannot reasonably be used.[60]

Third, a covered entity may disclose PHI in response to a law enforcement official's request in order to identify or locate a suspect, fugitive, material witness, or missing person, provided that the covered entity discloses only the following information of the individual: (1) name and address, (2) date and place of birth, (3) Social Security number, (4) blood type and Rh factor, (5) type of injury, (6) date and time of treatment, (7) date and time of death (if applicable), and (8) a description of physical characteristics including height, weight, gender, race, hair and eye color, facial hair, scars, and tattoos.[61]

Fourth, a covered entity may disclose PHI in response to a law enforcement official's request for such information about an individual who is or is suspected to be a victim of a crime if the individual agrees to the disclosure or, if the covered entity is unable to obtain permission due to the individual's incapacity or other emergency circumstances, the covered entity determines that the disclosure is in the best interest of the individual where the law enforcement official represents that the information is needed to determine whether a violation of the law by a person other than the individual occurred *and* the law enforcement official represents that it would be adverse to the immediate law enforcement activity to wait for the permission of the individual.[62]

Fifth, a covered entity may disclose PHI to a law enforcement official about an individual who died provided that the purpose of disclosure is to alert the law enforcement official of the death of the individual if the covered entity suspects that the death may have resulted from criminal conduct.[63]

Sixth, a covered entity may disclose PHI to a law enforcement official where the covered entity has a good faith belief that the PHI constitutes evidence of criminal activity that occurred on the covered entity's premises.[64]

Seventh, a covered entity that provides emergency health care in a medical emergency may disclose PHI to a law enforcement official if the disclosure is necessary to alert the enforcement official to (1) the commission and nature of a crime, (2) the location of a crime, and (3) the identity, description, and location of the perpetrator of such crime.[65] However, if the covered entity believes that the individual in need of emergency health care is the victim of abuse, neglect, or domestic violence, the covered entity may disclose PHI provided that the covered entity meets certain specific criteria as listed in the section "Victims of Abuse, Neglect, or Domestic Violence," below. [66]

Public Health Activities

A covered entity may disclose PHI for "public health purposes" to certain recipients.[67] The PHI may be disclosed to (1) a public health official to prevent or control disease, injury or disability; (2) an official who is authorized to receive reports of child abuse or neglect; (3) the Food and Drug Administration, provided that the covered entity discloses the information for the purpose of activities related to the quality, safety, or effectiveness of a product or activity;[68] (4) a person who may have been exposed to a communicable disease or may otherwise be at risk of contracting or spreading a disease or condition;[69] (5) an employer[70] (only under certain strict criteria that protect the workplace); and (6) a public health authority that may use the PHI for public health activities.[71]

Victims of Abuse, Neglect, or Domestic Violence

A covered entity may disclose PHI to a *public health authority* or other appropriate government authority allowed by law to receive reports of child abuse or neglect.[72]

Additionally, a covered entity may disclose PHI about an individual that the covered entity reasonably believes to be a victim of abuse, neglect, or domestic violence as long as it reports the PHI to a *government authority,* including a social service or protective services agency, authorized by law to receive reports of abuse, neglect, or domestic violence.[73] The disclosure must be required by law, comply with such law, and be limited to the relevant requirements of such law. Either the individual must agree to the disclosure *or* the disclosure must be expressly authorized by statute or regulation *and,* in the covered entity's professional judgment, it believes the disclosure is needed to prevent serious harm to the individual or other potential victims.[74]

If the individual is unable to agree because of incapacity, a public official must indicate that the PHI is not intended to be used against the individual and that an urgent enforcement activity would be adversely affected by waiting until the individual is able to agree to the disclosure. The covered entity must promptly inform the individual that such a report has been or will be made. However, if the covered entity believes that informing the individual would place the individual at risk for harm *or* if the covered entity would be informing the individual's personal representative, whom the covered entity believes to be the source of the abuse, neglect, or domestic violence, then HIPAA does not mandate that the covered entity inform the individual or the personal representative.[75]

For example, at a local hospital social workers receive a call from the Department of Social Services, requesting that the hospital staff give them a "heads up" when a particular individual arrives there to deliver her baby. The hospital has no direct knowledge of any abuse. The hospital has no history with either the patient or previous Department of Social Services complaints. The hospital basically knows nothing about the pregnant woman except that the Department of Social Services said they had removed other children from this patient's custody for abuse. The hospital staff has no firsthand knowledge of any concerns for the unborn child and no positive drug or alcohol toxicity screen for the mother. The mother appropriately presents to the hospital for delivery of her child. There may be a state mandatory reporting law that requires disclosure, under which HIPAA permits disclosure of the PHI.[76] Absent a state mandatory reporting law, these circumstances permit the hospital staff to use their professional judgment to determine that there is no choice but to withhold the PHI from the Department of Social Services. There is no good faith basis to determine that this particular baby is a potential victim of abuse as allowed under 45 C.F.R. § 164.512(c). However, there is nothing in the Privacy Rule that prevents the Department of Social Services from phoning the hospital daily to determine whether the hospital directory lists the woman as being admitted to the facility.

In summary, a covered entity may use or disclose PHI to the extent that the law requires such use or disclosure and it complies with and is limited to the relevant requirements of such law.[77] A covered entity must meet the requirements as described above in disclosures for (1) victims of abuse, neglect, or domestic violence;[78] (2) judicial and administrative proceedings;[79] and (3) law enforcement purposes.[80]

LAWFUL OVERSIGHT ACTIVITIES

The government acknowledged that covered entities may become subject to a variety of organizational activities that are necessary for compliance with federal and state regulations. These activities require the disclosure of PHI; however, obtaining an authorization is not feasible. HIPAA allows disclosures of PHI without authorizations when supervision of the health care system, determination of eligibility for government benefits program, determination of compliance with government regulatory programs, and determination of compliance with civil rights laws involves the PHI.

The covered entity may disclose PHI to a health oversight agency for oversight activities authorized by law, including audits; civil, administrative, or criminal investigations; inspection; licensure or disciplinary actions; and civil, administrative, or criminal proceedings or actions.[81] For example, HIPAA allows disclosure of PHI where the public health department seeks medical records during the investigation of a psychiatrist for unscrupulous activities with his or her patients. If it is necessary and relevant, PHI may be used or disclosed for oversight of other activities needed for appropriate monitoring of the health care system, government benefit programs, government regulatory programs, and civil rights laws.[82]

A health oversight activity does *not* include an investigation or other activity in which the individual is the subject of the investigation and the investigation does *not* arise out of and is *not* directly related to the receipt of health care, a claim for public benefits related to health, or qualification for or receipt of public benefits or services when a patient's health is integral to the claim for public benefits or services. But if there is an investigation or oversight activity that is not associated with a claim for public benefits related to health and that is done in conjunction with an investigation or oversight activity related to health, the joint investigation is considered a health oversight activity that falls within the exception and no authorization is required under HIPAA.[83]

If a covered entity is also a health oversight agency, the covered entity may use PHI for health oversight activities provided it meets the above criteria.[84]

JUDICIAL AND ADMINISTRATIVE PROCEEDINGS

During the course of any judicial or administrative proceeding, a covered entity may disclose PHI in response to (1) an order of a court or administrative tribunal or (2) a subpoena, discovery request, or other lawful process.[85] The covered entity may disclose PHI in response to an order of a court or administrative tribunal, provided that the covered entity discloses only the PHI expressly authorized by the order.[86]

In regards to a subpoena, discovery request, or other lawful process that is not accompanied by an order of the court or administrative tribunal, the covered entity must receive certain *satisfactory assurances* from the party seeking the PHI. If a party to an action propounds a request for discovery of PHI to a covered entity without a court order or a duly signed authorization, the covered entity must have satisfactory assurance from the party seeking the PHI that reasonable efforts were made by the party to ensure that the individual who is the subject of the PHI was given notice of the request or that reasonable efforts were made to secure a qualified protective order.[87]

A covered entity receives satisfactory assurance when he or she receives a written statement and accompanying documentation demonstrating that

1. The party requesting the information made a good faith attempt to provide written notice to the individual or, if the individual's location is unknown, to mail a notice to the individual's last known address;
2. The notice included sufficient information about the litigation or proceeding in which the PHI is requested to permit the individual to raise an objection to the court or administrative tribunal; and
3. The time for the individual to raise objections to the court or administrative tribunal has elapsed, and
   a. No objections were filed; or
   b. All objections filed by the individual have been resolved by the court or the administrative tribunal and the disclosures being sought are consistent with such resolution.[88]

Alternatively, the covered entity may receive a written statement from the party seeking the PHI that reasonable efforts were made by the party to secure a qualified protective order. The written statement and accompanying documentation must demonstrate that (1) the parties to the dispute giving rise to the request for information agreed to a qualified protective order and presented it to the court or tribunal with jurisdiction over the dispute; or (2) the party seeking the PHI requested a qualified protective order from such court or administrative tribunal.[89]

A "qualified protective order" is an order of a court or an administrative tribunal or a stipulation by the parties to the litigation or administrative proceeding that

- Prohibits the parties from using or disclosing the PHI for any purpose other than the litigation or proceeding for which such information was requested; and

- Requires the return to the covered entity or destruction of the PHI (including all copies made) at the end of the litigation or proceeding.[90]

Notwithstanding the above requirements, a covered entity may disclose PHI in response to a subpoena, discovery request, or other lawful process *without reasonable assurances from the party seeking the PHI if* the covered entity itself makes reasonable efforts to provide written notice to the individual as described above or makes reasonable efforts to seek a qualified protective order as described above.[91]

In light of the duties under HIPAA, many covered entities will not disclose PHI without a court order. Even with a subpoena, discovery request, or other lawful process, covered entities are mindful of the provisions in HIPAA requiring court intervention and are reluctant to disclose PHI absent a duly authorized release of medical information. It is common practice in some jurisdictions for the party seeking PHI to request a court-ordered subpoena when a duly signed authorization is not available. In that instance, the medical records are delivered to the court in a sealed envelope. Prior to disclosure to the party seeking the PHI, the court reviews the PHI to determine whether it is pertinent to the litigation or administrative proceeding. Under these circumstances, the covered entity properly responds to the court order under Section 164.512(e).

INFORMATIONAL AND PROMOTIONAL DISCLOSURES

Facility Directories

A covered entity may use or disclose PHI for facility directories without the written authorization of the individual provided that (1) the individual is notified *in advance* of the use or disclosure *and* the individual has the opportunity to *agree or object* (opt out) to having his or her name published in the directory. The agreement can be oral. The only information that can be published in the directory is the individual's name, location in the facility, general condition (no specific medical information), and religious affiliation. The information can be released only to people who ask for the individual by name or to members of the clergy. If an emergency exists in which the individual does not have the opportunity to agree or object, the information may be published in the facility's directory *if* (1) it is consistent with prior expressed consent of the individual and (2) the covered entity determines that it is in the best interest of the individual.[92]

For example, when a patient is admitted to the hospital for elective surgery, the hospital admissions staff must ask that patient if he or she would like to be listed in the hospital's patient directory. If the patient agrees, the hospital may list only the individual's name, location in the facility, general condition (no specific medical information), and religious affiliation. The hospital may release the information only if an individual asks for it. The hospital may not disclose the information if the patient opts out of having his or her name listed in the directory.

Friends and Relatives

A covered entity may disclose relevant PHI to a family member, other relative, or a close personal friend of the individual, or any other person identified by the individual who is involved in the individual's health care and treatment or payment related to the individual's health care, provided that if the individual is present and has the ability to form his or her own health care decisions, the covered entity gives the individual an opportunity to object or agree to the disclosure.[93] If the permission cannot be obtained due to the individual's incapacity or an emergency or if the individual is not present, disclosure to the next of kin is permitted if the covered entity can reasonably infer, based on professional judgment under the circumstances and on its experience with common practice, that the individual does not object. For example, a husband is permitted to pick up prescriptions for his wife at the pharmacy. However, if the individual objects, the covered entity is prohibited from sharing the individual's PHI with the individual's friends or relatives.[94]

Additionally, the individual may restrict the amount or type of information that the covered entity can share.[95] The individual can request that the covered entity release only certain PHI to family or friends. For example, a provider may believe that a patient's sexually transmitted disease status is directly relevant to providing care for the patient's pregnancy. The patient may agree to release information to her family pertaining to her pregnancy, but may request that the provider not disclose PHI related to her sexually transmitted disease. The covered entity does not have to agree to this restriction. If the provider does not agree to this restriction, the patient retains the right to prohibit the disclosure of *any* PHI to her family and friends. If the covered entity enters into an agreement to disclose only select information, it must abide by the agreement, except for emergency situations.

Marketing

HIPAA requires a covered entity to obtain an individual's written authorization to use or disclose PHI for marketing purposes.[96] The rule defines "marketing" as a communication about a product or service that encourages the recipient of the communication to purchase or use the product or service *unless* the communication is made (1) to describe a health-related product or service (or payment for such service) that is provided by the covered entity making the communication, (2) for treatment of the individual, or (3) for case management or care coordination for the individual or to direct or recommend alternative treatments, therapies, health care providers, or settings of care to the individual.[97] Essentially, the rule requires an individual's authorization for communications that encourage an individual to use or purchase a product or service that is not health related.

Generally, communications that promote the sale of products or services that are related to health care do not qualify as "marketing" under the rule and those communications do not require the individual's authorization. For example, a physician who recommends a brand-name medication does not engage in "marketing" for the purposes of HIPAA. Along those same lines, there is no need for an authorization where a pharmacist who receives financial incentives from a drug manufacturer recommends that an individual switch to a particular medication manufactured by that particular drug company. The communication is not marketing because, under the rule, recommending alternative treatments is not considered marketing and therefore no authorization is needed.

The rule also provides that there is no need for an authorization if the communication is made face to face by the covered entity to the individual *or* the communication is in the form of a promotional gift of nominal value provided by the covered entity.[98] For example, a physician does not need your authorization to give you a pen with his or her business address printed on it. On the other hand, a covered entity does need an individual's authorization for any other activity not listed under the rule, such as selling lists of patients to third parties. Additionally, if any marketing activity involves direct or indirect monetary compensation to the covered entity from a third party, the authorization must state that such remuneration exists.[99]

Fundraising

A covered entity may use or disclose PHI to a business associate or to an institutionally related foundation without an individual's authorization for the purpose of raising funds for its own benefit provided that the PHI contains only demographic information relating to an individual and dates of health care provided to the individual.[100] In its notice of privacy practices (previously discussed above), the covered entity must specifically note that it uses information for fundraising purposes. The covered entity must include in any fundraising materials that it sends to an individual a description of how the individual may opt out of (object to) receiving any further fundraising communications. Additionally, the covered entity must make reasonable efforts to ensure that individuals who opt out of receiving future fundraising communications are not sent such communications. "Fundraising" is included in the definition of "health care operations" and an individual has the right to request in advance that the covered entity restrict uses and disclosures for fundraising purposes. Under the rule, the covered entity has no obligation to agree to the restriction.

RESEARCH

HIPAA allows a covered entity to disclose PHI to researchers *without* patient authorization if either an institutional review board or a privacy board approves a waiver of the authorization or an alteration of the authorization.[101] The institutional review board must be established according to federal laws. The privacy board must have members with varying backgrounds and appropriate professional competency to review the effect of the research protocol on the individual's privacy rights and related interests. The privacy board must be comprised of at least one member who is not affiliated with the covered entity or with any entity conducting or sponsoring the research, and not related to any person who is affiliated with any of such entities. No member of the privacy board may have a conflict of interest.

The covered entity may disclose PHI to a researcher for review in preparation for research.[102] However, the covered entity must obtain the following information from the researcher: (1) The use or disclosure is sought solely to review PHI as needed to prepare a research protocol (or similar purposes in preparation for research); (2) no PHI will be removed from the covered entity by the researcher in the course of the review; and (3) the PHI is necessary for the research purposes.[103]

See 45 C.F.R. §§ 164.512(i) and 164.514(e) for other specific restrictions pertaining to research.

WORKERS' COMPENSATION

A covered entity may disclose PHI without the written authorization of the individual (or the opportunity for the individual to object) to the extent necessary to comply with laws relating to workers' compensation or other similar programs, established by law, that provide benefits for work-related injuries or illness without regard to fault.[104] Under HIPAA, a covered entity does not need an individual's authorization to disclose PHI in order to comply with workers' compensation laws.

Under HIPAA, individuals do not have a right to request that a covered entity restrict a disclosure of PHI about them for workers' compensation purposes when that disclosure is required by law or authorized by, and necessary to comply with, a workers' compensation or similar law.[105]

The government did not intend for HIPAA to impede the flow of health information to those who need it to process or adjudicate claims, or coordinate care, for injured or ill workers under workers' compensation systems. The minimum necessary standard generally requires covered entities to make reasonable efforts to limit uses and disclosures of, as well as requests for, PHI to the minimum necessary to accomplish the intended purpose. For disclosures of PHI made for workers' compensation purposes under 45 C.F.R. § 164.512(l), the minimum necessary standard permits covered entities to disclose information to the full extent authorized by state or other law. Additionally, where a state workers' compensation board or other public official (for workers' compensation purposes) requests PHI, covered entities are permitted reasonably to rely on the official's representations that the information requested is the minimum necessary for the intended purpose.[106] For disclosures of PHI for payment purposes, covered entities may disclose the type and amount of information necessary to receive payment for any health care provided to an injured or ill worker. The minimum necessary standard does not apply to disclosures required by state or other law or made pursuant to the individual's authorization.[107]

NOTES

1. Health Insurance Portability and Accountability Act of 1996 (HIPAA), 45 C.F.R. § 164.506 (2003).
2. *Id.*

3. *Id.*
4. *Id.*
5. *Id.*
6. *Id.*
7. *See id.* § 164.501.
8. U.S. Department of Health and Human Services (HHS), Privacy of Health Information/HIPAA, Treatment/Payment/Healthcare Operations, *available at* http://answers.hhs.gov; accessed Dec. 28, 2003 [hereinafter HHS, HIPAA Treatment/Payment/Healthcare Operations].
9. HIPAA, 45 C.F.R. § 164.510(b).
10. HHS, HIPAA Treatment/Payment/Healthcare Operations, *supra* note 6.
11. HIPAA, 45 C.F.R. § 164.506.
12. *Id.*
13. *See id.* § 164.506(c) and the definition of "payment" at § 164.501.
14. HIPAA, 45 C.F.R. §§ 164.502(b), 164.514(d), and 164.522.
15. HHS, HIPAA Treatment/Payment/Healthcare Operations, *supra* note 6.
16. See the definition of "payment" at HIPAA, 45 C.F.R. § 164.501.
17. HHS, HIPAA Treatment/Payment/Healthcare Operations, *supra* note 6.
18. *Id.*
19. *Id.*
20. HHS, HIPAA Treatment/Payment/Healthcare Operations, *supra* note 6.
21. *Id.*
22. HIPAA, 45 C.F.R. § 164.506.
23. *Id.*
24. *See id.* § 164.502(a)(1)(ii) and the definition of "health care operations" at § 164.501.
25. Business associates and business associate agreements are discussed in subsequent chapters.
26. HIPAA, 45 C.F.R. § 160.103.
27. *Id.*
28. HHS, HIPAA Treatment/Payment/Healthcare Operations, *supra* note 6.
29. *Id.*
30. HIPAA, 45 C.F.R. § 164.502(a)(1) (1993).
31. HHS, HIPAA Treatment/Payment/Healthcare Operations, *supra* note 6.
32. *Id.*
33. *Id.*
34. HIPAA, 45 C.F.R. § 160.103.
35. *See id.* § 164.502(a)(1).
36. HHS, HIPAA Treatment/Payment/Healthcare Operations, *supra* note 6.
37. *Id.*
38. See the definition of "business associate" at HIPAA, 45 C.F.R. § 160.103.
39. *See id.* § 164.514(e).
40. HHS, HIPAA Treatment/Payment/Healthcare Operations, *supra* note 6.
41. HIPAA, 45 C.F.R. § 164.308(b)(1).
42. *See id.* §§ 164.308(b)(1) and 164.314.

43. *Id.*
44. HIPAA Treatment/Payment/Healthcare Operations, *supra* note 6.
45. HIPAA, 45 C.F.R. § 314(a)(2)(i)(B).
46. *See id.* § 164.314(a)(2)(i)(C).
47. *See id.* § 164.306(b).
48. *Id.*
49. *See id.* § 164.306(b)(2)(iii).
50. *See id.* § 164.314(a)(2)(i)(D).
51. HHS, HIPAA Treatment/Payment/Healthcare Operations, *supra* note 6.
52. *Id.*
53. *Id.*
54. HIPAA, 45 C.F.R. § 164.504(e)(4).
55. *See id.* § 164.504(e)(2)(i)(D).
56. *See id.* § 164.512(j).
57. *Id.*
58. *See id.* § 164.512(f).
59. *See id.* § 164.512(f)(1)(i).
60. HIPAA, 45 C.F.R. § 164.512(f)(1)(i).
61. *See id.* § 164.512(f)(2)(i).
62. *See id.* § 164.512(f)(3).
63. *See id.* § 164.512(f)(4).
64. *See id.* § 164.512(f)(5).
65. *See id.* § 164.512(f)(6).
66. HIPAA, 45 C.F.R. § 164.512(f)(6).
67. *See id.* §§ 164.512(b) and 164.514(e).
68. *See id.* § 164.512(b)(1)(iii).
69. *See id.* § 164.512(b)(1)(iv).
70. *See id.* § 164.512(b)(1)(v).
71. *See id.* § 164.512(b)(2).
72. HIPAA, 45 C.F.R. § 164.512(b)(1)(ii).
73. *See id.* § 164.512(c).
74. *See id.* § 164.512(c)(1).
75. *See id.* § 164.512(c)(1)(iii).
76. *See id.* § 160.203.
77. *See id.* § 164.512(a).
78. HIPAA, 45 C.F.R. § 164.512(c).
79. *See id.* § 164.512(e).
80. *See id.* § 164.512(f).
81. *See id.* § 164.512(d).
82. *See id.* § 164.512(d).
83. *See id.* § 164.512(d)(4).
84. HIPAA, 45 C.F.R. § 164.512(d)(4).
85. *See id.* § 164.512(e).
86. *See id.* § 164.512(e)(1)(i).

87. *See id.* § 164.512(e)(ii).
88. *See id.* § 164.512(e)(1)(iii).
89. *See id.* § 164.512(e)(1)(iv).
90. HIPAA, 45 C.F.R. § 164.512(e)(1)(v).
91. *See id.* § 164.512(e)(1)(vi).
92. *See id.* § 164.510(a).
93. U.S. Department of Health and Human Services, Privacy of Health Information/HIPAA, Authorizations, *available at* http://answers.hhs.gov; accessed December 6, 2003.
94. HIPAA, 45 C.F.R. § 164.510(b).
95. *See id.* § 164.522.
96. *See id.* §§ 164.501 and 164.508(a)(3).
97. *See id.* § 164.501.
98. *See id.* § 164.508(a)(3).
99. *Id.*
100. HIPAA, 45 C.F.R. §§ 164.501, 164.514(f), and 164.522.
101. *See id.* §§ 164.512(i) and 164.514(e).
102. *See id.* § 164.512(i).
103. *Id.*
104. *See id.* § 164.512(l).
105. *See id.* §§ 164.522(a) and 164.512(a) and (l).
106. HIPAA, 45 C.F.R. § 164.514(d)(3)(iii)(A).
107. U.S. Department of Health and Human Services, Privacy of Health Information/HIPAA, Workers' Compensation Disclosures, *available at* http://answers.hhs.gov; accessed January 3, 2004.

CHAPTER 4

Administrative Requirements for Covered Entities

HIPAA mandates that covered entities engage in certain administrative functions. These functions require the covered entity to provide information to their clients regarding HIPAA as well as certain protections of PHI.

NOTICE

The covered entity must provide individuals with a written notice describing the entity's privacy practices.[1] An individual has a right to adequate notice of the uses and disclosure of PHI that the covered entity may make.[2] The individual is also entitled to know his or her rights and the covered entity's legal duties with respect to PHI.[3]

An individual enrolled in a group health plan who does not receive health benefits through an insurance contract with a health insurer or HMO is entitled to receive a notice of privacy practices from the group health plan.[4] If the individual receives health benefits under a group health plan through an HMO or health insurance insurer, the individual has a right to receive the notice of privacy practices from the health insurance issuer or HMO.[5] A group health plan that provides health benefits only through an insurance contract with a health insurance issuer or HMO and who creates or receives PHI or information about an individual participating or information about the enrollment status of the individual must maintain a notice of privacy practice and provide the notice to the individual upon request.[6]

A person who is incarcerated or otherwise confined to a correctional institution does not have a right to notice of privacy practices.[7]

The requirements for notice of privacy practices for PHI do not apply to any covered entity that is a correctional facility, jail, reformatory, detention center, work farm, halfway house, or residential community program center operated by or under contract to the United States, a state, a territory, or a political subdivision of a state or territory. Similarly, the requirements for notice of privacy practices do not apply to a facility used for the confinement or rehabilitation of a person charged with or convicted of a criminal offense or other persons held in lawful custody by an Indian tribe.[8]

Required Elements of Notice of Privacy Practices

The covered entity must provide a notice to the individual that is written in plain language and contains specific elements.[9] The following elements must be listed in the notice of privacy practices.

Header

The notice must prominently display the following header: "This notice describes how medical information about you may be used and disclosed and how you can get access to this information. Please review it carefully."[10]

Uses and Disclosures

The notice must contain a description and at least one example of each of the types of uses and disclosures that the covered entity is permitted to make for (1) treatment, (2) payment, and (3) health care operations.[11] It also must contain a description of each of the other purposes for which the covered entity is either allowed or required to use or disclose PHI without the individual's written authorization.[12] The description must include enough detail to place the individual on notice of the required or permitted uses and disclosures.[13] If a more stringent law controls disclosures that the covered entity is either required or permitted to perform, the description of that law must be included in the notice.[14]

The notice must also contain a statement that other uses and disclosures will be made by the covered entity only with the individual's written authorization.[15] Additionally, the notice must state that the individual has a right to revoke an authorization, provided that the covered entity did not rely on the authorization and that the authorization was not obtained as a condition of securing insurance coverage.[16]

Separate Statements for Specific Uses or Disclosures

The notice must include the following separate statements if the covered entity engages in any of the following activities: [17]

- The covered entity may contact the individual to provide appointment reminders or information about treatment alternatives or other health-related benefits and services that may be of interest to the individual;
- The covered entity may contact the individual to raise funds for the covered entity; or
- If the covered entity is a group health plan, or a health insurance issuer or HMO with respect to a group health plan, it may disclose PHI to the sponsor of the plan.

Rights of the Individual

The notice of privacy practices must include a statement of the individual's rights with respect to the PHI *and* a brief description of how the individual may exercise these rights.[18] The individual has the following rights under HIPAA.

The Right to Request Restrictions on Certain Uses and Disclosures of PHI

A covered entity must permit an individual to request that the covered entity restrict the following uses:[19] (1) uses or disclosures of PHI to carry out treatment, payment, or health care operations; and (2) disclosures permitted for facility directories or to family and friends for involvement in the individual's health care.

Even though the individual is allowed to request restrictions, the covered entity is not *required* to agree to a restriction.[20] If the covered entity agrees to the restriction, it may not use or disclose PHI in violation of such restriction, except under emergency situations that involve treatment to the individual.[21] If the PHI is disclosed for emergency reasons, the covered entity must request that the health care provider make no further use or disclosure of the information.[22]

A restriction agreed to by the individual and the covered entity does not prevent the covered entity from making required or permitted disclosures for investigation of the covered entity's compliance with HIPAA;[23] in emergency circumstances;[24] and for disclosures that are required by law, for public health activities, for victims of abuse, neglect or domestic violence, for health oversight activities, for judicial and administrative proceedings, for law enforcement purposes, for decedents, for averting a serious threat to health or safety, for workers' compensation, and for other activities listed under 45 C.F.R. § 164.512.[25]

Individuals do not have a right to request that a covered entity restrict a disclosure of PHI about them for workers' compensation purposes when that disclosure is required by law or authorized by, and necessary to comply with, a workers' compensation or similar law.[26]

The notice of privacy practices must include a statement that the covered entity is not required to agree to a restriction requested by an individual.[27]

The Right to Receive Confidential Communications of PHI

The *health care provider* who is a covered entity must permit the individual to request and must accommodate reasonable requests by individuals to receive communications of PHI by alternative means or at alternative locations.[28] A *health plan* that is a covered entity must permit individuals to request and must accommodate reasonable requests by individuals to receive communications of PHI from the health plan by alternative means or alternative locations, *if the individual clearly states that the disclosure of all or part of the information could endanger the individual.*[29]

In situations where a patient requested that the covered entity communicate with him or her in a confidential manner, such as by alternative means or at an alternative location, the covered entity must accommodate that request, if reasonable. For example, a request to receive mailings from the covered entity in a closed envelope rather than by postcard is a reasonable request that should be accommodated. Similarly, a request to receive mail from the covered entity at a post office box rather than at a home address or to receive calls at the office rather than at home are also reasonable requests, absent extenuating circumstances.[30]

The Right to Inspect and Copy His or Her Own PHI

The right exists as long as the covered entity keeps the PHI in the individual's record.[31] The individual does not have the right to copy or inspect (1) psychotherapy notes (notes recorded by the professional mental health care provider of the contents of conversations during counseling sessions that are separated from the rest of the individual's medical record); (2) information compiled in reasonable anticipation of, or for use in, a civil, criminal, or administrative action or proceeding; or (3) PHI maintained by a covered entity for which access by the individual is prohibited by law, such as under the Clinical Laboratory Improvements Amendments of 1988 (CLIA) (42 U.S.C. § 263a) or exempt from CLIA pursuant to 42 C.F.R. § 493.3(a)(2).[32]

The Right to Request Amendment of PHI

At the individual's request, the covered entity must amend the individual's PHI *unless* the covered entity determines that the information (1) was not created by the covered entity, (2) was not part of the individual's record, (3) would not be available for inspection (under 45 C.F.R § 164.524), or (4) the individual's PHI is already accurate and complete.[33]

The Right to Receive an Accounting of Disclosures of PHI[34]

The accounting includes any disclosures made by the covered entity in the six years prior to the date that the individual requests the accounting.[35] The accounting does not include disclosures (1) to carry out treatment, payment, and health care operations, (2) to the individual, (3) that are incidental or otherwise permitted under 45 C.F.R. § 164.502, (4) pursuant to an authorization, (5) for the facility's directory or to persons involved in the individual's care, (6) for national security or intelligence purposes, (7) to correctional institutions, and (8) that are part of a limited data set that excludes certain identifying information (under 45 C.F.R. § 164.514 (e)) for research, public health, or health care operations purposes.[36]

The Right to Receive a Paper Copy of the Notice of Privacy Practices[37]

This right extends to those individuals who agreed to receive the notice electronically via e-mail or on the covered entity's Web site. Receipt of electronic forms of the covered entity's notice of privacy practices does not waive the individual's right to receive a paper copy of the notice.[38]

Duties of the Covered Entity

The notice must also contain information regarding the duties of the covered entity. Specifically, the notice must contain the following:[39]

- A statement that the covered entity is required by law to maintain the privacy of PHI and to provide individuals with notice of its legal duties and privacy practices with respect to PHI;
- A statement that the covered entity is required to abide by the terms of the notice currently in effect; and
- A statement that the covered entity reserves the right to change the terms of its notice and to make the new notice provisions effective for all PHI that it maintains. The statement must also describe how it will provide individuals with a revised notice.

Complaints

The notice must contain a statement that individuals may complain to the covered entity and to the secretary of the U.S. Department of Health and Human Services (or any other officer or employee of HHS who has authority) if the individuals believe their privacy rights were violated.[40] The notice must also include a brief description of how the individual may file a complaint with the covered entity.[41] Lastly, the notice must contain a statement that the individual will not be retaliated against for filing a complaint.[42]

Contact Information

The notice must also contain the name, or title, and telephone number of a person or office to contact for further information.[43] The contact person must be responsible for receiving complaints and be able to provide further information about the notice of privacy practice.[44]

Effective Date

The notice must contain the date on which it is first in effect.[45] The date may not be earlier than the date on which the notice is printed or otherwise published.[46]

Optional Elements of Notice of Privacy Practices

If a covered entity chooses to limit the uses or disclosures that it is permitted to make, the covered entity may describe the more limited uses or disclosures in its notice of privacy practices.[47] However, the covered entity may not include in the notice a limitation that affects its right to make a use or disclosure that is required by law or permitted to avert a serious threat to health or safety to a person reasonably able to prevent or lessen the threat.[48]

If the covered entity intends to change the more limited uses and disclosures prior to revising the notice of privacy practices, the notice must contain a statement that it reserves the right to change the terms of its notice and to make the new notice provisions effective for all PHI that it maintains. The statement must also explain how the covered entity will provide the individuals with a revised notice.[49]

Revisions to the Notice of Privacy Practices

Whenever there is a material change to the uses or disclosures, the individual's rights, the covered entity's legal duties, or other privacy practices stated in the notice, the covered entity must promptly revise and distribute the revised version of its notice of privacy practices.[50] Except when required by law, the material change to any term contained in the notice may not be implemented before the effective date of the revised notice.[51]

Availability of the Notice of Privacy Practices

If a covered entity has a direct treatment relationship with an individual, the covered entity must provide the notice of privacy practices to the individual on the first day of service to the individual or, during an emergency situation, as soon as reasonably practicable following the emergency treatment situation.[52] The covered entity must make a good faith effort to obtain a written acknowledgment of receipt of the notice of privacy practices.[53] If it is not possible to obtain a written receipt, the covered entity must document its good faith efforts and the reason why it did not obtain the acknowledgment.[54]

If a covered entity is a health plan, it must provide its notice of privacy practices to individuals covered by the health plan on or before the compliance date deadline and thereafter at the time of enrollment of new enrollees and within sixty days of a material revision to the notice to individuals covered by the health plan at the time of the revision.[55] Every three years or more frequently, the health plan must provide notification to covered individuals (e.g., the named insured of a policy) of the availability of the notice of privacy practices and how to obtain it.[56]

If a covered entity maintains a Web site that provides information about the covered entity's customer services or benefits, it must prominently post its notice of privacy practices on the Web site and make the notice of privacy practices available electronically through the Web site.[57] The covered entity may provide the notice of privacy practices via e-mail if the individual agrees to electronic notice and the agreement has not been withdrawn.[58] However, if the covered entity knows that the e-mail transmission failed, a paper copy of the notice must be provided to the individual.[59] Additionally, if the first delivery to an individual is made electronically, the covered health care provider must supply electronic notice automatically and contemporaneously in response to the individual's first request for service from the health care provider and must make a good faith effort to obtain written acknowledgment of the receipt of the electronic notice.[60] The individual retains the right to obtain a paper copy of the notice of privacy practices.[61]

Joint Notice of Privacy Practices by Separate Covered Entities

A joint notice of privacy practices may be drafted by covered entities that participate in organized health care arrangements provided that[62]

- All the covered entities participating in the organized health care arrangement agree to abide by the notice;
- The joint notice of privacy practices meets all of the required and optional elements of the notice as previously discussed;
- The notice is altered to reflect that the notice covers more than one covered entity; and
- The notice describes with reasonable specificity the covered entities and the service delivery sites and (if applicable) states that the covered entities participating in the organized health care arrangement will share PHI with each other to carry out treatment, payment, or health care operations related to the organized health care arrangement.

The provision of the joint notice of privacy practices to an individual by any one of the covered entities included in the joint notice will satisfy the notice requirement with respect to all other covered entities included in the joint notice.[63]

Documentation of Notice

A covered entity must document its compliance with the requirements of notice of privacy practices by retaining copies of the notices issued by the covered entity and any written acknowledgments of receipt of the notice or documentation of good faith efforts to obtain such written acknowledgment.[64]

A sample of a Notice of Privacy Practices is included in Appendix E.

SAFEGUARDS

A covered entity must have appropriate administrative, technical, and physical safeguards in place to protect the privacy of PHI.[65] A covered entity must also reasonably safeguard PHI from any intentional or unintentional use or disclosure.[66] Last, a covered entity must reasonably safeguard PHI to limit incidental uses or disclosures made pursuant to an otherwise permitted or required use or disclosure.[67]

Covered entities may need to make certain adjustments to their facilities to minimize access to PHI, such as isolating and locking file cabinets or records rooms, or providing additional security (such as passwords and firewalls) on computers maintaining personal information.[68] Some safeguards may be more elaborate than others. Covered entities need to evaluate and analyze their ability to configure their record-keeping systems to allow their personnel access to only those fields needed to perform their job functions. The covered entity should be cognizant of the practical aspects of organizing its systems to allow this capacity. For example, it may not be reasonable for a small, solo practitioner who has a paper-based records system to limit access of employees with certain functions to only limited fields in a patient record, while other employees have access to the complete record. In this case, appropriate training of employees may be sufficient. Alternatively, a hospital with an electronic patient record system may reasonably implement such controls, and therefore may choose to limit access in this manner to comply with HIPAA.[69]

HIPAA does not prevent covered entities from practicing ordinary and essential health care procedures, nor does it provide the specific actions that must be used in order to protect an individual's privacy. Covered entities must implement reasonable safeguards to protect an individual's privacy.[70] In addition, covered entities must reasonably restrict how much information is used and disclosed, as well as who within the entity has access to PHI.[71] Covered entities must consider what measures make sense in their environment and tailor their practices and safeguards to their particular circumstances.[72]

Covered entities must apply reasonable safeguards to limit incidental and avoid prohibited uses and disclosures. HIPAA does not require that covered entities eliminate all risk of disclosing PHI. Covered entities must evaluate their own practices and determine what actions are reasonable to safeguard their patient information. Covered entities should examine potential risks to patient privacy, as well as bear in mind such issues as the potential effects on patient care and any administrative or financial burden to be incurred from implementing particular safeguards. Covered entities also may take into consideration the steps that other prudent health care and health information professionals take to protect patient privacy.[73]

The Department of Health and Human Services advises that HIPAA does not prohibit covered entities from engaging in the following practices, where reasonable precautions have been taken to protect an individual's privacy:

- Maintaining patient charts at bedside or outside of exam rooms, displaying patient names on the outside of patient charts, or displaying patient care signs (e.g., "high fall risk" or "diabetic diet") at patient bedside or at the doors of hospital rooms. However, the covered entity should implement certain safeguards, including reasonably limiting access to these areas, ensuring that the area is supervised, escorting nonemployees in the area, or placing patient charts in their holders with identifying information facing the wall or otherwise covered, rather than have health information about the patient visible to anyone who walks by.
- Announcing patient names and other information over a facility's public announcement system. Possible safeguards include limiting the information disclosed over the system, such as referring the patients to a reception desk where they can receive further instructions in a more confidential manner.
- Using X-ray lightboards or in-patient logs, such as whiteboards, at a nursing station. Possible safeguards include placing the X-ray lightboard in an area generally not accessible to the public, or placing the nursing station whiteboard in an area that is not readily visible to the public, or any other safeguard that reasonably limits incidental disclosures to the general public.

Other safeguards could include the following:

- Pharmacies could ask waiting customers to stand a few feet back from a counter used for patient counseling.
- In an area where multiple patient-staff communications routinely occur, use of cubicles, dividers, shields, curtains, or similar barriers may constitute a reasonable safeguard. For example, a large clinic intake area may reasonably use cubicles or shield-type dividers, rather than separate rooms, or providers could add curtains or screens to areas where discussions often occur between doctors and patients or among professionals treating the patient.

- Hospitals could ensure that areas housing patient files are supervised or locked.

The above examples are not the only applicable methods of safeguarding PHI. Covered entities may use any method that reasonably safeguards PHI to limit incidental uses and disclosures.[74] However, HIPAA does *not* require the following types of structural or systems changes:[75]

- Private rooms
- Soundproof rooms
- Encryption of wireless or other emergency medical radio communications that can be intercepted by scanners
- Encryption of telephone systems

HIPAA clearly permits certain incidental disclosures that occur as a by-product of an otherwise permitted disclosure.[76] Some examples of incidental disclosure include (1) calling the first name of a patient in a covered entity's waiting room when other patients are present; (2) posting patient names on the wall outside of the patients' hospital rooms if the use or disclosure is for treatment (for example, to ensure that patient care is provided to the correct individual) or health care operations purposes (for example, as a service for patients and their families); and (3) using a sign-in sheet at the doctor's office as long as it does not display medical information that is not necessary for the purpose of signing in (e.g., the medical problem for which the patient is seeing the physician).[77]

HIPAA permits incidental disclosures only to the extent that the covered entity applied reasonable and appropriate safeguards and implemented the minimum necessary standard, where appropriate.[78] In the examples listed in the previous paragraph, the disclosure of names is the minimum necessary for the purposes of the permitted uses or disclosures described above, and there does not appear to be additional safeguards that would be reasonable to take in these circumstances. However, each covered entity must evaluate what measures are reasonable and appropriate in its environment. Covered entities may customize reasonable measures to their particular circumstances.[79]

HIPAA allows health care providers to communicate with patients regarding their health care. This includes communicating with patients at their homes, whether through the mail or by phone or in some other manner. Additionally, HIPAA does not prohibit covered entities from leaving messages for patients on their answering machines. However, in order to fulfill their obligation to reasonably safeguard the individual's privacy, covered entities should limit the amount of information disclosed on the patient's answering machine to promote discrete communication. For example, a covered entity may need to leave no more than its name, number, and other information necessary to confirm an appointment or ask the individual to call back.[80]

A covered entity also may leave a message with a family member or other person who answers the phone when the patient is not home. As discussed previously, HIPAA allows covered entities to disclose limited information to family members, friends, or other persons regarding an individual's care when the individual is not present.[81] However, covered entities should use professional judgment to ensure that such disclosures are in the best interest of the individual and limit the information disclosed in order to provide reasonably confidential communications.[82]

POLICIES AND PROCEDURES

A covered entity must implement policies and procedures with respect to PHI that are designed to comply with the privacy rule.[83] The policies and procedures must be reasonably designed in order to ensure compliance, taking into account the size and type of activities that relate to the PHI controlled by the covered entity.[84] The covered entity must revise its policies and procedures when needed to comply with the changes in the law.[85] The changes must be documented prior to being implemented.[86]

The covered entity must provide a method for individuals to file complaints concerning the covered entity's policies and procedures.[87] The covered entity must document all complaints it receives and what steps, if any, it took to respond to the complaints.[88]

A covered entity must have and apply appropriate sanctions against members of its workforce who fail to comply with the privacy policies and procedures.[89] There are three exceptions. First, this requirement does not apply to whistleblowing: that is, the disclosure of PHI to a health oversight agency or public health authority by workforce members who believe in good faith that the covered entity is engaging in conduct that is unlawful or otherwise violates professional or clinical standards, or that the covered entity's care, services, or conditions potentially endanger one or more patients, workers, or the public.[90]

Second, sanctions also do not apply to disclosures made by members of the covered entity's workforce who are victims of a crime, provided that the disclosures were made to a law enforcement official; that the PHI disclosed is about the suspected perpetrator of the criminal act; and that the PHI disclosed is limited to the name, address, date and place of birth, Social Security number, blood type and Rh factor, type of injury, date and time of treatment, date and time of death, and a description of distinguishing physical characteristics, including weight, height, gender, race, hair and eye color, facial hair, scars, and tattoos.[91]

Third, the covered entity cannot sanction a workforce member who files a complaint with the secretary of HHS or testifies, assists, or participates in an investigation, compliance review, proceeding, or hearing.[92]

The covered entity must document any sanctions it applies to its workforce members.[93]

TRAINING

A covered entity must train all members of its workforce on the policies and procedures with respect to PHI that are necessary and appropriate for the members of the workforce to carry out their function within the covered entity.[94] HIPAA requires that the covered entity document the training it provides to its workforce.[95] The training requirement may be satisfied by a small physician practice's providing each new member of the workforce with a copy of its privacy policies and documenting that new members have reviewed the policies, whereas a large health plan may provide training through live instruction, video presentations, or interactive software programs.[96]

The covered entity must provide the training to each member of the covered entity's workforce no later than the compliance date for the covered entity.[97] Each new member of the workforce must be trained within a reasonable period of time after the person joins the covered entity's workforce.[98] HIPAA does not define "reasonable time" for purposes of training new personnel. Arguably, a "reasonable time" may be the same time frame that the new staff member is trained for the functions of his or her primary role in the covered entity's workforce.

If there is a material change in the policies or procedures of the functions of a member of the covered entity's workforce, the covered entity must train the workforce member within a reasonable time after the material change becomes effective.[99] Again, the rule does not specify what a "reasonable time" is for purposes of training members of the covered entity's workforce of revised policies or procedures. However, common sense dictates that the workforce member should be trained on or before the covered entity implements the material change.

PRIVACY OFFICIAL

A covered entity must designate a privacy official (also known as the privacy officer) who is responsible for the development and implementation of the policies and procedures of the entity.[100] Every covered entity must also designate a contact person or official who is responsible for receiving complaints and who is able to provide further information about the covered entity's notice of privacy practice.[101] The privacy official may be the same person as the contact person. HIPAA does not require that these functions serve as the only designated role of the person. For instance, in a small covered entity, the business manager may also be the privacy official as well as the contact person for complaints and information about the notice of privacy practices.

ACCOUNTING

The covered entity must keep an accounting of the disclosures of PHI. An individual has the right to receive an accounting of disclosures made anytime within six years prior to the individual's request.[102]

Exceptions

The covered entity does not need to account for disclosures

- To carry out treatment, payment or health care operations[103]
- To individuals of PHI about themselves[104]
- That are incidental, permitted, or required[105]
- That are made pursuant to an authorization[106]
- For the facility's directory or to persons involved in the individual's care or other notification purposes[107]
- For national security or intelligence purposes[108]
- To correctional institutions or law enforcement officials[109]
- That are made as part of a limited data set[110]

- That occurred prior to the compliance date for the covered entity[111]

The individual's right to receive an accounting "shall be" suspended by the covered entity when the disclosure is made to a health oversight agency or law enforcement official and the agency or official provides the covered entity with a written statement that such an accounting to the individual is reasonably likely to impede the agency's activities.[112] The agency must specify the time for which such a suspension is required.[113] The agency or official may give an oral statement, as long as the covered entity documents the statement (including the identity of the agency or official making the statement); temporarily suspends the individual's rights to an accounting of the disclosures subject to the statement; and limits the suspension to no longer than thirty days from the date of the oral statement (unless the agency submits a written statement during that time).[114]

Contents of the Accounting

The accounting must include disclosures of PHI that occurred during the six years (or shorter period per the request of the individual) prior to the date of the request for an accounting, including disclosures to or by business associates of the covered entity.[115]

The accounting must include

- The date of the disclosure
- The name of the entity or person who received the PHI and, if known, the address of such entity or person
- A brief description of the PHI disclosed
- A brief statement of the purpose of the disclosure that reasonably informs the individual of the basis for the disclosure or, in lieu of such statement, a copy of a written request for disclosure[116]

If the covered entity made multiple disclosures of PHI to the same person or entity for a single purpose, the accounting may provide all of the information required for the first disclosure *plus* the number or frequency of the disclosures made during the accounting period (e.g., seven total disclosures; a disclosure every two weeks) and the date of the last such disclosure.[117]

Accounting of Disclosures for Research

If the covered entity made disclosures of PHI for research purposes for fifty or more individuals, the accounting *may* provide

- The name of the protocol or other research activity
- A description, in plain language, of the research protocol or other research activity, including the purpose of the research and the criteria for selecting particular records
- A brief description of the type of PHI disclosed
- The date or period of time during which such disclosures occurred, or may have occurred, including the date of the last such disclosure during the accounting period
- The name, address, and telephone number of the entity that sponsored the research and of the researcher to whom the information was disclosed
- A statement that the PHI of the individual may or may not have been disclosed for a particular protocol or other research activity[118]

At the request of the individual, the covered entity shall assist in contacting the entity that sponsored the research and the researcher if the accounting provides the above stated particulars of disclosures for research purposes and if it is reasonably likely that the covered entity disclosed the individual's PHI for research purposes.[119]

Time to Respond to Request for Accounting

The covered entity must provide the individual with the accounting within sixty days after the covered entity receives the individual's request for an accounting.[120] If the covered entity is unable to provide the accounting within sixty days, it may extend the time to provide the accounting by no more than thirty days as long as it provides the individual with a written statement of the reasons for the delay and the date by which the covered entity will provide the accounting.[121] The covered entity may be granted only one such extension of time per request.[122]

Fees

The covered entity must supply the first accounting to the individual free of charge in any twelve-month period.[123] Thereafter, the covered entity may charge a reasonable, cost-based fee for each subsequent request for an accounting by the same individual within the twelve month period.[124] However, the covered entity must inform the individual in advance of the fee and provide the individual with an opportunity to withdraw or modify the request for the subsequent accounting in order to avoid or reduce the fee.[125]

Documentation of the Accounting

A covered entity must document and keep records of the following: (1) the information in the accounting, (2) the written accounting provided to the individual, and (3) the titles of the persons or offices responsible for receiving and processing requests for an accounting by individuals.[126] The records must be kept for six years from the date of its creation or the date when it was last in effect, whichever is later.[127]

Other Areas of Concern

Public Health Department

Under the Privacy Rule, making a set of records available for review by a third party constitutes a "disclosure" of the PHI in the entire set of records, regardless of whether the third party actually reviews any particular record.[128] By definition, mere access by a third party, such as a public health authority, to PHI is a disclosure and subject to an accounting for disclosures.

Public health departments commonly monitor certain public health concerns using a retrospective review by the public health authority of a collection of patient records to identify reportable events. When the public health authority identifies a reportable case, specific PHI pertinent to the monitoring activity is obtained and reported to the public health authority.[129] For example, "retrospective review of the medical charts for all patients treated by a health care provider or all charts of patients treated in the entity's emergency department may be required to identify cases of new or previously unknown infectious agents, clinical conditions associated with the use or abuse of illicit or prescription drugs, or adverse events or reactions associated with pharmaceuticals or medical devices."[130]

By definition, all records in the above example are deemed to have been disclosed under the Privacy Rule. The covered entity must keep an accounting but because of the universal nature of the access provided, the covered entity need document only the identity (and address if known) of the public health authority to which access was provided, a description of the records and PHI subject to access, the purpose for the disclosure, and when access was provided.[131] The covered entity need not note the disclosure in each record.[132] It is satisfactory for the covered entity to maintain a separate notation of such disclosures that is applicable to all records that were so accessed.[133] If an individual requests an accounting, the covered entity need determine only whether the individual's records were among the set of records to which the public health authority was granted access.[134] All individuals whose records were accessed in this fashion would receive the same accounting for the disclosure.[135]

For example, on August 1, 2003, a hospital began providing a public health authority ongoing access to the medical charts of all patients treated in its emergency department to identify reportable cases and extract relevant information required for a particular surveillance activity. It would be satisfactory, under 45 C.F.R. § 164.528(b)(2), for the accounting to include the following:

- The identity, and address, if known, of the public health authority
- A statement that the public health authority had access to medical charts for patients treated in the emergency department
- The date (or approximate range of dates) when the individual's record was subject to access (e.g., access provided within a week of treatment in the emergency room on [fill in date of individual visit])
- A statement of the purpose of the access (that is, identify the particular public health surveillance activity)

The same basic statement could then be provided in response to a request for an accounting by any individual who was seen in the emergency department of the hospital on or after August 1, 2003.[136]

Unknown Date of Service

As previously mentioned, accounting for disclosures requires an individual to be informed of the date the disclosure was made[137]

> If access to a universe of records was provided for a discrete period of time, OCR [Office for Civil Rights] interprets this provision to permit the accounting to include the range of dates (e.g., access was provided from August 1 to August 3, 2003; or during the week of August 10,

2003). If the disclosure is routinely made within a set period from an event, OCR, likewise, interprets this provision to permit the accounting to provide the date of the event and the normal interval (e.g., gun shot wound reported within 48 hours of treatment and provide date of treatment; hospital discharges reported on 15th of the following month and provide date of discharge; or access provided to public health authorities within 30 days of treatment in emergency department and provide the date of treatment).[138]

Business Associates

HIPAA regulates covered entities, not business associates.[139] The Privacy Rule requires covered entities to include specific provisions in agreements with business associates to safeguard PHI, and addresses how covered entities may share this information with business associates.[140] Covered entities have a duty to fulfill HIPAA requirements with respect to individual rights, including the rights of access, amendment, and accounting, as provided for by 45 C.F.R. §§ 164.524, 164.526, and 164.528. With a few exceptions, HIPAA mandates a covered entity to provide an individual access to his or her PHI in a designated record set.[141] This includes information in a designated record set of a business associate, unless the information held by the business associate merely duplicates the information maintained by the covered entity. Therefore, the Privacy Rule requires covered entities to specify in the business associate contract that the business associate must make such PHI available if and when needed by the covered entity to provide an individual with access to the information.

However, HIPAA does not prevent the parties from agreeing through the business associate contract that the business associate will provide access to individuals, as may be appropriate where the business associate is the only holder of the designated record set or part thereof.

If a request for an amendment is granted, a covered entity must amend PHI about an individual in a designated record set, including any designated record sets (or copies thereof) held by a business associate.[142] Therefore, the Privacy Rule requires covered entities to specify in the business associate contract that the business associate must amend PHI in such records (or copies) when requested by the covered entity. The covered entity itself is responsible for addressing requests from individuals for amendment and coordinating such requests with its business associate. However, HIPAA also does not prevent the parties from agreeing through the contract that the business associate will receive and address requests for amendment on behalf of the covered entity.

HIPAA requires a covered entity to provide an accounting of certain disclosures, including certain disclosures by its business associate, to the individual upon request.[143] The business associate contract must provide that the business associate will make such information available to the covered entity in order for the covered entity to fulfill its obligation to the individual. As with access and amendment, the parties can agree through the business associate contract that the business associate will provide the accounting to individuals, as may be appropriate given the PHI held by, and the functions of, the business associate.[144]

NOTES

1. Health Insurance Portability and Accountability Act of 1996 (HIPAA), 45 C.F.R. § 164.500 and § 164.520 (2003).
2. *See id.* § 164.520.
3. *Id.*
4. *See id.* § 164.520(a)(2).
5. *Id.*
6. *Id.*
7. HIPAA, 45 C.F.R. § 164.520(a)(3).
8. *See id.* §§ 164.500 and 164.520.
9. *See id.* § 164.520(b).
10. *See id.* § 164.520(b)(1)(i).
11. *See id.* § 164.520(b)(1)(ii).
12. *Id.*
13. HIPAA, 45 C.F.R. § 164.520(b)(1)(ii).
14. *Id.*
15. *See id.* § 164.520(b)(1)(ii).
16. *See id.* § 164.520(b)(1)(ii) and § 164.508(b)(5).
17. *See id.* § 164.520(b)(1)(iii).
18. *See id.* § 164.520(b)(1)(iv).
19. HIPAA, 45 C.F.R. § 164.522(a)(1).
20. *Id.*
21. *Id.*
22. *Id.*
23. *See id.* § 164.502(a)(2)(ii).
24. *See id.* § 164.510(a).
25. HIPAA, 45 C.F.R. § 164.522(a)(1)(v).
26. *See id.* §§ 164.522(a) and 164.512(a) and (l).
27. *See id.* § 164.520(b)(1)(iv)(A).
28. *See id.* § 164.522(b).
29. *See id.* § 164.522(b)(1)(ii).

30. 45 C.F.R. 164.522(b) and U.S. Department of Health and Human Services (HHS), Privacy of Health Information/HIPAA, Safeguards, http://answers.hhs.gov; accessed Jan. 2, 2004 [hereinafter HHS, HIPAA Safeguards].
31. HIPAA, 45 C.F.R. § 164.524.
32. *See id.* § 164.524.
33. *See id.* § 164.526(a)(2).
34. *See id.* § 164.528.
35. *Id.*
36. *See id.* § 164.514 (e) and § 164.520(b)(1)(iv)(E).
37. HIPAA, 45 C.F.R. § 164.520(b)(1)(iv)(F).
38. *See id.* § 164.520(c)(3).
39. *See id.* § 164.520(b)(1)(v).
40. *See id.* § 164.520(b)(1)(vi).
41. *Id.*
42. *Id.*
43. HIPAA, 45 C.F.R. § 164.520(b)(1)(vii).
44. *See id.* § 164.530(a)(1)(ii).
45. *See id.* § 164.520(b)(1)(viii).
46. *Id.*
47. *See id.* § 164.520(b)(2).
48. *Id.*
49. HIPAA, 45 C.F.R. § 164.520(b)(2).
50. *See id.* § 164.520(b)(3).
51. *Id.*
52. *See id.* § 164.520(c)(2).
53. *Id.*
54. *See id.* § 164.520(c)(2)(ii).
55. HIPAA, 45 C.F.R. § 164.520(c)(1).
56. *Id.*
57. *See id.* § 164.520(c)(3).
58. *Id.*
59. *Id.*
60. *Id.*
61. HIPAA, 45 C.F.R. § 164.520(c)(3).
62. *See id.* § 164.520(d).
63. *Id.*
64. *See id.* § 164.520(e).
65. *See id.* § 164.530(c)(1).
66. *See id.* § 164.530(c)(2).
67. HIPAA, 45 C.F.R. § 164.530(c)(2).
68. HHS, HIPAA Safeguards, *supra* note 30.
69. *Id.*
70. HIPAA, 45 C.F.R. § 164.530(c)(2)(i).
71. *See id.* §§ 164.502(b) and 164.514(d).

72. HHS, HIPAA Safeguards, *supra* note 30.
73. *Id.*
74. *Id.*
75. *Id.*
76. HIPAA, 45 C.F.R. § 164.502(a).
77. *See id.* § 164.502(a)(1)(iii).
78. *Id.*
79. HHS, HIPAA Safeguards, *supra* note 30.
80. *Id.*
81. HIPAA, 45 C.F.R. § 164.522(b).
82. *See id.* § 164.510(b)(3).
83. *See id.* § 164.530(i).
84. *Id.*
85. *Id.*
86. *Id.*
87. HIPAA, 45 C.F.R. § 164.530(d)(1).
88. *Id.*
89. *See id.* § 164.530(e).
90. *See id.* § 164.502(j).
91. *Id.*
92. *See id.* § 164.530(g)(2).
93. HIPAA, 45 C.F.R. § 164.530(e)(2).
94. *See id.* § 164.530(b).
95. *Id.*
96. U.S. Department of Health and Human Services, Privacy of Health Information/HIPAA, All Sub-Categories, *available at* http://answers.hhs.gov; accessed Jan. 3, 2004 [hereinafter HHS, HIPAA (All Sub-Categories)].
97. HIPAA, 45 C.F.R. § 164.530(b)(2).
98. *Id.*
99. *Id.*
100. *See id.* § 164.530(a).
101. *Id.*
102. *Id.*
103. HIPAA, 45 C.F.R. § 164.506.
104. *See id.* § 164.502.
105. *Id.*
106. *See id.* § 164.508.
107. *See id.* § 164.510.
108. *See id.* § 164.512(k)(2).
109. HIPAA, 45 C.F.R. § 164.512(k)(5).
110. *See id.* § 164.514(e).
111. *See id.* § 164.528(a)(1).
112. *See id.* §§ 164.512(d), 164.512(f), and 164.528(a)(2)(i).
113. *See id.* § 164.528(a)(2)(i).

114. *See id.* § 164.528(a)(2)(ii).
115. HIPAA, 45 C.F.R. § 164.528(b).
116. *Id.*
117. *See id.* § 164.528(b)(3).
118. *See id.* § 164.528(b)(4)(i).
119. *See id.* § 164.528(b)(4)(ii).
120. *See id.* § 164.528(c)(1).
121. HIPAA, 45 C.F.R. § 164.528(c)(1).
122. *Id.*
123. *See id.* § 164.528(c)(2).
124. *Id.*
125. *Id.*
126. *Id.*
127. HIPAA, 45 C.F.R. § 164.530(j).
128. *See id.* and definition of "Disclosures" under 45 C.F.R. § 164.501.
129. HHS, HIPAA (All Sub-Categories), *supra* note 96.
130. *Id.*
131. *Id.*
132. *Id.*
133. HHS, HIPAA (All Sub-Categories), *supra* note 96.
134. *Id.*
135. *Id.*
136. *Id.*
137. HIPAA, 45 C.F.R. § 164.528(b)(2).
138. HHS, HIPAA (All Sub-Categories), *supra* note 96.
139. HIPAA, 45 C.F.R. § 160.102.
140. *See id.* §§ 164.502(e) and 164.504(e).
141. *See id.* § 164.524.
142. *See id.* § 164.526.
143. *See id.* § 164.528.
144. HHS, HIPAA (All Sub-Categories), *supra* note 96.

CHAPTER 5

Penalties and Enforcement

Whenever possible, the government will work cooperatively with covered entities to achieve compliance with the Health Insurance Portability and Accountability Act of 1996 (HIPAA).[1] The secretary of the U.S. Department of Health and Human Services (HHS) may even provide technical assistance to covered entities to help them comply voluntarily with the requirements.[2] If an individual believes that his or her rights or someone else's rights under HIPAA were violated, the individual may file a complaint with the Office for Civil Rights (OCR) at the HHS regional office that covers the state where the alleged violation took place.[3] A list of regional offices may be found on the OCR Web site at http://www.hhs.gov/ocr/hipaa or at the end of this chapter. Any person who believes that a covered entity is not complying with the requirements under the HIPAA Privacy Rule has standing to file a complaint.[4] A complaint may be filed by an individual, a patient, a relative, a friend, an office staff member, a physician, an allied health professional, or any person who believes that someone's medical privacy rights under HIPAA were violated.

ENFORCEMENT

The OCR has the authority to receive and investigate complaints based on violations of the HIPAA Privacy Rule. The secretary of HHS delegated the authority to the OCR.[5] A person who believes a covered entity violated a requirement of the rule may file a written complaint with the OCR, either on paper or electronically. The complaint must be filed within 180 days of when the complainant knew or should have known that the act occurred. HHS may waive this 180-day time limit if good cause is shown by the complainant.[6] The Office for Civil Rights provides further information about how to file a complaint on its Web site at http://www.hhs.gov/ocr/hipaa.

Additionally, individuals have a right to file a complaint directly with the covered entity. Individuals should refer to the particular covered entity's notice of privacy practices for more information about how to file a complaint with the covered entity.

Requirements for Filing a Complaint to OCR

A complaint with OCR filed by an individual must meet certain criteria.[7] First, the complaint must be filed in writing, either on paper or electronically. Second, the complaint must name the entity that is the subject of the complaint and describe the acts or omissions that are believed to be in violation of the applicable requirements of the privacy rule. Third, the complaint must be filed within 180 days of when the complainant knew or should have known that the act or omission complained of occurred (unless HHS waives this time limit for good cause). The secretary of HHS may develop additional procedures for filing complaints and the place and manner of filing. If there are changes, they would be published in the *Federal Register.*

The complaint can be submitted in any written format. However, the OCR has a complaint form, which it encourages complainants to use, that may be downloaded from its Web site at http://www.hhs.gov/ocr/hipaa. An individual may also obtain an OCR complaint form at any regional office. If the individual does not utilize the OCR form, he or she must provide the following information in the complaint:

- The complainant's name, full address, home and work telephone numbers, and e-mail address
- If the complaint is being filed on someone else's behalf, the name of the person on whose behalf the complaint is being filed
- The name, full address, and phone number of the person, agency or organization that allegedly violated the health information privacy rights
- A description of what happened (i.e., how, why, and when the privacy rights were allegedly violated)
- Any other relevant information

The complainant must sign and date the letter. The following information is optional: (1) what, if any, special accommodations the complainant needs in order to communicate with OCR about the complaint;

(2) the name of an alternate person to contact in the event that OCR cannot reach the complainant; and (3) whether the complainant filed a complaint somewhere else and where the prior complaint was filed.

Compliance Reviews and Investigations

The Office for Civil Rights may conduct compliance reviews to determine whether covered entities comply with the requirements under the HIPAA Privacy Rule.[8] A covered entity has certain responsibilities to the OCR during a compliance review or complaint investigation.[9] First, the covered entity must provide records and compliance reports to the OCR in a timely fashion to allow the OCR to determine whether the covered entity is complying or complied with the privacy rule.[10] Second, the covered entity must cooperate with the OCR during compliance reviews and investigations.[11] Third, the covered entity must allow the OCR access to information.[12] The OCR may gain access to the covered entity's facilities, books, records, accounts, and other sources of information, including PHI, relevant to determining compliance with the HIPAA privacy rule.[13] If the OCR determines that special circumstances exist (e.g., suspicions that documents may be hidden or destroyed), a covered entity must give the OCR access at any time and without notice.[14] Additionally, if any information is in the exclusive possession of any other agency, institution, or person, and that agency, institution, or person fails or refuses to furnish the information, the covered entity must so certify and explain the efforts it made to obtain the information.[15]

Any PHI obtained by the OCR in connection with an investigation or compliance review will not be disclosed by the agency, except where necessary to enforce compliance with the Privacy Rule or if otherwise required by law.[16] The secretary of HHS will notify the covered entity of the outcome of the compliance review or complaint investigation.[17]

Resolution by the Office for Civil Rights

Whenever possible, the OCR will seek to resolve matters by informal means before issuing findings of noncompliance to the covered entity.[18] If an investigation or compliance review demonstrates that the covered entity is noncompliant with the Privacy Rule, and the secretary of HHS determines that the matter cannot be resolved by informal means, the secretary may issue written findings to the covered entity as well as to the complainant, documenting the noncompliance.[19] Conversely, after a complaint investigation or a compliance review, if it is determined that further action is not warranted, the secretary of HHS will notify the covered entity and the complainant accordingly in writing.[20]

CIVIL PENALTIES

If the OCR finds that the covered entity violated the requirements under the HIPAA Privacy Rule, the OCR may impose civil penalties.[21]

Monetary Fines

Civil monetary fines may be imposed by OCR in the amount of $100 per violation up to $25,000 for each calendar year for each identical requirement or prohibition that is violated.[22] The covered entity has a right to a notice and hearing before the civil monetary penalty becomes final.

There are a number of substantive limitations on the OCR's authority to impose civil monetary penalties.[23] First, a civil monetary penalty may not be imposed with respect to an act that "constitutes an offense punishable" under the criminal penalty provision.[24] Second, a civil monetary penalty may not be imposed "if it is established to the satisfaction of the Secretary that the person liable for the penalty did not know, and by exercising reasonable diligence would not have known, that such person violated the provision."[25] Third, a civil monetary penalty may not be imposed if the failure to comply was due "to reasonable cause and not to willful neglect" and is corrected within a certain time.[26] Finally, a civil monetary penalty may be reduced, if not waived entirely, "to the extent that the payment of such penalty would be excessive relative to the compliance failure involved."[27]

Procedural Limitations

There are a number of procedural requirements that limit the OCR's ability to impose civil penalties.[28] The OCR may not initiate an action for a civil monetary penalty later than six years after the date of the occurrence that forms the basis for the civil monetary penalty. The OCR may initiate a civil monetary action by serving notice "in any manner authorized by Rule 4 of the Federal Rules of Civil Procedure."[29] Rule 4 allows the commencement of an action via a summons and complaint.[30]

A person upon whom the OCR seeks to impose civil monetary penalties must be given written notice and allowed an opportunity for a determination to be made "on the record after a hearing at which the person is entitled to be represented by counsel, to present witnesses, and to cross-examine witnesses against the person."[31] The hearing officer may impose sanctions for misconduct in connection with the civil monetary proceeding, judicial review of the OCR's determination in the United States Court of Appeals for the circuit in which the person resides, and the issuance of subpoenas by HHS and the enforcement of those subpoenas.[32]

Fines Apply to the Covered Entity

Only covered entities are subject to penalties. There is no provision for civil penalties for persons, organizations, companies, or other entities that are not covered entities. Therefore, although business associates may be contractually bound to the covered entity via the business associate agreement, those business associates who are not covered entities are not subject to civil penalties.[33]

CRIMINAL PENALTIES

The OCR refers potential criminal violations of the law to the U.S. Department of Justice for further investigation and appropriate action.[34] Criminal penalties are imposed for certain wrongful disclosures of health information. The Department of Justice has the authority to enforce criminal penalties. The criminal penalties are graduated and reflect the seriousness of the infraction.

Knowingly Obtaining or Disclosing

The minimum criminal penalty is imposed where the covered entity knowingly obtained or disclosed PHI. Under those circumstances, the covered entity is subject to a fine of $50,000 and one year in prison.

False Pretenses

Where the covered entity obtained or disclosed PHI under false pretenses, it is subject to a fine of $100,000 and five years in prison.

Intent to Sell or Use for Personal Gain or Harm

For the most severe violations, where a covered entity obtained or disclosed PHI with the intent to sell, transfer, or use PHI for commercial advantage, personal gain, or malicious harm, the covered entity is subject to fines of up to $250,000 and ten years in prison.[35]

Business Associates and Others

The Department of Justice may seek to prosecute business associates and other individuals for HIPAA violations. In the Second Circuit case of *U.S. v. Lucien*,[36] the court held that the health care fraud statute, 18 U.S.C. § 1347, authorizes the Department of Justice to prosecute any individual, not just health care providers, for health care fraud. In the *Lucien* case, three individuals were found guilty for defrauding their auto insurers by staging motor vehicle collisions. Defendants argued that the health care fraud statute applies only to health care professionals. They also argued that the auto insurers that received the fraudulent claims were not "health care benefit programs" within the meaning of the statute. The court rejected both arguments.

First, the court stated that the language of the fraud provision itself (18 U.S.C. § 1347), which authorizes the prosecution of "whoever" carries out a scheme to "defraud any health care benefit program," encompasses individuals beyond the scope of just medical professionals. Second, the court found that the health care fraud statute defines the term "health care benefit program" as "any public or private *plan or contract* . . . under which *any medical benefit*, item or service is provided to any individual."[37] Since the defendants "received a medical benefit as a result of the vehicle owners' no-fault insurance contracts, a health care benefit program is . . . plainly implicated." The court recognized that its holding "authorizes the application of the federal health care fraud statute to circumstances that are atypical of the health care fraud case law, which to date has concerned itself more exclusively with conduct within the medical community."[38] It is clear that the Department of Justice may prosecute covered entities as well as business associates and individuals for HIPAA violations.

CASE LAW

In re PPA Litigation; New Jersey

On September 23, 2003, the Superior Court of New Jersey released its decision that "HIPAA is an express but selective preemption of New Jersey law"[39] that does not conflict with New Jersey law and the informal discovery techniques permitted under *Stempler v. Speidell*.[40] *Stempler* allows ex parte interviews of physicians who are involved in the health care of injured plaintiffs.[41] Prior to HIPAA, the New Jersey Supreme Court allowed the defense counsel to conduct ex parte interviews with plaintiffs' treating physicians, reasoning that by virtue of filing a suit for personal injury, the plaintiff placed his or her medical condition at issue and consequently waived some of his or her privacy privilege.[42] The *Stempler* court found that the time and costs incurred during trial preparation gave good reason for personal interviews as an informal method of obtaining facts and documents prior to trial. After *Stempler,* defendants routinely conducted informal personal interviews of physicians outside of the presence of plaintiff's counsel. However, prior to the interview the defendants must (1) provide the plaintiff's counsel with reasonable notice of the time and place of the proposed interview; (2) provide the physician with a description of the anticipated scope of the interview; and (3) communicate with unmistakable clarity the fact that the physician's participation in an ex parte interview is voluntary.

HIPAA's requirement for authorization by the patient of release of PHI appeared to conflict with *Stempler.* However, the New Jersey court adamantly stated that HIPAA does not preempt the informal discovery techniques allowed under *Stempler,* citing a "strong federal policy against federal court intervention against pending state judicial proceedings absent extraordinary circumstances."[43] "Because informal discovery is not expressly addressed under HIPAA, the courts should be governed by state law or as in the case of New Jersey as set forth by our Supreme Court."[44] The court reasoned that "because the disclosure is limited in scope, the *Stempler* interviews do not conflict with the general principles of HIPAA."[45] Therefore, ex parte interviews as part of informal discovery may proceed as permitted under New Jersey law.

Campos v. Payne; New York

In *Campos v. Payne,*[46] the New York court declined to sign a judicial subpoena *duces tecum* submitted by the defendants for the purpose of obtaining production of "all medical records relating to plaintiff's medical treatment" at Staten Island University Hospital pertaining to a certain automobile accident. The court based its decision on HIPAA as well as the recently enacted New York state law[47] that requires "any subpoena served upon a medical provider requesting the medical records of a patient shall state in conspicuous bold-faced type that the records shall not be provided unless the subpoena is accompanied by a written authorization by the patient."[48]

The court determined that even though the New York law is directed primarily to the discovery phase of litigation, the same safeguards must be continued through the trial stage. The court held that it cannot "so order" a subpoena for medical records without the authorization of the party whose records are sought. The court was careful to clarify that production of the records can be accomplished by complying with state law[49] or by bringing a motion on notice to all parties.

> Recent amendments to CPLR 3122(a) affect discovery of protected health information in the context of a subpoena duces tecum served upon a health care provider (CPLR 3122[a] as amended by L 2002, ch. 575, § 3, eff. 9/1/03). The amendments require, first, that any subpoena seeking the disclosure of medical information be accompanied by an authorization executed by the patient. Second, the subpoena itself must set forth in conspicuous boldfaced type that if it is not accompanied by the required authorization, it must be disregarded by the health care provider. Third, the statute implies that there is an affirmative obligation on the provider to refuse to provide the information if the requirements of the statute are not met. The Courts have also required that the authorization accompanying the subpoena comply with the federal Health Insurance Portability and Accountability Act (known as "HIPAA") and the regulations promulgated thereunder by the United States Secretary of Health and Human Services.[50]

Lemieux v. Tandem Health Care of Florida, Inc.; Florida

In a Florida case,[51] the defendant sought to have ex parte discussions of the plaintiff's preexisting medical conditions and medical conditions that arose prior to, during, and subsequent to plaintiff's treatment at the defendant's medical facility.

The appellate state court denied defendant's request for ex parte discussions with the plaintiff's treating physicians. The court reasoned that substantive provisions of Florida state law[52] for disclosure of PHI were more stringent than HIPAA and, therefore, state statutes control. HIPAA did not preempt state law in this matter.

National Abortion Federation v. Ashcroft

In *National Abortion Federation v. Ashcroft*, the New York Federal District Court granted the defendant's motion to enforce a subpoena against the New York-Presbyterian Hospital for release of medical records of women on whom the plaintiff physicians performed certain abortion procedures.[53] The dispute between the parties centered around the meaning of HIPAA's antipreemption provision. Plaintiff hospital argued that the HIPAA *incorporates* more stringent state laws, thus requiring the court to abide by New York's more stringent law that mandates patient consent before disclosure. The New York law provides in relevant part that "unless the patient waives the privilege, a person authorized to practice medicine . . . shall not be allowed to disclose any information which he acquired in attending a patient in a professional capacity, and which was necessary to enable him to action that capacity."[54]

Defendant Attorney General of the United States argued that HIPAA's antipreemption provision permits more stringent state laws to retain the same force that they had before HIPAA was enacted. "Because state medical privacy regulations lacked any effect on rules of discovery and evidence in federal court proceedings before HIPAA, Defendant contends that those state regulations have no such effect after HIPAA."[55]

The court determined that HIPAA does not allow for the application of state law to federal programs or activities where state law did not apply prior to HIPAA. HIPAA does not give an effect to state law that it would not otherwise have in the absence of HIPAA. The court held that the "privacy provisions promulgated under HIPAA therefore control the enforceability of the subpoena . . . the regulations permit disclosure of health information without patient consent pursuant to a qualified protective order."[56] The significance of this case is that HIPAA, not state law, governs the release of PHI in federal court proceedings. On March 29, 2004, a federal appeals court in Manhattan temporarily stopped the lower court's order for release of New York-Presbyterian Hospital's medical records.[57]

Similar issues surfaced in a series of related cases involving the Justice Department's attempt to subpoena medical records of abortions from at least six hospitals in New York City, Philadelphia, Chicago, and elsewhere.[58] Federal judges in Philadelphia, Chicago, and San Francisco refused to order the release of abortion records.[59]

HIPAA OPENS THE DOOR TO LITIGATION

Although HIPAA does not create a private cause of action, the Privacy Rule has the potential to dramatically increase the number of lawsuits against health care providers and payers for wrongful disclosures. Some experts believe that private litigation will play a more significant role in enforcement than government agencies will.[60] Some even consider the potential magnitude of HIPAA litigation to be in the same class with tobacco litigation, breast implant litigation, and asbestos litigation.[61] In any event, HIPAA expands opportunities for civil lawsuits that are intended to protect the individual's right to privacy of PHI.

There are two major reasons for the anticipated increase in litigation. First, HIPAA does not preempt state privacy actions, unfair trade practice actions, or tort laws that create a private right of action.[62] Consequently, civil litigation based on any of those causes of action may be brought in state court. Second, HIPAA establishes a national "standard of care" that health care providers are obligated to follow.[63] HIPAA sets the standard for privacy of PHI that all health care providers must follow. Additionally, HIPAA establishes duties and contracts between patients and health care providers. Any breach of the duties or contracts justifies a viable cause of action for an injured patient.

Many experts foresee both low-stakes litigation exposures, involving a single plaintiff and an isolated breach, and high-stakes litigation exposures, involving inadvertent mass disclosures due to poor security, failure to follow one's own privacy policies and procedures, or medical data abuses.[64] HIPAA also sets the scene for mass-torts litigation, involving a large number of plaintiffs harmed by a single defendant. The ease of disclosure of electronic information and the personal nature of the information create a potentially high incidence for high stakes litigation.

The private and sensitive nature of the PHI creates an emotionally charged atmosphere that, when handled improperly and without discretion, can ignite a firestorm of litigation. Covered entities are wise to be proactive in preventing unauthorized disclosures by ensuring that a strong privacy policy is in place and actively enforced.

Office for Civil Rights Regional Addresses

Region I: CT, ME, MA, NH, RI, VT
Office for Civil Rights
U.S. Department of Health & Human Services
JFK Federal Building, Room 1875
Boston, MA 02203
(617) 565-1340 (voice)
(617) 565-1343 (TDD)
(617) 565-3809 (fax)

Region II: NJ, NY, PR, VI
Office for Civil Rights
U.S. Department of Health & Human Services
26 Federal Plaza, Ste. 3313
New York, NY 10278
(212) 264-3313 (voice)
(212) 264-2355 (TDD)
(212) 264-3039 (fax)

Region III: DE, DC, MD, PA, VA, WV
Office for Civil Rights
U.S. Department of Health & Human Services
150 S. Independence Mall West, Ste. 372
Philadelphia, PA 19106-3499
(215) 861-4441 (voice)
(215) 861-4440 (TDD)
(215) 861-4431 (fax)

Region IV: AL, FL, GA, KY, MS, NC, SC, TN
Office for Civil Rights
U.S. Department of Health & Human Services
61 Forsyth St., SW., Ste. 3B70
Atlanta, GA 30323
(404) 562-7886 (voice)
(404) 331-2867 (TDD)
(404) 562-7881 (fax)

Region V: IL, IN, MI, MN, OH, WI
Office for Civil Rights
U.S. Department of Health & Human Services
233 N. Michigan Ave., Ste. 240
Chicago, IL 60601
(312) 886-2359 (voice)
(312) 353-5693 (TDD)
(312) 886-1807 (fax)

Region VI: AR, LA, NM, OK, TX
Office for Civil Rights
U.S. Department of Health & Human Services
1301 Young St., Ste. 1169
Dallas, TX 75202

(214) 767-4056 (voice)
(214) 767-8940 (TDD)
(214) 767-0432 (fax)

Region VII: IA, KS, MO, NE
Office for Civil Rights
U.S. Department of Health & Human Services
601 East 12th St., Room 248
Kansas City, MO 64106
(816) 426-7278 (voice)
(816) 426-7065 (TDD)
(816) 426-3686 (fax)

Region VIII: CO, MT, ND, SD, UT, WY
Office for Civil Rights
U.S. Department of Health & Human Services
1961 Stout St., Room 1426
Denver, CO 80294
(303) 844-2024 (voice)
(303) 844-3439 (TDD)
(303) 844-2025 (fax)

Region IX: AZ, CA, HI, NV, AS, GU, The U.S. Affiliated Pacific Island Jurisdictions
Office for Civil Rights
U.S. Department of Health & Human Services
50 United Nations Plaza, Room 322
San Francisco, CA 94102
(415) 437-8310 (voice)
(415) 437-8311 (TDD)
(415) 437-8329 (fax)

Region X: AK, ID, OR, WA
Office for Civil Rights
U.S. Department of Health & Human Services
2201 Sixth Ave., Mail Stop RX-11
Seattle, WA 98121
(206) 615-2290 (voice)
(206) 615-2296 (TDD)
(206) 615-2297 (fax)

NOTES

1. Health Insurance Portability and Accountability Act of 1996 (HIPAA), 45 C.F.R. § 160.304(a) (2003).

2. *See id.* § 160.304(b).

3. *See id.* § 160.306(a) and http://www.hhs.gov/ocr/privacyhowtofile.htm, accessed Jan. 11, 2004.

4. *Id.*

5. HIPAA, 65 Fed. Reg. 82,381 (Dec. 28, 2000).

6. HIPAA, 45 C.F.R. §§ 160.306 and 164.534.

7. *See id.* § 160.306(b).

8. *See id.* § 160.308.

9. *See id.* § 160.310.

10. *See id.* § 160.310(a).

11. *See id.* § 160.310(b).

12. HIPAA, 45 C.F.R. § 160.310(c).

13. *See id.* § 160.310(c)(1).

14. *Id.*

15. *See id.* § 160.310(c)(2).

16. *See id.* § 160.310(c)(3).

17. *See id.* § 160.312.

18. HIPAA, 45 C.F.R. § 160.312(a)(1).

19. *See id.* § 160.312(a)(2).

20. *See id.* § 160.312(b).

21. *See id.* § 160.506; and delegation of authority to impose civil monetary penalties, 65 Fed. Reg. 82,381 (Dec. 28, 2000).

22. Social Security Act, 42 U.S.C. § 1320d-5(a).

23. *See id.* § 1320d-5.

24. *See id.* § 1320d-5(b)(1).

25. *See id.* § 1320d-5(b)(2).

26. *See id.* § 1320d-5(b)(3).

27. *See id.* § 1320d-5(b)(4).

28. Social Security Act, 42 U.S.C. § 1320a-7(a).

29. *See id.* § 1320a-7(a)(c)(1).

30. Fed. R. Civ. P. 4.

31. Social Security Act, 42 U.S.C. § 1320a-7a(c)(2).

32. *See id.* § 1320a-7a(c)(4).

33. United States Department of Health and Human Services, Privacy of Health Information/HIPAA, Authorizations, *available at* http://answers.hhs.gov; accessed Jan. 18, 2004.

34. United States Department of Health and Human Services, Fact Sheet: Protecting the Privacy of Patients' Health Information, released Apr. 14, 2003, *available at* http://www.hhs.gov/news/facts/privacy.html; accessed Jan. 18, 2004.

35. Social Security Act, 42 U.S.C. § 1320d-6.

36. U.S. v. Lucien, 347 F.3d 45 (2nd Cir., Oct. 14, 2003).

37. *Id.* at 52 (emphasis in original case).

38. *Id.*

39. *In re* PPA Litigation, Superior Court of New Jersey, Law Division Middlesex County, Civil Action Case Code 264, Opinion on HIPAA Preempting *Stempler v. Speidell,* Sept. 23, 2003.

40. Stempler v. Speidell, 100 N.J. 368 (1985).

41. *Id.*

42. *Id.*

43. Middlesex County Ethic Committee v. Garden State Bar Ass'n, 457 U.S. 423, 431, 102 S. Ct. 2515, 2521 (1982).

44. *In re* PPA Litigation, Superior Court of New Jersey, Law Division Middlesex County, Civil Action Case Code 264, Opinion on HIPAA Preempting *Stempler v. Speidell,* Sept. 23, 2003.

45. *Id.*

46. N.Y.City Civ. Ct., 766 N.Y.S.2d 535 (2003), N.Y. slip op. 23810.

47. CPLR 3122-a (effective Sept. 1, 2003).

48. *Id.*

49. CPLR 3120 and 3122.

50. *In re Carella,* 2004 N.Y. slip op. 50185(u) (N.Y. Sur., 2004), 2 Misc.3d 1007(A), 2004 WL 727094 (N.Y. Sur.) (citing Campos v. Payne, NYLJ, Oct. 14, 2003, at 17, col. 2) (March 25, 2004).

51. Lemieux v. Tandem Health Care of Florida, Inc., 2003 WL 22438605 (Fla.App. 2 Dist. 2003).

52. FLA. STAT. § 456.057(6) (2002).

53. National Abortion Federation v. Ashcroft, No. 03 Civ. 8695(RCC), 2004 WL 555701 (S.D.N.Y. Mar. 19, 2004).

54. CPLR § 101.

55. *Id.* at *4.

56. *Id.* at *6.

57. Susan Saulny, "Trials Open Across Nation on Abortion-Procedure Ban," N.Y. TIMES, Mar. 30, 2004, at 2, *available at* http://www.nytimes.com/2004/03/30/national/30ABOR.html.

58. *Id.*

59. *Id.*

60. Evan Hendricks, 22(22) PRIVACY TIMES 6 (Dec. 2, 2002), http://www.privacytimes.com/buttons/b8_HIPAA.htm; Bob Brewin, "HIPAA Could Open Door to Litigation," Bio IT Bulletin, BIO IT WORLD, (Feb. 21, 2003), at http://www.bio-itworld.com/news/022103_report2052.html.

61. Hendricks, *supra* note 59, quoting Leigh-Ann M. Patterson, Esq., Fifth National HIPAA Summit, Baltimore, MD, Nov. 1, 2002.

62. Hendricks, *supra* note 59.

63. *Id.*

64. Hendricks, *supra* note 59; Brewin, *supra* note 59.

DO I NEED A HIPAA AUTHORIZATION?

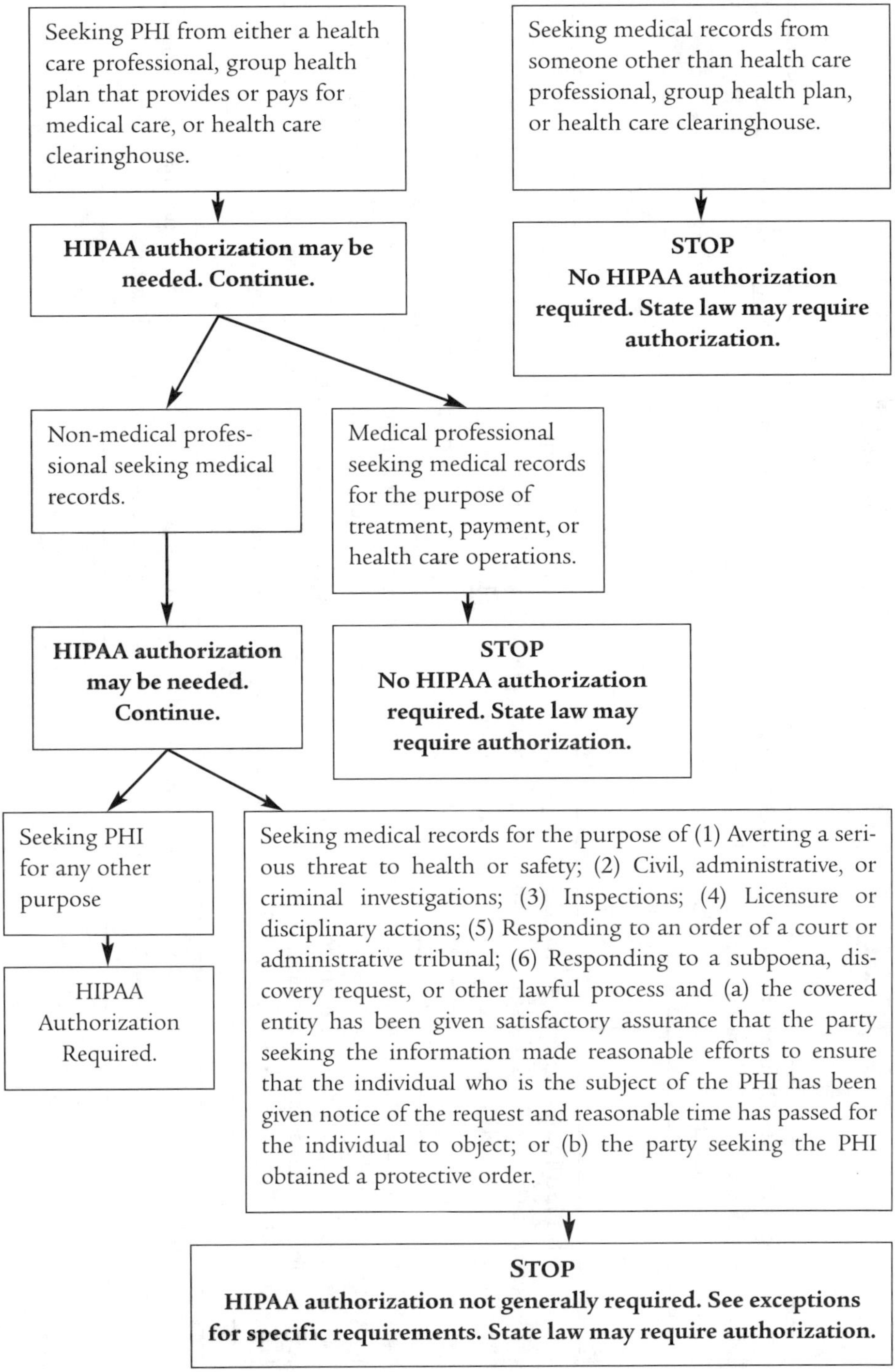

IS MY BUSINESS A COVERED ENTITY?

Covered entities are (1) **Health Plans,** (2) **Health Care Clearinghouses,** or (3) **Health Care Providers** that transmit any health information in electronic form.

All other entities are **not** covered entities and HIPAA does not apply to them. Examples: health plan sponsors (e.g., employers) and auto insurance issuers.

↓

A **Health Plan** is an entity that provides or pays the cost of medical care. Examples: health insurance issuer; HMO; Medicare Part A or B; Medicaid; issuer of a Medicare supplemental policy; issuer of a long term care policy (excluding a nursing home fixed-indemnity policy); employee welfare benefit plan; plans that provide or pay for the cost of medical care.

A **Health Care Clearinghouse** is a billing service, repricing company, community health management information system, community health information system, or "value-added" network or switch, that does either or both of the following: (1) processes or facilitates the processing of PHI received from another entity in a nonstandard format or with nonstandard data into standard data or a standard transaction or (2) receives a standard transaction and processes or facilitates the processing of PHI into nonstandard format or nonstandard data content for the receiving entity.

A **Health Care Provider** is a person or entity that furnishes, bills, or is paid for health care in the normal course of business. Examples: psychiatrists, physicians, hospitals, clinics, therapists, dentists, pharmacies, and urgent care centers.

WHO IS A BUSINESS ASSOCIATE?

Business associates are persons or entities (who are not members of the covered entity's workforce) that perform a function or activity on behalf of a covered entity involving the use or disclosure of PHI.

Examples include claims processing or administration; data analysis, processing, or administration, utilization review; quality assurance; accreditation; billing; benefits management; practice management, and repricing. Business associates may also provide legal, actuarial, accounting, consulting, data aggregation, management, administrative, accreditation, or financial services to or for a covered entity, or to or for an organized health care arrangement in which the covered entity participates, where the provision of the service involves the disclosure of PHI from such covered entity or from another business associate of such covered entity.

All other entities that perform work on behalf of a covered entity that does *not* involve the use or disclosure of PHI are *not* business associates.

Examples include janitorial services, computer software vendors, plumbers, electricians, photo copier repair persons, mail carriers, and deliver companies.

APPENDIX A

Background Information

In order to improve the efficiency of the health care system, the 104th Congress enacted Public Law 104-191, better known as the Health Insurance Portability and Accountability Act of 1996 (HIPAA). The act contains two major parts: Title I, which provides for the portability of health care insurance; and Title II, which provides for administrative simplification of health care, including privacy and confidentiality. The act mandated the secretary of the U.S. Department of Health and Human Services (HHS) to adopt standards to support electronic data interchange for a variety of administrative and financial health care transactions as well as health information privacy. Specifically, the law required the secretary of HHS to submit recommendations for federal health information privacy legislation to the Congress. Secretary Shalala forwarded these recommendations to the Congress on September 11, 1997. Several health information privacy bills were subsequently introduced in Congress. Congress did not enact health information privacy legislation by August 1999, and the secretary of HHS was required to issue final regulations to protect the information transmitted in connection with the HIPAA administrative transaction standards by February 2000.

UNDERSTANDING THE NEED FOR PROTECTION OF HEALTH INFORMATION

This book focuses on the privacy issues of Title II. A brief explanation of Title I is provided in the following section, which may be passed over for those of you who have no interest in the portability aspect of HIPAA.

Title I: Health Insurance Portability

Title I of HIPAA protects health insurance coverage for workers and their families when they change or lose their jobs. Under most group health plans, Title I of HIPAA works in four ways. First, it may increase employees' ability to get health insurance coverage for themselves or for their dependents when the employees start a new job. Second, it may lower the chance of losing existing health care coverage. Third, it may help maintain health care coverage for employees and their dependents when they change jobs. Fourth, it may help employees buy health care coverage on their own if they lose coverage under an employer's group health plan and no other health coverage is available.[1]

Prior to HIPAA, a health plan could control the length of time that it excluded a person from coverage due to a preexisting condition. HIPAA provides safeguards to prevent that from happening in most instances. Specifically, Title I of HIPAA limits the length of preexisting conditions exclusions that can keep employees or their dependents from getting full health care insurance coverage. It also prohibits the health plan from denying coverage or charging higher premiums based on an employee's or dependent's current health or health history. Additionally, it may give the employee a special enrollment period for enrolling in the group health plan when the employee loses other coverage if the employee declined to enroll in the health plan when first eligible or when the employee has a new dependent. However, HIPAA protections may be more limited for workers who are employed with a church, state or local governmental employer, or a very small employer.[2]

The purpose of Title I of HIPAA is to protect the health insurance coverage of employees and their dependents. It is important to note that it does not protect employees or their dependents in the following ways. It does not require employers to offer health insurance coverage or to pay for health coverage for employees or family coverage for dependents. It does not guarantee health coverage for all workers. It does not control the amount an insurer may charge for health care coverage. It does not require group health plans to offer specific benefits. It does not permit people to keep the same health coverage they had in their old job when they move to a new job. It does not eliminate all use of preexisting condition exclusions. Finally, and most importantly, it does not replace each state as the primary regulator of health insurance.[3]

Group health plans and insurers are affected by provisions of HIPAA. Under HIPAA, an individual's eligibility for enrollment in a group health plan is determined by the terms of the health plan and the rules of the issuer, not by the individual's or the dependent's health status. The rules and the terms of the group health plan or issuer must comply with all applicable state laws. The plan or issuer may not exclude coverage for any preexisting condition for more than twelve months after an individual's enrollment date (eighteen months for a late enrollee), regardless of whether this date occurred before the HIPAA effective date for the plan. This period may have already passed. If this period has not passed, the plan or issuer is required to count the time individuals have already served under the plan toward satisfaction of the preexisting condition exclusion period. In addition, the plan must use any creditable coverage that an individual accumulated prior to his or her enrollment date to reduce the individual's remaining preexisting condition exclusion period.[4]

The "portability" part of HIPAA provides that once an individual has health coverage, this coverage may be used to reduce or eliminate any preexisting condition exclusion that might be applied to an individual who moves to another employer's group health plan. The concept of portability is really one of an individual receiving credit for maintaining health coverage, even though it may be under different health plans or policies. "Portability" does not mean that individuals can carry current health benefits or their current plan or policy with them when moving from one health plan or policy to another, such as when changing or losing jobs.[5]

An example of portability is where an employee receives health insurance coverage that does not pay for preexisting conditions. Prior to HIPAA, it was legal for a health plan to exclude coverage for preexisting conditions. Under HIPAA, the health plan may no longer exclude coverage for the employee's preexisting condition as long as the employee satisfies the preexisting exclusion time period. Another example is where an employee works for one entity and is covered under its health plan for less than the preexisting exclusion period; for example, three months. When the employee changes jobs, the new health plan must use the employee's prior three months of creditable coverage from the prior employer to reduce the current health plan's preexisting condition exclusion time period. For instance, if the current health plan's preexisting exclusion period is twelve months, the plan must credit the employee for the three months from the prior job, resulting in a current preexisting condition exclusion period of nine months.[6]

A "preexisting condition exclusion" is a limitation or exclusion of health benefits due to the fact that a physical or mental condition was present before the first day of health insurance coverage. During the preexisting condition exclusion period, the plan or issuer may opt not to cover or pay for treatment of a physical or mental condition based on the fact that the employee received medical advice, diagnosis, care, or treatment within six months prior to an individual's enrollment date under the new plan or policy. (The plan or issuer must, however, pay for any *unrelated* covered services or conditions that arise once coverage has begun.) The enrollment date is the first day of coverage, or if there is a waiting period before coverage takes effect, the first day of the waiting period.

A group health plan can apply a preexisting condition exclusion for no more than twelve months (eighteen months for a late enrollee) after an individual's enrollment date. However, one of the main purposes of HIPAA is to limit the degree to which a plan or issuer can apply the preexisting condition exclusion. Under HIPAA, any preexisting condition exclusion must be reduced by an individual's prior creditable coverage. No preexisting condition may be applied to an individual who maintains continuous creditable coverage (without a break of sixty-three or more days) for twelve months (eighteen months for a late enrollee).

Title II: Administrative Simplification

Intent and Purpose of Administrative Simplification

Title II of HIPAA requires HHS to establish national standards for electronic health care transactions and national identifiers for providers, health plans, and employers. It also addresses the security and privacy of health data.

The standards are meant to improve the efficiency and effectiveness of the nation's health care system by encouraging the widespread use of electronic data interchange in health care.[7]

The intent of Title II is to reduce the costs and administrative burdens of health care by standardizing the electronic transmission of certain administrative and financial transactions that had been carried out manually on paper in the past. In its quest to restrain health care costs, the government determined that a high percentage of every health care dollar spent was on administrative overhead, including processing for enrollment, payment, eligibility, authorizations, filing a claim, supporting a claim, coordination of payments between more than one insurance company, and notifying the provider about payment.[8]

In order to resolve these issues, Congress enacted the Administrative Simplification portion of HIPAA. The health care industry estimates that full implementation of the simplification provisions of HIPAA could save up to $9 billion per year from administrative overhead alone, without a reduction in the amount or quality of health care services.[9]

HEALTH CARE PRIVACY

Concerns about the Security of Confidential Information

Congress had concerns about the security and confidentiality of health information that require electronic processing, particularly the protection of transmission of sensitive information contained in a person's medical record such as personal information, diagnosis, prognosis, and treatment.[10] In enacting HIPAA, Congress recognized the fact that administrative simplification could not be successful if it did not also protect the privacy and confidentiality of personal health information. The provision of high-quality health care requires the exchange of personal, often sensitive information between an individual and a skilled practitioner. Vital to that interaction is the patient's ability to trust that the information shared is protected and kept confidential. Yet there are concerns by many patients that their information is not protected. Among the factors adding to this concern are the growth of the number of organizations involved in the provision of care and the processing of claims, the growing use of electronic information technology, increased efforts to market health care and other products to consumers, and the increasing ability to collect highly sensitive information about a person's current and future health status as a result of advances in scientific research.[11]

Prior to HIPAA, no federal rules existed to protect the privacy of health information and guarantee patient access to such information. HIPAA establishes, for the first time, a set of basic national privacy standards that provides all Americans with a basic level of protection that is essential to their full participation in their health care. HIPAA sets a floor of ground rules for health care providers, health plans, and health care clearinghouses to follow, in order to protect patients and encourage them to seek needed care. The regulation seeks to balance the needs of the individual with the needs of the society. It creates a framework of protection that is strengthened by enforcement of both the federal government and by states as health information systems continue to evolve.[12]

The Impact of the Internet

Prior to advancements in electronic data, physicians, nurses, hospitals, and other health care professionals and institutions recorded and maintained health information on paper and in storage archives. In some ways, this imperfect system of record keeping created a false sense of privacy among patients, providers, and others. Patients' health information was never completely confidential. Until recently, however, a breach of confidentiality involved a physical exchange of paper records or an oral exchange of information. Currently, more and more health care providers, plans, and others use electronic means of storing and transmitting health information.[13] The electronic information revolution is transforming the recording of health information so that the disclosure of information may require only the push of a button. In a matter of seconds, a person's most profoundly private information can be shared with hundreds, thousands, even millions of individuals and organizations at a time. While the majority of medical records still are in paper form, information from those records is often copied and transmitted through electronic means.[14]

The relative ease of information collection, organization, retention, and exchange that is made possible by the advances in computer and other electronic technology bestows many benefits to individuals as well as to the health care industry. The use of electronic information helps to speed the delivery of effective care and the processing of billions of dollars worth of health care claims. Greater use of electronic data has increased our ability to identify and treat those who are at risk for disease, conduct vital research, detect fraud and abuse, and measure and improve the quality of care delivered in the United States.[15]

Simultaneously, these information technology advances reduced or eliminated many of the financial and logistical obstacles that previously protected the confidentiality of health information and the privacy interests of individuals. Additionally, the information technology advances made individuals' private information available to many more people, beyond the individuals' control. With this in mind, the shift from paper to electronic health information records increases the need for legal protections related to the right to privacy in health information. Prior to those advances, it was far more expensive to access and use medical records and the risk of harm to individuals was relatively low. In the very near future, technology may make it almost free to send a lifetime of medical records over the Internet. The risks to the loss of privacy will grow rapidly. It will become cost effective, for instance, for companies to offer services that allow purchasers to obtain the details of a person's physical and mental treatments.[16]

In addition to legitimate uses for such information, malicious or curious persons may be able to download medical records for purposes ranging from identity theft to embarrassment to curiosity about a celebrity or neighbor. Many people believe that they have a right to live in society without having these details of their lives laid open to unknown and possibly adversarial eyes. These changes in information technology may provide a reason for initiating federal privacy protections in situations where the risk of harm did not previously justify writing such protections into law.[17]

The growing level of concern about privacy in general followed the rise in the widespread use of electronic information technology. Americans have embraced the use of the Internet and other forms of electronic information as a way to provide greater access to information, save time, and save money.[18] A recent survey by the California Health Care Foundation reported that 75 percent of consumers seeking health information on the Internet are concerned or very concerned about the health sites they visit sharing their personal health information with a third party without their permission.[19]

Unless the public is reassured that their fears are unwarranted, the full benefits of information technology cannot be realized. Without national standards for the confidentiality of health information, the health care industry and the population in general are uncomfortable about this primarily financially driven expansion in the use of electronic information. Prior to the enactment of HIPAA, several plans, providers, and clearinghouses took measures to safeguard the privacy of individually identifiable health information. Yet they were constrained by a patchwork of state laws and regulations that were incomplete and, at times, inconsistent. In the past, states attempted, in varying degrees, to enhance confidentiality by establishing laws governing at least some aspects of medical record privacy. In the federal government's opinion, this approach, though a step in the right direction, was woefully inadequate because the state laws failed to provide a consistent or comprehensive legal foundation of health information privacy. For example, there was considerable variation among the states in the type of information protected and the scope of the protections.[20]

More importantly, electronic health data continue to become available nationally. As more information becomes available in electronic form, it can reach far beyond the immediate community where the patient resides. Prior to HIPAA, neither private action nor state laws provided an adequately comprehensive and rigorous legal structure to sufficiently allay public concerns, protect the right to privacy, and correct the market failures caused by the absence of privacy protections. Therefore, the federal government developed a national policy with consistent rules that encouraged the health care industry to increase the proper use of electronic information while also protecting the very real needs of patients to safeguard their privacy.[21]

Public Disclosures of Private Information

The concern of the American people about the security of their confidential health information had a basis in fact. Without a federal law of health privacy protections, consumers were increasingly vulnerable to the exposure of their personal health information to unauthorized persons. After a review of literature, it was found that disclosures of individually identifiable information could occur deliberately or accidentally and could occur within an organization or be the result of an external breach of security. Examples of privacy breaches include[22]

- A Michigan-based health system accidentally posted the medical records of thousands of patients on the Internet (*Ann Arbor News,* February 10, 1999).
- A Utah-based pharmaceutical benefits management firm used patient data to solicit business for its owner, a drug store (Kiplinger's, February 2000).
- An employee of the Tampa, Florida, health department took a computer disk containing the names of 4,000 people who had tested positive for HIV (*USA Today,* October 10, 1996).
- The health insurance claims forms of thousands of patients blew out of a truck on its way to a recycling center in East Hartford, Connecticut (*Hartford Courant,* May 14, 1999).
- A patient in a Boston-area hospital discovered that her medical record had been read by more than 200 of the hospital's employees (*Boston Globe,* August 1, 2000).
- A Nevada woman who purchased a used computer discovered that the computer still contained the prescription records of the customers of the pharmacy that had previously owned the computer. The pharmacy data base included names, addresses, Social Security numbers, and a list of all the medicines the customers had purchased (*New York Times,* April 4, 1997, and April 12, 1997).
- A speculator bid $4,000 for the patient records of a family practice in South Carolina. Among the businessman's uses of the purchased records was selling them back to the former patients (*New York Times,* August 14, 1991).
- In 1993, the *Boston Globe* reported that Johnson & Johnson marketed a list of 5 million names and addresses of elderly incontinent women (ACLU Legislative Update, April 1998).
- A few weeks after an Orlando woman had her doctor perform some routine tests, she received a letter from a drug company promoting a treatment for her high cholesterol (*Orlando Sentinel,* November 30, 1997).

Despite the reasons behind the disclosure of personal information, whether it is intentional or accidental, the harm to the individual remains the same.

In light of the push to improve the efficiency and economy of the health care industry, the potential benefits of the evolving health care system, and the true risks and occurrences of harm, protection of privacy needed to be built into the routine operations of the American health care system.[23]

THE PROMOTION OF PRIVACY PROTECTION

Government Influences

Over the past several decades, there were many federal initiatives aimed at protecting the privacy of sensitive personal information. While HIPAA is likely the largest single federal initiative to protect privacy, it is by no means the only federal attempt to control the security of private information. The government drafted HIPAA in light of fairly recent legislative activity dealing with advances in technology, in addition to a formerly established body of law granting federal protections for personal privacy.[24]

In 1965, the House of Representatives created a Special Subcommittee on Invasion of Privacy. In 1973, the Department of Health, Education, and Welfare (predecessor of the Department of Health and Human Services) issued *The Code of Fair Information Practice Principles,* which established an important baseline for information privacy in the United States. These basic principles formed the foundation for the federal Privacy Act of 1974, a body of law that regulates the government's use of personal information by limiting the disclosure of personally identifiable information, allows consumers access to information about them, requires federal agencies to specify the purposes for collecting personal information, and provides civil and criminal penalties for misuse of information.[25]

In the several years preceding HIPAA, federal laws, regulations, and legislative proposals were made in areas ranging from financial privacy to genetic privacy to the safeguarding of children on the Internet. When considering the new developments in the law, the legislature was mindful of the rapid expansion in electronic technology and simultaneous concerns about individual privacy. For example, the Children's Online Privacy Protection Act was enacted in 1998, providing protection for children when interacting at Web sites. In February 2000, President Clinton signed Executive Order 13,145, banning the use of genetic information in federal hiring and promotion decisions. The landmark financial modernization bill, signed by President Clinton in November 1999, likewise contained financial privacy protections for consumers. At that same time, there was also legislative activity on establishing legal safeguards for the privacy of individuals' Social Security numbers and calls for regulation of online privacy in general.[26]

Prior to HIPAA, and against the backdrop of decades of privacy-enhancing statutes passed at the federal level, the government drafted laws, regulations, and legislative proposals to enact safeguards in fields ranging from government data files to video rental records. In the 1970s, individual privacy was paramount in the passage of the Fair Credit Reporting Act (1970), the Privacy Act (1974), the Family Educational Rights and Privacy Act (1974), and the Right to Financial Privacy Act (1978). These key laws were followed in the next decade by another series of statutes, including the Privacy Protection Act (1980), the Electronic Communications Privacy Act (1986), the Video Privacy Protection Act (1988), and the Employee Polygraph Protection Act (1988). Ten years before HIPAA, Congress and the president passed legal privacy protection through the Telephone Consumer Protection Act (1991), the Driver's Privacy Protection Act (1994), the Telecommunications Act (1996), the Children's Online Privacy Protection Act (1998), the Identity Theft and Assumption Deterrence Act (1998), and Title V of the Gramm-Leach-Bliley Act (1999) governing financial privacy.[27]

But what about health information? In 1997, a presidential advisory commission, the Advisory Commission on Consumer Protection and Quality in the Health Care Industry, recognized the need for patient privacy protection in its recommendations for a Consumer Bill of Rights and Responsibilities (November 1997). In 1997, Congress enacted the Balanced Budget Act (Public Law 105-34), which added language to the Social Security Act (18 U.S.C. § 1852) requiring Medicare + Choice organizations to establish safeguards for the privacy of individually identifiable patient information. Similarly, the Veterans Benefits Section of the United States Code provides for confidentiality of medical records in cases involving drug abuse, alcoholism or alcohol abuse, HIV infection, or sickle cell anemia (38 U.S.C. § 7332).[28]

Congress recognized the importance of protecting the privacy of health information by enacting the Health Insurance Portability and Accountability Act of 1996. The act required Congress to enact a medical privacy statute and asked the secretary of Health and Human Services to provide Congress with recommendations for protecting the confidentiality of health care information. Congress further recognized the importance of such standards by providing the secretary with authority to promulgate regulations on health care privacy in the event that lawmakers were unable to act within the allotted three years.[29]

Additionally, Congress recognized the importance of the United States' joining the rest of the developed world in establishing basic medical privacy protections. In 1995, the European Union (EU) adopted a Data Privacy Directive requiring its fifteen member states to adopt consistent privacy laws by October 1998. The EU urged all other nations to do the same or face the potential loss of access to information from EU countries.[30]

Congress addressed the opportunities and challenges presented by the rapid evolution of health information systems in the Health Insurance Portability and Accountability Act of 1996, Public Law 104-191, which was enacted on August 21, 1996. Sections 261 through 264 of HIPAA are the Administrative Simplification provisions. The major part of these provisions are in Section 262 of HIPAA, which enacted a new part C of Title XI of the Social Security Act.[31]

In Section 262, Congress primarily facilitated the efficiencies and cost savings for the health care industry by increasing the use of electronic technology. Thus, Section 262 directs HHS to issue standards to facilitate the electronic exchange of information with respect to financial and administrative transactions carried out by health plans, health care clearinghouses, and health care providers who transmit information electronically in connection with such transactions.[32]

Simultaneously, Congress recognized the challenges to the confidentiality of health information presented by the increasing complexity of the health care industry, and by advances in health information systems technology and communications. Accordingly, Section 262 also directs HHS to develop standards to protect the security, including the confidentiality and integrity, of health information.[33]

As mentioned previously, Congress recognized the need for protection of health information privacy generally, as well as the privacy implications of electronic data interchange and the increased ease of transmitting and sharing individually identifiable health information. Prior to HIPAA, Congress worked on broad health privacy legislation for many years and found it important to enact such legislation. A significant portion of the first Administrative Simplification Section debated on the floor of the Senate in 1994 (as part of the Health Security Act) consisted of privacy provisions. In the version of HIPAA passed by the House of Representatives in 1996, the requirement for the issuance of privacy standards was located in the same section of the bill (Section 1173) as the requirements for issuance of the other HIPAA administrative simplification standards. In conference, the requirement for privacy standards was moved to a separate section in the same part of HIPAA, Section 264, so that Congress could link the privacy standards to congressional action.[34]

HIPAA Section 264(b) requires the secretary of HHS to develop and submit to the Congress recommendations for

- The rights that an individual who is a subject of individually identifiable health information should have
- The procedures that should be established for the exercise of such rights
- The uses and disclosures of such information that should be authorized or required[35]

The secretary's recommendations were submitted to the Congress on September 11, 1997. Section 264(c)(1) provides that

> If legislation governing standards with respect to the privacy of individually identifiable health information transmitted in connection with the transactions described in Section 1173(a) of the Social Security Act (as added by Section 262) is not enacted by [August 21, 1999],

> the Secretary of Health and Human Services shall promulgate final regulations containing such standards not later than [February 21, 2000]. Such regulations shall address at least the subjects described in subsection (b).[36]

Since Congress did not enact legislation regarding the privacy of individually identifiable health information prior to August 21, 1999, HHS published proposed rules setting forth such standards on November 3, 1999 (64 Fed. Reg. 59,918), and published the mandated final regulation in the *Federal Register* on December 28, 2000 (65 Fed. Reg. 82,761–82,810).[37]

Consumer Influences

Today, it is nearly impossible for any person to be truly "let alone." The average American is inundated with requests for information from potential employers, retail shops, telephone marketing firms, electronic marketers, banks, insurance companies, hospitals, physicians, health plans, and others. In a 1998 national survey, 88 percent of consumers said they were "concerned" by the amount of information being requested, including 55 percent who said they were "very concerned."[38] These worries are based in reality. Consumers who use the Internet to make purchases or request "free" information often are asked for personal and financial information. Companies making such requests routinely promise to protect the confidentiality of that information. Yet several firms have tried to sell this information to other companies even after promising not to do so.[39]

Americans' concern about the privacy of their health information is part of a broader anxiety about their lack of privacy in a variety of areas.[40] In a *Wall Street Journal*/ABC poll on September 16, 1999, 29 percent of respondents stated that what concerned them most in the coming century was the *loss of privacy.* Twenty-three percent or less of the respondents expressed serious concerns about other issues such as terrorism, world war, and global warming.[41]

This growing concern stems from several trends, including the rising use of interconnected electronic media for business and personal activities, the increasing ability to know an individual's genetic make-up, and, in health care, the increasing complexity of the system. Each of these trends brings the potential for tremendous benefits to individuals and society generally. At the same time, each also brings new potential for invasions of individuals' privacy.[42]

NOTES

1. U.S. Department of Health and Human Services, Health Care Financing Administration, Protecting Your Health Insurance Coverage, *available at* http://www.cms.hms.gov/hipaa/hipaa1/content/protect.pdf.
2. *Id.*

3. *Id.*

4. Centers for Medicare and Medicaid Services, HIPAA Insurance Reform, Employer Questions and Answers About HIPAA, *available at* http://www.cms.gov/hipaa/hipaa1/content/qa-emp.asp#4; accessed Nov. 2, 2003.

5. *Id.*

6. *Id.*

7. Centers for Medicare & Medicaid Services, Health Insurance Portability and Accountability Act of 1996 (HIPAA), *available at* www.cms.hhs.gov/hipaa; last modified Oct. 16, 2002; accessed Nov. 15, 2003.

8. Centers for Medicare & Medicaid Services, Health Insurance Portability and Accountability Act of 1996 (HIPAA), *available at* www.cms.hhs.gov/hipaa/hipaa2/general/background/kkimpl.asp.

9. *Id.*

10. *Id.*

11. Centers for Medicare & Medicaid Services, Health Insurance Portability and Accountability Act of 1996 (HIPAA), Final Privacy Rule Preamble, *available at* http://www.cms.hhs.gov/hipaa/hipaa2/regulations/privacy/finalrule; accessed Nov. 15, 2003 [hereinafter Final Privacy Rule Preamble].

12. *Id.*

13. In 1996 the health care industry invested an estimated $10 billion to $15 billion in information technology. National Research Council, Computer Science and Telecommunications Board, *For the Record: Protecting Electronic Health Information* (1997), *cited in* Final Privacy Rule Preamble, *supra* note 11.

14. Final Privacy Rule Preamble, *supra* note 11.

15. "[T]he Internet has great potential to improve Americans' health by enhancing communications and improving access to information for care providers, patients, health plan administrator, public health officials, biomedical researchers, and other health professionals." National Research Council, Computer Science and Telecommunications Board, *Networking Health: Prescriptions for the Internet* (2000), *cited in* Final Privacy Rule Preamble, *supra* note 11.

16. Final Privacy Rule Preamble, *supra* note 11.

17. *Id.*

18. Sixty percent of Americans surveyed in 1999 reported that they have a computer in their home; 82 percent reported that they have used a computer; 64 percent say that they have used the Internet and 58 percent have sent an e-mail. Among those who are under the age of sixty, those percentages are even higher. Additionally, 59 percent of Americans worry that an unauthorized person will gain access to their personal information. Henry J. Kaiser Family Foundation, *National Survey of Adults on Technology* (Feb. 2000), *cited in* Final Privacy Rule Preamble, *supra* note 11.

19. California Health Care Foundation, *Ethics Survey of Consumer Attitudes About Health Web Sites* 3 (Jan. 2000), *cited in* Final Privacy Rule Preamble, *supra* note 11.

20. Lawrence O. Gostin, Zita Lazzarini, & Kathleen M. Flaherty, *Legislative Survey of State Confidentiality Laws, with Specific Emphasis on HIV and Immunization,* Report to Centers for Disease Control, Council of State and Territorial Epidemiologists, and Task Force for Child Survival and Development, Carter Presidential Center (1996), cited in Final Privacy Rule Preamble, *supra* note 11.

21. Final Privacy Rule Preamble, *supra* note 11.

22. *Id.*

23. *Id.*

24. *Id.*

25. *Id.*

26. *Id.*

27. Final Privacy Rule Preamble, *supra* note 11.

28. *Id.*

29. *Id.*

30. *Id.*

31. *Id.*

32. *Id.*

33. Final Privacy Rule Preamble, *supra* note 11.

34. *Id.*

35. *Id.*

36. *Id.*

37. *Id.*

38. Privacy and American Business, *1998 Privacy Concerns & Consumer Choice Survey* (http://www.pandab.org), *cited in* Final Privacy Rule Preamble, *supra* note 11.

39. Final Privacy Rule Preamble, *supra* note 11.

40. Final Privacy Rule Preamble, *supra* note 11, citing a series of national public opinion polls conducted by Louis Harris & Associates that documents a rising level of public concern about privacy, growing from 64 percent in 1978 to 82 percent in 1995. Over 80 percent of persons surveyed in 1999 agreed with the statement that they had "lost all control over their personal information." See Harris Equifax, *Health Information Privacy Study* (1993), http://www.epic.org/privacy/medical/polls.html.

41. Final Privacy Rule Preamble, *supra* note 11.

42. *Id.*

APPENDIX B

Authorization for Release of Protected Health Information

MEDICAL AUTHORIZATION

____________________	____________________	____________________
Patient's Name	Date of Birth	Social Security Number (optional)

I authorize ____________________________ (the "Keeper of the Records") to disclose my protected health information as specified below. I understand that signing this Authorization is voluntary and that my treatment may not be conditioned on the signing of this authorization. I understand that I have the right to revoke this Authorization at any time by providing a signed, written notice of such revocation to the Keeper of the Records. I understand that I cannot revoke this Authorization to the extent this Authorization has been relied upon. I understand that information released pursuant to this Authorization may no longer be protected by law or regulation and may be redisclosed by the recipient.

1) (a) Please disclose the entire medical record including any and all medical information and opinions (whether written or oral), office notes pertaining to my physical or mental condition and physical or medical treatment rendered therefore, and allow ________________ (insert name of recipient) or their representative to see and obtain copies of all records, notes, reports, X-rays, medical tests, studies, and correspondence, including correspondence to and from other medical providers and insurance companies regarding my condition and/or treatment.

   (b) The Keeper of the Records cannot use or disclose certain information unless the patient specifically authorizes such use or disclosure. **Please initial next to each item below if you specifically authorize the release** of health information relating to the testing, diagnosis, or treatment for:

   _______ HIV/AIDS
   _______ Drug and alcohol abuse
   _______ Mental health/psychiatric disorders

2) All information maintained at any time by the Keeper of the Records may be disclosed.

3) The information requested by this Authorization may be received by ____________________ (insert name and address of recipient).

4) The information is being requested for the purposes of discovery during litigation between ____ (insert parties' names).

5) Unless revoked earlier, this Authorization will expire at the resolution of the litigation, whether by settlement, verdict or judgment, inclusive of the period of time for any appeal.

By signing below, I understand and acknowledge the following:

- I have read and understand this Authorization
- I have been given a copy of this Authorization
- I am authorizing the Keeper of the Records to use or disclose my health information to the persons and for the purposes identified in this Authorization; and
- If I have any questions about disclosure of my protected health information pursuant to this Authorization, I may contact the Keeper of the Records.
- **A photocopy of this authorization shall be considered as effective and valid as the original.**

______________________	______________________	______________
Print name	Signature of Patient or Personal Representative	Date

If signed by the patient's personal representative, describe the legal authority of the representative to act on behalf of the patient ______________________ .

Legal authority of representative verified by ____________________________ .

APPENDIX C

Business Associate Agreement

THIS AGREEMENT is executed this _____ day of ____________, 20__, by ___________ ("**Covered Entity**") and ___________ ("**Business Associate**").

RECITALS

A. Business Associate and Covered Entity have a business relationship by virtue of ______________________ services provided by Business Associate to Covered Entity.

B. Business Associate must use and/or disclose Protected Health Information received from, or created or received on behalf of, Covered Entity in its performance of Services related to the legal representation of Covered Entity.

C. Covered Entity is required by the Privacy Rule and the Security Rule issued pursuant to the Health Insurance Portability and Accountability Act of 1996 ("HIPAA") to obtain satisfactory assurance that Business Associate will appropriately safeguard the Protected Health Information received from, or created or received on behalf of, Covered Entity.

In consideration of the receipt of Protected Health Information and other good and valuable consideration, Business Associate agrees as follows:

SECTION 1
Definitions

Capitalized terms used, but not otherwise defined, in this Agreement shall have the meanings given those terms in the Privacy Rule and the Security Rule.

1.1 ***Business Associate:*** "Business Associate" shall mean ___________ (insert name of business associate).

1.2 ***Covered Entity:*** "Covered Entity" shall mean the health care provider.

1.3 ***Individual:*** "Individual" shall have the same meaning as the term "Individual" in 45 C.F.R. § 164.501 and shall include a person who qualifies as a personal representative in accordance with 45 C.F.R. § 164.502(g).

1.4 ***Privacy Rule:*** "Privacy Rule" shall mean the Standards for Privacy of Individually Identifiable Health Information at 45 C.F.R. Parts § 160 and § 164, Subparts A and E.

1.5 ***Security Rule:*** "Security Rule" shall mean the Standards for Security of Electronic Protected Health Information at 45 C.F.R. Parts § 160 and § 164, Subparts A and C.

1.6 ***Protected Health Information:*** Protected Health Information (PHI) shall have the same meaning as the term "Protected Health Information" in 45 C.F.R. § 164.501, limited to the information received from, or created or received by Business Associate on behalf of, Covered Entity.

1.7 ***Secretary:*** "Secretary" shall mean the Secretary of the Department of Health and Human Services or his/her designee.

SECTION 2
Obligations and Activities of Business Associate

Business Associate agrees to the following:

2.1 ***Not to Use or Disclose PHI Unless Permitted or Required.*** Business Associate agrees not to use or disclose Protected Health Information other than as permitted or required by this Agreement, or as Required By Law, or as otherwise authorized by Covered Entity.

2.2 ***Use Safeguards.*** Business Associate agrees to use appropriate safeguards to prevent use or disclosure of Protected Health Information other than as provided for by this Agreement. Business Associate will implement administrative, physical, and technical safeguards that reasonably and appropriately protect the confidentiality, integrity and availability of any electronic Protected Health Information that Business Associate creates, receives, maintains, or transmits on behalf of Covered Entity.

2.3 ***Mitigate Harmful Effects.*** Business Associate agrees to mitigate, to the extent practicable, any harmful effect that is known to Business Associate of a use or disclosure of Protected Health Information by Business Associate in violation of this Agreement.

2.4 ***Report Unpermitted Disclosures of PHI.*** Business Associate agrees to report to Covered Entity any use or disclosure of Protected Health Information not permitted or required by this Agreement of which Business Associate becomes aware. Business Associate also agrees to report to Covered Entity any Security Incident related to Protected Health Information of which Business Associate becomes aware.

2.5 ***Compliance of Agents.*** Business Associate agrees to require any agents, including subcontractors, to whom it provides Protected Health Information to agree to the same restrictions and conditions that apply to Business Associate through this Agreement with respect to such Protected Health Information.

2.6 ***Provide Access.*** Business Associate agrees to provide access, during normal business hours, to Protected Health Information in a Designated Record Set of Covered Entity to Covered Entity in order to meet the requirements of 45 C.F.R. § 164.524, provided Covered Entity delivers written notice to Business Associate, at least five business days in advance, requesting such access. This provision does not apply if Business Associate and its employees, subcontractors, and agents have no Protected Health Information in a Designated Record Set of Covered Entity or if the Protected Health Information held by Business Associate merely duplicates information held by Covered Entity.

2.7 ***Incorporate Amendments.*** Business Associate agrees to incorporate any amendment(s) to Protected Health Information in a Designated Record Set of Covered Entity that Covered Entity directs pursuant to 45 C.F.R. § 164.526. This provision does not apply if Business Associate and its employees, subcontractors, and agents have no Protected Health Information from a Designated Record Set of Covered Entity.

2.8 ***Disclose Practices, Books, and Records.*** Unless otherwise protected or prohibited from discovery or disclosure by law, Business Associate agrees to make internal practices, books, and records relating to the use and disclosure of Protected Health Information available to the Secretary for purposes of determining Covered Entity's compliance with the Privacy Rule or the Security Rule. Business Associate shall have a reasonable time within which to comply with requests for such access and in no case shall access be required in less than five (5) business days after Business Associate's receipt of such request, unless otherwise designated by the Secretary.

2.9 ***Document Disclosures.*** Business Associate agrees to maintain sufficient documentation of such disclosures of Protected Health Information by Business Associate as would be required for Covered Entity to respond to a request by an Individual for an accounting of disclosures of Protected Health Information in accordance with 45 C.F.R. § 164.528.

2.10 ***Release Documentation of Disclosures.*** On request of Covered Entity, Business Associate agrees to provide to Covered Entity documentation made in accordance with Section 2.9 of this Agreement to permit Covered Entity to respond to a request by an Individual for an accounting of disclosures of Protected Health Information in accordance with 45 C.F.R. § 164.528. Business Associate shall have a reasonable time within which to comply with such a request from Covered Entity and in no case shall Business Associate be required to provide such documentation in less than five (5) business days after Business Associate's receipt of such request.

2.11 ***Respond to Requests from Individuals.*** Except as this Agreement or any other agreement between Covered Entity and Business Associate may otherwise provide, in the event Business Associate receives an access, amendment, accounting of disclosure, or other similar request directly from an Individual, Business Associate will redirect the Individual to Covered Entity.

SECTION 3
Permitted Uses and Disclosures by Business Associates

3.1 ***Functions and Activities on Behalf of Covered Entity***

Under the ________________ Agreement, Business Associate provides Covered Entity with __________ services ("Services") that involve the use and disclosure of Protected Health Information. These Services may include ____.

Except as otherwise limited by this Agreement, Business Associate may make any uses and disclosures of Protected Health Information necessary to perform Services and meet its obligations under this Agreement, if such use or disclosure would not violate the Privacy Rule if done by Covered Entity. All other uses or disclosures by Business Associate not authorized by this Agreement or by specific instruction of Covered Entity are prohibited.

3.2 ***Business Associate's Management and Administration.*** Except as otherwise limited by this Agreement, Business Associate may use Protected Health Information for the proper management and administration of Business Associate and to carry out the responsibilities of Business Associate.

3.3 ***Disclosure by Business Associate Required by Law or With Reasonable Assurances.*** Except as otherwise limited by this Agreement, Business Associate may disclose Protected Health Information for the proper management and administration of the Business Associate and to carry out its responsibilities, provided that disclosure is Required By Law, or provided that the Business Associate obtains reasonable assurances from the person or entity to whom the Protected Health Information is disclosed that: (1) the Protected Health Information will be held confidentially; (2) the Protected Health Information will be used or further disclosed only as Required By Law or for the purpose(s) for which it was disclosed to the person or entity; and (3) the person or entity will notify Business Associate of any instances of which the person or entity is aware in which the confidentiality of the information has been breached.

SECTION 4
Term and Termination

4.1 ***Term.*** The Term of this Agreement shall begin April 14, 2003, or the effective date of the agreement between Business Associate and Covered Entity, whichever is later. This Agreement shall terminate when all of the Protected Health Information provided by Covered Entity to Business Associate, or created or received by Business Associate on behalf of Covered Entity, is destroyed or returned to Covered Entity, or, if it is not feasible in the determination of the Business Associate to return or destroy Protected Health Information, protections are extended to such information, in accordance with the termination provisions in this section.

4.2 ***Termination for Cause.*** Upon Covered Entity's reasonable determination that Business Associate has breached or violated a material term of this Agreement, Covered Entity shall give Business Associate written notice of such breach and provide reasonable opportunity for Business Associate to cure the breach or end the violation. Covered Entity may terminate the Agreement, and Business Associate agrees to such termination, if Business Associate has breached a material term of this Agreement and does not cure the breach or cure is not possible.

4.3 ***Effect of Termination.*** Upon termination of the business relationship between Business Associate and Covered Entity and receipt of written demand from Covered Entity, Business Associate agrees to, if feasible, return or destroy all Protected Health Information received from, or created or received by Business Associate on behalf of, Covered Entity. In the event the return or destruction of such Protected Health Information is not feasible in the determination of Business Associate, the protections of this Agreement will remain in force and Business Associate shall make no further uses and disclosures of Protected Health Information except for the proper management and administration of its business or to carry out its legal responsibilities or as Required By Law.

SECTION 5
Miscellaneous Provisions

5.1.1 ***Regulatory References.*** A reference in this Agreement to a section in the Privacy Rule means the Section in effect or as amended and for which compliance is required.

5.1.2 ***Amendment.*** Business Associate agrees to take such action as is necessary to amend this Agreement from time to time as is necessary for Covered Entity to comply with the requirements of the Privacy Rule and HIPAA.

5.2 ***Survival.*** The rights and obligations of Business Associate under Section 4.3 of this Agreement shall survive the termination of this Agreement.

5.2.1 ***Interpretation.*** Any ambiguity in this Agreement shall be resolved in favor of a meaning that permits Covered Entity to comply with the Privacy Rule.

Covered Entity	**Business Associate**
Signature: ____________________	Signature: ____________________
Print Name: ____________________	Print Name: ____________________

APPENDIX D

Reasonable Assurances Agreement

THIS ASSURANCES AGREEMENT, REQUIRED BY THE HEALTH INSURANCE PORTABILITY AND ACCOUNTABILITY ACT (HIPAA), (this "Agreement") is made by and between ____________ ("Person or Entity") and ________________ (insert name of Business Associate), each individually a "Party" and together the "Parties."

WHEREAS, _________ (insert name of Business Associate) is a party to a Business Associate Agreement under HIPAA for which it receives protected health information (PHI) regarding ________________________________, (insert name of parties to the litigation) and under which _________ (insert name of Business Associate) agrees to secure reasonable assurances from subcontractors or vendors _________ (insert name of Business Associate) engages to assist in providing services to a covered entity under HIPAA.

WHEREAS, _________ (insert name of Business Associate) and Person or Entity have entered into an agreement (the "Service Agreement") under which Person or Entity uses Protected Health Information in its performance of services under the Service Agreement; and

WHEREAS, _________ (insert name of Business Associate) and Person or Entity intend to comply with the Standards for Privacy of Individually Identifiable Health Information codified at 45 C.F.R. Parts 160 and 164 (the "Privacy Rule") under the Health Insurance Portability and Accountability Act of 1996 ("HIPAA"); and

WHEREAS, this Agreement sets forth the terms and conditions pursuant to which _________ (insert name of Business Associate) and Person or Entity will handle Protected Health Information ("PHI") that is provided by, or created or received by, Person or Entity from or on behalf of _________ (insert name of Business Associate) during the term of the Service Agreement and after its termination.

NOW THEREFORE, the Parties agree as follows:

1. Definitions. Terms used in this Agreement that are not defined herein shall have the meaning as set forth in the Privacy Rule.

2. Permitted Uses and Disclosures. *Services.* Pursuant to the Service Agreement, Person or Entity provides services for _________ (insert name of

Business Associate) that involves the use or disclosure of PHI. Except as otherwise specified herein, Person or Entity may make any uses of PHI necessary to perform its obligations under the Service Agreement in a manner consistent with the Privacy Rule.

Unless otherwise limited herein, Person or Entity may:

a. Use the PHI in its possession for its own proper management and administration, or to fulfill any present or future legal responsibilities of Person or Entity, provided that such uses are permitted under applicable state and federal laws.
b. Under no circumstances may Person or Entity disclose PHI of a covered entity, absent the explicit authorization of _________ (insert name of Business Associate).

3. Responsibilities of Person or Entity. With regard to its use and disclosure of Protected Health Information, Person or Entity agrees to:

a. **Keep the Protected Health Information confidential.**
b. Use or disclose Protected Health Information only as permitted or required by the Service Agreement and this Agreement or as required by law.
c. Use appropriate security safeguards as required by current law to prevent the use or disclosure of PHI other than as provided for by the Service Agreement and this Agreement.
d. Report to _________ (insert name of Business Associate), any use or disclosure of the PHI not permitted or required by the Service Agreement or this Assurances Agreement of which Person or Entity becomes aware within 15 days of Person or Entity's discovery of such unauthorized use or disclosure.
e. Ensure that any agent, including a subcontractor, to whom Person or Entity provides PHI received from or created or received by Person or Entity on behalf of _________ (insert name of Business Associate) agrees to the same restrictions and conditions that apply through the Service Agreement or this Agreement to Person or Entity with respect to such information.
f. Make internal practices, books, and records relating to the use and disclosure of PHI received from, or created by Person or Entity on behalf of _________ (insert name of Business Associate) available to the Secretary of the federal Department of Health and Human Services, Office for Civil Rights for purposes of monitoring compliance with the Privacy Rule.
g. Make an individual's PHI accessible to _________ (insert name of Business Associate) by such date as mutually agreed upon by the Parties for individual access requirements in accordance with 45 C.F.R. § 164.524.

h. Make any amendments to an individual's PHI as requested by _________ (insert name of Business Associate) by such date as mutually agreed upon by the Parties for amendment of PHI requirements in accordance with 45 C.F.R. § 164.526.
i. Document such disclosure of PHI and information related to such disclosures as would be required for _________ (insert name of Business Associate) for an accounting of disclosures of PHI in accordance with 45 C.F.R. § 164.528.
j. Provide to _________ (insert name of Business Associate) by such date as mutually agreed upon by the Parties, information collected in accordance with Section 3.h of this Agreement, to permit to respond to a request for an accounting of disclosures of PHI in accordance with 45 C.F.R. § 164.528.

4. Term and Termination.

4.1 Term. This Agreement will become effective on April 14, 2003, or the effective date of the Retainer Agreement between the Covered Entity and _________ (insert name of Business Associate), whichever is later, and will remain effective until all of the PHI provided by _________ (insert name of Business Associate) to Person or Entity, or created or received by Person or Entity on behalf of _________ (insert name of Business Associate) is destroyed or returned to _________ (insert name of Business Associate). If it is not feasible to return or destroy the PHI, in the determination of Person or Entity, the protections of this Agreement will remain in force. Person or Entity shall make no further uses of PHI, except for the proper management and administration of its business or to carry out its legal responsibilities or as required by law.

4.2 Effect of Termination. Upon termination of the Service Agreement, Person or Entity shall return to _________ (insert name of Business Associate) all PHI received from _________ (insert name of Business Associate) for the purpose of performing obligations under the Service Agreement. Person or Entity will comply with the requirements of this Agreement for as long as Person or Entity retains the information and will limit further uses and disclosures to those purposes that are required to fulfill the obligations under the Service Agreement. Person or Entity shall remain bound by the provisions of this Agreement; even after termination of the Agreement, until such time as all PHI has been returned to _________ (insert name of Business Associate) or destroyed.

5. Miscellaneous.

5.1 Survival. The respective rights and obligations of Person or Entity and _________ (insert name of Business Associate) under the provisions of Section 4.2 will survive termination of this Agreement.

5.2 Amendments: Waive. This Agreement constitutes the entire agreement between the Parties with respect to its subject matter. It may not be modified, nor will any provision be waived or amended, except in a writing duly signed by authorized representatives of the Parties. A waiver with respect to one event will not be construed as continuing, or as a bar to or waiver of any right or remedy as to subsequent events. The Parties agree to take such action as is necessary to amend this Agreement for _________ (insert name of Business Associate) to comply with the requirements of the Privacy Rule.

5.3 No Third-Party Beneficiaries. Except as provided in Section 2, nothing express or implied in this Agreement is intended to confer, nor shall anything herein confer, upon any person other than the Parties and the respective successors and permitted assigns of the Parties, any rights, remedies, obligation or liabilities whatsoever.

5.4 Notices. Any notice to be given under this Agreement to a Party shall be made via U.S. Mail, commercial courier, or hand delivery to such Party at its address given below, or to such other address as shall hereinafter be specified by notice from the Party. Any such notice shall be deemed given when so delivered to or received at the proper address.

(insert name of Business Associate)
(insert business address of Business Associate)

5.5 Inconsistencies. If any terms of this Agreement conflict with or are inconsistent with the terms of any other agreements in existence between _________ (insert name of Business Associate) and Person or Entity, the terms of this Agreement will prevail.

IN WITNESS THEREOF, each of the parties have caused this Agreement to be executed in its name and on its behalf.

BUSINESS ASSOCIATE	**PERSON OR ENTITY**
Signature: ______________________	Signature: ______________________
Print Name: ____________________	Print Name: ____________________
Title: __________________________	Title: __________________________
Date: ____________________	Date: ____________________

APPENDIX E

Notice of Privacy Practices

Reader please take note: Reproduction and use of this form by physicians and their staff is permitted. Any other use, duplication, or distribution of this form by any other party requires the prior written approval of the American Medical Association, Health Law Division.

[This form does not constitute legal advice and is for educational purposes only. This form is based on current federal law and subject to change based on changes in federal law or subsequent interpretative guidance. This form is based on federal law and must be modified to reflect state law where that state law is more stringent than the federal law or other state law exceptions apply.]

[INSERT NAME OF PRACTICE]
NOTICE OF PRIVACY PRACTICES

THIS NOTICE DESCRIBES HOW MEDICAL INFORMATION ABOUT YOU MAY BE USED AND DISCLOSED AND HOW YOU CAN GET ACCESS TO THIS INFORMATION. PLEASE REVIEW IT CAREFULLY.

If you have any questions about this Notice please contact our Privacy Officer, who is [Insert Name of Privacy Officer]

This Notice of Privacy Practices describes how we may use and disclose your protected health information to carry out treatment, payment, or health care operations and for other purposes that are permitted or required by law. It also describes your rights to access and control your protected health information. "Protected health information" is information about you, including demographic information, that may identify you and that relates to your past, present, or future physical or mental health or condition and related health care services.

We are required to abide by the terms of this Notice of Privacy Practices. We may change the terms of our notice, at any time. The new notice will be effective for all protected health information that we maintain at that time.

Upon your request, we will provide you with any revised Notice of Privacy Practices. You may request a revised version by accessing our Web site, or calling the office and requesting that a revised copy be sent to you in the mail or asking for one at the time of your next appointment.

1. Uses and Disclosures of Protected Health Information

Your protected health information may be used and disclosed by your physician, our office staff, and others outside of our office who are involved in your care and treatment for the purpose of providing health care services to you. Your protected health information may also be used and disclosed to pay your health care bills and to support the operation of your physician's practice.

Following are examples of the types of uses and disclosures of your protected health information that your physician's office is permitted to make. These examples are not meant to be exhaustive, but to describe the types of uses and disclosures that may be made by our office.

Treatment: We will use and disclose your protected health information to provide, coordinate, or manage your health care and any related services. This includes the coordination or management of your health care with another provider. For example, we would disclose your protected health information, as necessary, to a home health agency that provides care to you. We will also disclose protected health information to other physicians who may be treating you. For example, your protected health information may be provided to a physician to whom you have been referred to ensure that the physician has the necessary information to diagnose or treat you. In addition, we may disclose your protected health information from time to time to another physician or health care provider (e.g., a specialist or laboratory) who, at the request of your physician, becomes involved in your care by providing assistance with your health care diagnosis or treatment to your physician.

Payment: Your protected health information will be used and disclosed, as needed, to obtain payment for your health care services provided by us or by another provider. This may include certain activities that your health insurance plan may undertake before it approves or pays for the health care services we recommend for you, such as making a determination of eligibility or coverage for insurance benefits, reviewing services provided to you for medical necessity, and undertaking utilization review activities. For example, obtaining approval for a hospital stay may require that your relevant protected health information be disclosed to the health plan to obtain approval for the hospital admission.

Health Care Operations: We may use or disclose, as needed, your protected health information in order to support the business activities of your physician's practice. These activities include, but are not limited to, quality assessment activities, employee review activities, training of medical students, licensing, fundraising activities, and conducting or arranging for other business activities.

We will share your protected health information with third party "business associates" that perform various activities (for example, billing or transcription services) for our practice. Whenever an arrangement between our office and a business associate involves the use or disclosure of your protected health information, we will have a written contract that contains terms that will protect the privacy of your protected health information.

We may use or disclose your protected health information, as necessary, to provide you with information about treatment alternatives or other health-related benefits and services that may be of interest to you. You may contact our Privacy Officer to request that these materials not be sent to you.

We may use or disclose your demographic information and the dates that you received treatment from your physician, as necessary, in order to contact you for fundraising activities supported by our office. If you do not want to receive these materials, please contact our Privacy Officer and request that these fundraising materials not be sent to you.

Other Permitted and Required Uses and Disclosures That May Be Made without Your Authorization or Opportunity to Agree or Object

We may use or disclose your protected health information in the following situations without your authorization or providing you the opportunity to agree or object. These situations include

Required by Law: We may use or disclose your protected health information to the extent that the use or disclosure is required by law. The use or disclosure will be made in compliance with the law and will be limited to the relevant requirements of the law. You will be notified, if required by law, of any such uses or disclosures.

Public Health: We may disclose your protected health information for public health activities and purposes to a public health authority that is permitted by law to collect or receive the information. For example, a disclosure may be made for the purpose of preventing or controlling disease, injury, or disability.

Communicable Diseases: We may disclose your protected health information, if authorized by law, to a person who may have been exposed to a communicable disease or may otherwise be at risk of contracting or spreading the disease or condition.

Health Oversight: We may disclose protected health information to a health oversight agency for activities authorized by law, such as audits, investigations, and inspections. Oversight agencies seeking this information include government agencies that oversee the health care system, government benefit programs, other government regulatory programs, and civil rights laws.

Abuse or Neglect: We may disclose your protected health information to a public health authority that is authorized by law to receive reports of child abuse or neglect. In addition, we may disclose your protected health information if we believe that you have been a victim of abuse, neglect, or domestic violence to the governmental entity or agency authorized to receive such information. In this case, the disclosure will be made consistent with the requirements of applicable federal and state laws.

Food and Drug Administration: We may disclose your protected health information to a person or company as required by the Food and Drug Administration for the purpose of quality, safety, or effectiveness of FDA-regulated products or activities, including to report adverse events, product defects or problems, or biologic product deviations; to track products; to enable product recalls; to make repairs or replacements; or to conduct post marketing surveillance.

Legal Proceedings: We may disclose protected health information in the course of any judicial or administrative proceeding, in response to an order of a court or administrative tribunal (to the extent such disclosure is expressly authorized), or in certain conditions in response to a subpoena, discovery request, or other lawful process.

Law Enforcement: We may also disclose protected health information, so long as applicable legal requirements are met, for law enforcement purposes. These law enforcement purposes include (1) legal processes and otherwise required by law, (2) limited information requests for identification and location purposes, (3) pertaining to victims of a crime, (4) suspicion that death has occurred as a result of criminal conduct, (5) in the event that a crime occurs on the premises of our practice, and (6) medical emergency (not on our practice's premises) and it is likely that a crime has occurred.

Coroners, Funeral Directors, and Organ Donation: We may disclose protected health information to a coroner or medical examiner for identification purposes, determining cause of death or for the coroner or medical examiner to perform other duties authorized by law. We may also disclose protected health information to a funeral director, as authorized by law, in order to permit the funeral director to carry out their duties. We may disclose such information in reasonable anticipation of death. Protected health information may be used and disclosed for cadaveric organ, eye, or tissue donation purposes.

Research: We may disclose your protected health information to researchers when their research has been approved by an institutional review board that has reviewed the research proposal and established protocols to ensure the privacy of your protected health information.

Criminal Activity: Consistent with applicable federal and state laws, we may disclose your protected health information if we believe that the use or disclosure is necessary to prevent or lessen a serious and imminent threat to the health or safety of a person or the public. We may also disclose protected health information if it is necessary for law enforcement authorities to identify or apprehend an individual.

Military Activity and National Security: When the appropriate conditions apply, we may use or disclose protected health information of individuals who are Armed Forces personnel (1) for activities deemed necessary by appropriate military command authorities, (2) for the purpose of a determination by the Department of Veterans Affairs of your eligibility for benefits, or (3) to a foreign military authority if you are a member of that foreign military service. We may also disclose your protected health information to authorized federal officials for conducting national security and intelligence activities, including for the provision of protective services to the President or others legally authorized.

Workers' Compensation: We may disclose your protected health information as authorized to comply with workers' compensation laws and other similar legally established programs.

Inmates: We may use or disclose your protected health information if you are an inmate of a correctional facility and your physician created or received your protected health information in the course of providing care to you.

Uses and Disclosures of Protected Health Information Based upon Your Written Authorization

Other uses and disclosures of your protected health information will be made only with your written authorization, unless otherwise permitted or required by law as described below. You may revoke this authorization in writing at any time. If you revoke your authorization, we will no longer use or disclose your protected health information for the reasons covered by your written authorization. Please understand that we are unable to take back any disclosures already made with your authorization.

Other Permitted and Required Uses and Disclosures That Require Providing You the Opportunity to Agree or Object

We may use and disclose your protected health information in the following instances. You have the opportunity to agree or object to the use or disclosure of all or part of your protected health information. If you are not present or able to agree or object to the use or disclosure of the protected health information, then your physician may, using professional judgment, determine whether the disclosure is in your best interest.

Facility Directories: Unless you object, we will use and disclose in our facility directory your name, the location at which you are receiving care, your general condition (such as "fair" or "stable"), and your religious affiliation. All of this information, except religious affiliation, will be disclosed to people that ask for you by name. Your religious affiliation will be given only to a member of the clergy, such as a priest or rabbi.

Others Involved in Your Health Care or Payment for Your Care: Unless you object, we may disclose to a member of your family, a relative, a close friend, or any other person you identify, your protected health information that directly relates to that person's involvement in your health care. If you are unable to agree or object to such a disclosure, we may disclose such information as necessary if we determine that it is in your best interest based on our professional judgment. We may use or disclose protected health information to notify or assist in notifying a family member, personal representative, or any other person that is responsible for your care of your location, general condition, or death. Finally, we may use or disclose your protected health information to an authorized public or private entity to assist in disaster relief efforts and to coordinate uses and disclosures to family or other individuals involved in your health care.

2. Your Rights

Following is a statement of your rights with respect to your protected health information and a brief description of how you may exercise these rights.

You have the right to inspect and copy your protected health information. This means you may inspect and obtain a copy of protected health information about you for so long as we maintain the protected health information. You may obtain your medical record that contains medical and billing records and any other records that your physician and the practice uses for making decisions about you. As permitted by federal or state law, we may charge you a reasonable copy fee for a copy of your records.

Under federal law, however, you may not inspect or copy the following records: psychotherapy notes; information compiled in reasonable anticipation of, or use in, a civil, criminal, or administrative action or proceeding; and laboratory results that are subject to law that prohibits access to protected health information. Depending on the circumstances, a decision to deny access may be reviewable. In some circumstances, you may have a right to have this decision reviewed. Please contact our Privacy Officer if you have questions about access to your medical record.

You have the right to request a restriction of your protected health information. This means you may ask us not to use or disclose any part of your protected health information for the purposes of treatment, payment, or health care operations. You may also request that any part of your protected health information not be disclosed to family members or friends who may be involved in your care or for notification purposes as described in this Notice of

Privacy Practices. Your request must state the specific restriction requested and to whom you want the restriction to apply.

Your physician is not required to agree to a restriction that you may request. If your physician does agree to the requested restriction, we may not use or disclose your protected health information in violation of that restriction unless it is needed to provide emergency treatment. With this in mind, please discuss any restriction you wish to request with your physician. You may request a restriction by **[describe how patient may obtain a restriction]**.

You have the right to request to receive confidential communications from us by alternative means or at an alternative location. We will accommodate reasonable requests. We may also condition this accommodation by asking you for information as to how payment will be handled or specification of an alternative address or other method of contact. We will not request an explanation from you as to the basis for the request. Please make this request in writing to our Privacy Officer.

You may have the right to have your physician amend your protected health information. This means you may request an amendment of protected health information about you in a designated record set for so long as we maintain this information. In certain cases, we may deny your request for an amendment. If we deny your request for amendment, you have the right to file a statement of disagreement with us and we may prepare a rebuttal to your statement and will provide you with a copy of any such rebuttal. Please contact our Privacy Officer if you have questions about amending your medical record.

You have the right to receive an accounting of certain disclosures we have made, if any, of your protected health information. This right applies to disclosures for purposes other than treatment, payment, or health care operations as described in this Notice of Privacy Practices. It excludes disclosures we may have made to you if you authorized us to make the disclosure, for a facility directory, to family members or friends involved in your care, or for notification purposes, for national security or intelligence, to law enforcement (as provided in the privacy rule) or correctional facilities, as part of a limited data set disclosure. You have the right to receive specific information regarding these disclosures that occur after April 14, 2003. The right to receive this information is subject to certain exceptions, restrictions, and limitations.

You have the right to obtain a paper copy of this notice from us, upon request, even if you have agreed to accept this notice electronically.

3. Complaints

You may complain to us or to the Secretary of Health and Human Services if you believe your privacy rights have been violated by us. You may file a complaint with us by notifying our Privacy Officer of your complaint. We will not retaliate against you for filing a complaint.

You may contact our Privacy Officer, **[Insert Name of Privacy Officer]**, at (___)____-_______ or **[Insert e-mail address of Privacy Officer]** for further information about the complaint process.

This notice was published and becomes effective on ____________ .

APPENDIX F

Health Insurance Portability and Accountability Act

U.S. Department of Health and Human Services
Office for Civil Rights

Standards for Privacy of Individually Identifiable Health Information

Security Standards for the Protection of Electronic Protected Health Information

General Administrative Requirements Including, Civil Money Penalties: Procedures for Investigations, Imposition of Penalties, and Hearings

Regulation Text

(Unofficial Version)

(45 CFR Parts 160 and 164)

December 28, 2000 as amended: May 31, 2002,
August 14, 2002, February 20, 2003, and April 17, 2003

TABLE OF CONTENTS

Section

PART 160—GENERAL ADMINISTRATIVE REQUIREMENTS

SUBPART A—GENERAL PROVISIONS
§ 160.101 Statutory basis and purpose
§ 160.102 Applicability
§ 160.103 Definitions
Act
ANSI
Business associate
Compliance date
Covered entity
Disclosure
EIN
Electronic protected health care information
Electronic media
Employer
Group health plan
HCFA
HHS
Health care
Health care clearinghouse
Health care provider
Health information
Health insurance issuer
Health maintenance organization (HMO)
Health plan
Implementation specification
Individual
Individually identifiable health information
Modify or modification
Organized health care arrangement
Protected health information
Secretary
Small health plan
Standard
Standard setting organization (SSO)
State
Trading partner agreement
Transaction
Use
Workforce
§ 160.104 Modifications

SUBPART B—PREEMPTION OF STATE LAW

§ 160.201 Applicability

§ 160.202 Definitions

Contrary
More stringent
Relates to the privacy of individually identifiable health information
State law

§ 160.203 General rule and exceptions

§ 160.204 Process for requesting exception determinations

§ 160.205 Duration of effectiveness of exception determinations

SUBPART C—COMPLIANCE AND ENFORCEMENT

§ 160.300 Applicability

§ 160.302 Definitions

§ 160.304 Principles for achieving compliance

(a) Cooperation
(b) Assistance

§ 160.306 Complaints to the Secretary

(a) Right to file a complaint
(b) Requirements for filing complaints
(c) Investigation

§ 160.308 Compliance reviews

§ 160.310 Responsibilities of covered entities

(a) Provide records and compliance reports
(b) Cooperate with complaint investigations and compliance reviews
(c) Permit access to information

§ 160.312 Secretarial action regarding complaints and compliance reviews

(a) Resolution where noncompliance is indicated
(b) Resolution when no violation is found

SUBPART E—CIVIL MONEY PENALTIES: PROCEDURES FOR INVESTIGATIONS, IMPOSITION OF PENALTIES, AND HEARINGS

§ 160.500 Applicability

§ 160.502 Definitions

ALJ
Entity
Penalty
Person
Respondent

§ 160.504 Investigational subpoenas and inquiries

§ 160.506 Basis for penalty

§ 160.508 Amount of penalty

§ 160.510 Authority to settle

§ 160.512 [Reserved]

§ 160.514 Notice of proposed determination
§ 160.516 Failure to request a hearing
§ 160.518 Collection of penalty
§ 160.520 [Reserved]
§ 160.522 Limitations
§ 160.524 [Reserved]
§ 160.526 Hearing before an ALJ
§ 160.528 Rights of parties
§ 160.530 Authority of the ALJ
§ 160.532 Ex parte contacts
§ 160.534 Prehearing conferences
§ 160.536 Settlement
§ 160.538 Discovery
§ 160.540 Exchange of witness lists, witness statements, and exhibits
§ 160.542 Subpoenas for attendance at hearing
§ 160.544 Fees
§ 160.546 Form, filing, and service of papers
§ 160.548 Computation of time
§ 160.550 Motions
§ 160.552 Sanctions
§ 160.554 The hearing
§ 160.556 Witnesses
§ 160.558 Evidence
§ 160.560 The record
§ 160.562 Post hearing briefs
§ 160.564 ALJ decision
§ 160.566 [Reserved]
§ 160.568 Judicial review
§ 160.570 Stay of ALJ decision
§ 160.572 [Reserved]

PART 162—ADMINISTRATIVE REQUIREMENTS

PART 164—SECURITY AND PRIVACY

SUBPART A—GENERAL PROVISIONS
§ 164.102 Statutory basis
§ 164.103 Definitions
Common control
Common ownership
Covered functions
Health care component
Hybrid entity
Plan sponsor
Required by law
§ 164.104 Applicability

§ 164.105 Organizational Requirements
§ 164.106 Relationship to other parts

SUBPART B—[RESERVED]

SUBPART C—SECURITY STANDARDS FOR THE PROTECTION OF ELECTRONIC PROTECTED HEALTH INFORMATION
§ 164.302 Applicability
§ 164.304 Definitions
- Access
- Administrative Safeguards
- Authentication
- Availability
- Confidentiality
- Encryption
- Facility
- Information system
- Integrity
- Malicious software
- Password
- Physical safeguards
- Security or Security measures
- Security incident
- Technical safeguards
- User
- Workstation

§ 164.306 Security standards: General rules
§ 164.308 Administrative safeguards
§ 164.310 Physical safeguards
§ 164.312 Technical safeguards
§ 164.314 Organizational requirements
§ 164.316 Policies and procedures and documentation requirements
§ 164.318 Compliance dates for initial implementation of security standards

SUBPART D—[RESERVED]

SUBPART E—PRIVACY OF INDIVIDUALLY IDENTIFIABLE HEALTH INFORMATION
§ 164.500 Applicability
§ 164.501 Definitions
- Correctional institution
- Data aggregation
- Designated record set
- Direct treatment relationship
- Health care operations

Health oversight agency
Indirect treatment relationship
Inmate
Law enforcement official
Marketing
Payment
Psychotherapy notes
Public health authority
Research
Treatment

§ 164.502 Uses and disclosures of protected health information: general rules

(a) Standard:
- (1) Permitted uses & disclosures
- (2) Required disclosures

(b) Standard: minimum necessary
- (1) Minimum necessary applies
- (2) Minimum necessary does not apply

(c) Standard: uses and disclosures of protected health information subject to an agreed upon restriction

(d) Standard: Uses and disclosures of de-identified protected health information
- (1) Uses and disclosures to create de-identified information
- (2) Uses and disclosures of de-identified information

(e) (1) Standard: disclosures to business associates
- (2) Implementation specification: documentation

(f) Standard: deceased individuals

(g) (1) Standard: personal representatives
- (2) Implementation specification: adults and emancipated minors
- (3) Implementation specification: unemancipated minors
- (4) Implementation specification: deceased individuals
- (5) Implementation specification: abuse, neglect, endangerment situations

(h) Standard: confidential communications

(i) Standard: uses and disclosures consistent with notice

(j) Standard: disclosures by whistleblowers and workforce member crime victims
- (1) Disclosures by whistleblowers
- (2) Disclosures by workforce members who are victims of a crime

§ 164.504 Uses and disclosures: organizational requirements

(a) Definitions
- Plan administration functions
- Summary health information

Paragraphs (b)-(d)–[Removed and Reserved]

(e) (1) Standard: business associate contracts
    (2) Implementation specifications: business associate contracts
    (3) Implementation specifications: other arrangements
    (4) Implementation specifications: other requirements for contracts and other arrangements
(f) (1) Standard: requirements for group health plans
    (2) Implementation specifications: requirements for plan documents
    (3) Implementation specifications: uses and disclosures
(g) Standard: requirements for a covered entity with multiple covered functions

§ 164.506 Uses and disclosures to carry out treatment, payment, or health care operations

(a) Standard: permitted uses and disclosures
(b) Standard: consent for uses and disclosures permitted
(c) Implementation specifications: treatment, payment, or health care operations

§ 164.508 Uses and disclosures for which an authorization is required

(a) Standard: authorizations for uses and disclosures
    (1) Authorization required: general rule
    (2) Authorization required: psychotherapy notes
    (3) Authorization required: marketing
(b) Implementation specifications: general requirements
    (1) Valid authorizations
    (2) Defective authorizations
    (3) Compound authorizations
    (4) Prohibition on conditioning of authorizations
    (5) Revocation of authorizations
    (6) Documentation
(c) Implementation specifications: core elements and requirements
    (1) Core elements
    (2) Required statements
    (3) Plain language requirement
    (4) Copy to the individual

§ 164.510 Uses and disclosures requiring an opportunity for the individual to agree or to object

(a) Standard: use and disclosure for facility directories
    (1) Permitted uses and disclosure
    (2) Opportunity to object
    (3) Emergency circumstances
(b) Standard: uses and disclosures for involvement in the individual's care and notification purposes
    (1) Permitted uses and disclosures
    (2) Uses and disclosures with the individual present

- (3) Limited uses and disclosures when the individual is not present
- (4) Use and disclosures for disaster relief purposes

§ 164.512 Uses and disclosures for which an authorization or opportunity to agree or object is not required

- (a) Standard: uses and disclosures required by law
- (b) Standard: uses and disclosures for public health activities
  - (1) Permitted disclosures
  - (2) Permitted uses
- (c) Standard: disclosures about victims of abuse, neglect, or domestic violence
  - (1) Permitted disclosures
  - (2) Informing the individual
- (d) Standard: uses and disclosures for health oversight activities
  - (1) Permitted disclosures
  - (2) Exception to health oversight activities
  - (3) Joint activities or investigations
  - (4) Permitted uses
- (e) Standard: disclosures for judicial and administrative proceedings
  - (1) Permitted disclosures
  - (2) Other uses and disclosures under this section
- (f) Standard: disclosures for law enforcement purposes
  - (1) Permitted disclosures: pursuant to process and as otherwise required by law
  - (2) Permitted disclosures: limited information for identification and location purposes
  - (3) Permitted disclosure: victims of a crime
  - (4) Permitted disclosure: decedents
  - (5) Permitted disclosure: crime on premises
  - (6) Permitted disclosure: reporting crime in emergencies
- (g) Standard: uses and disclosures about decedents
  - (1) Coroners and medical examiners
  - (2) Funeral directors
- (h) Standard: uses and disclosures for cadaveric organ, eye, or tissue donation purposes
- (i) Standard: uses and disclosures for research purposes
  - (1) Permitted uses and disclosures
    - (i) Board approval of a waiver of authorization
    - (ii) Reviews preparatory to research
    - (iii) Research on decedent's information
  - (2) Documentation of waiver approval
    - (i) Identification and date of action
    - (ii) Waiver criteria
    - (iii) Protected health information needed
    - (iv) Review and approval procedures
    - (v) Required signature

- (j) Standard: uses and disclosures to avert a serious threat to health or safety
  - (1) Permitted disclosures
  - (2) Use or disclosure not permitted
  - (3) Limit on information that may be disclosed
  - (4) Presumption of good faith belief
- (k) Standard: uses and disclosures for specialized government functions
  - (1) Military and veterans activities
    - (i) Armed Forces personnel
    - (ii) Separation or discharge from military service
    - (iii) Veterans
    - (iv) Foreign military personnel
  - (2) National security and intelligence activities
  - (3) Protective services for the President and others
  - (4) Medical suitability determinations
  - (5) Correctional institutions and other law enforcement custodial situations
    - (i) Permitted disclosures
    - (ii) Permitted uses
    - (iii) No application after release
  - (6) Covered entities that are government programs providing public benefits
- (l) Standard: disclosures for workers' compensation

§ 164.514 Other requirements relating to uses & disclosures of protected health information

- (a) Standard: de-identification of protected health information
- (b) Implementation specifications: requirements for de-identification of protected health information
- (c) Implementation specifications: re-identification
  - (1) Derivation
  - (2) Security
- (d) (1) Standard: minimum necessary requirements
  - (2) Implementation specifications: minimum necessary uses of protected health information
  - (3) Implementation specification: minimum necessary disclosures of protected health information
  - (4) Implementation specifications: minimum necessary requests for protected health information
  - (5) Implementation specification: other content requirement
- (e) (1) Standard: limited data set
  - (2) Implementation specification: limited data set
  - (3) Implementation specification: permitted purposes for uses and disclosures
  - (4) Implementation specifications: data use agreement
    - (i) Agreement required

(ii) Contents
(iii) Compliance
(f) (1) Standard: uses and disclosures for fundraising
(2) Implementation specifications: fundraising requirements
(g) Standard: uses and disclosures for underwriting and related purposes
(h) (1) Standard: verification requirements
(2) Implementation specifications: verification
(i) Conditions on disclosures
(ii) Identity of public officials
(iii) Authority of public officials
(iv) Exercise of professional judgment

§ 164.520 Notice of privacy practices for protected health information

(a) Standard: notice of privacy practices
(1) Right to notice
(2) Exception for group health plans
(3) Exception for inmates
(b) Implementation specifications: content of notice
(1) Required elements
(i) Header
(ii) Uses and disclosures
(iii) Separate statements for certain uses or disclosures
(iv) Individual rights
(v) Covered entity's duties
(vi) Complaints
(vii) Contact
(viii) Effective date
(2) Optional elements
(3) Revisions to the notice
(c) Implementation specifications: provision of notice
(1) Specific requirements for health plans
(2) Specific requirements for certain covered health care providers
(3) Specific requirements for electronic notice
(d) Implementation specifications: joint notice by separate covered entities
(e) Implementation specifications: documentation

§ 164.522 Rights to request privacy protection for protected health information

(a) (1) Standard: right of an individual to request restriction of uses and disclosures
(2) Implementation specifications: terminating a restriction
(3) Implementation specification: documentation
(b) (1) Standard: confidential communications requirements
(2) Implementation specifications: conditions on providing confidential communications

§ 164.524 Access of individuals to protected health information

(a) Standard: access to protected health information
  (1) Right of access
  (2) Unreviewable grounds for denial
  (3) Reviewable grounds for denial
  (4) Review of a denial of access
(b) Implementation specifications: requests for access and timely action
  (1) Individual's request for access
  (2) Timely action by the covered entity
(c) Implementation specifications: provision of access
  (1) Providing the access requested
  (2) Form of access requested
  (3) Time and manner of access
  (4) Fees
(d) Implementation specifications: denial of access
  (1) Making other information accessible
  (2) Denial
  (3) Other responsibility
  (4) Review of denial requested
(e) Implementation specification: documentation

§ 164.526 Amendment of protected health information

(a) Standard: right to amend
(1) Right to amend
(2) Denial of amendment
(b) Implementation specifications: requests for amendment and timely action
(1) Individual's request for amendment
(2) Timely action by the covered entity
(c) Implementation specifications: accepting the amendment
(1) Making the amendment
(2) Informing the individual
(3) Informing others
(d) Implementation specifications: denying the amendment
(1) Denial
(2) Statement of disagreement
(3) Rebuttal statement
(4) Recordkeeping
(5) Future disclosures
(e) Implementation specification: actions on notices of amendment
(f) Implementation specification: documentation

§ 164.528 Accounting of disclosures of protected health information

(a) Standard: right to an accounting of disclosures of protected health information
(b) Implementation specifications: content of the accounting

(c) Implementation specifications: provision of the accounting
(d) Implementation specification: documentation

§ 164.530 Administrative requirements

(a) (1) Standard: personnel designations
(2) Implementation specification: personnel designations
(b) (1) Standard: training
(2) Implementation specifications: training
(c) (1) Standard: safeguards
(2) Implementation specification: safeguards
(d) (1) Standard: complaints to the covered entity
(2) Implementation specification: documentation of complaints
(e) (1) Standard: sanctions
(2) Implementation specification: documentation
(f) Standard: mitigation
(g) Standard: refraining from intimidating or retaliatory acts
(1) Individuals
(2) Individuals and others
(h) Standard: waiver of rights
(i) (1) Standard: policies and procedures
(2) Standard: changes to policies or procedures
(3) Implementation specification: changes in law
(4) Implementation specifications: changes to privacy practices stated in the notice
(5) Implementation specification: changes to other policies or procedures
(j) (1) Standard: documentation
(2) Implementation specification: retention period
(k) Standard: group health plans

§ 164.532 Transition provisions

(a) Standard: effect of prior authorizations
(b) Implementation specification: effect of prior authorization for purposes other than research
(c) Implementation specification: effect of prior permission for research
(d) Standard: effect of prior contracts or other arrangements with business associates
(e) Implementation specification: deemed compliance
(1) Qualification
(2) Limited deemed compliance period
(3) Covered entity responsibilities

§ 164.534 Compliance dates for initial implementation of the privacy standards

(a) Health care providers

(b) Health plans
  (1) Health plans other than small health plans
  (2) Small health plans
(c) Health care clearinghouses

PART 160—GENERAL ADMINISTRATIVE REQUIREMENTS

SUBPART A—GENERAL PROVISIONS

160.101 Statutory basis and purpose.
160.102 Applicability.
160.103 Definitions.
160.104 Modifications.

SUBPART B—PREEMPTION OF STATE LAW

160.201 Applicability.
160.202 Definitions.
160.203 General rule and exceptions.
160.204 Process for requesting exception determinations.
160.205 Duration of effectiveness of exception determinations.

SUBPART C—COMPLIANCE AND ENFORCEMENT

160.3 Applicability.
160.302 Definitions.
160.304 Principles for achieving compliance.
160.306 Complaints to the Secretary.
160.308 Compliance reviews.
160.310 Responsibilities of covered entities.
160.312 Secretarial action regarding complaints and compliance reviews.

SUBPART E—CIVIL MONEY PENALTIES: PROCEDURES FOR INVESTIGATIONS, IMPOSITION OF PENALTIES, AND HEARINGS

160.5 Applicability.
160.502 Definitions.
160.504 Investigational subpoenas and inquiries.
160.506 Basis for penalty.
160.508 Amount of penalty.
160.510 Authority to settle.
160.512 [Reserved]
160.514 Notice of proposed determination.
160.516 Failure to request a hearing.
160.518 Collection of penalty.
160.520 [Reserved]
160.522 Limitations.
160.524 [Reserved]

160.526 Hearing before an ALJ.
160.528 Rights of parties.
160.530 Authority of the ALJ.
160.532 Ex parte contacts.
160.534 Prehearing conferences.
160.536 Settlement.
160.538 Discovery.
160.540 Exchange of witness lists, witness statements, and exhibits.
160.542 Subpoenas for attendance at hearing.
160.544 Fees.
160.546 Form, filing, and service of papers.
160.548 Computation of time.
160.550 Motions.
160.552 Sanctions.
160.554 The hearing.
160.556 Witnesses.
160.558 Evidence.
160.560 The record.
160.562 Post hearing briefs.
160.564 ALJ decision.
160.566 [Reserved]
160.568 Judicial review.
160.570 Stay of ALJ decision.
160.572 [Reserved]

Authority: 42 U.S.C. 1302(a), 42 U.S.C. 1320d–1320d-8, and sec. 264 of Pub. L. 104-191, 110 Stat. 20-2034 (42 U.S.C. 1320d-2(note)).

Subpart A—General Provisions

§ 160.101 Statutory basis and purpose.
The requirements of this subchapter implement sections 1171 through 1179 of the Social Security Act (the Act), as added by section 262 of Public Law 104-191, and section 264 of Public Law 104-191.

§ 160.102 Applicability.
(a) Except as otherwise provided, the standards, requirements, and implementation specifications adopted under this subchapter apply to the following entities:

(1) A health plan.

(2) A health care clearinghouse.

(3) A health care provider who transmits any health information in electronic form in connection with a transaction covered by this subchapter.

(b) To the extent required under the Social Security Act, 42 U.S.C. 1320a-7c(a)(5), nothing in this subchapter shall be construed to diminish the authority of any Inspector General, including such authority as provided in the Inspector General Act of 1978, as amended (5 U.S.C. App.).

§ 160.103 Definitions.

Except as otherwise provided, the following definitions apply to this subchapter:

Act means the Social Security Act.

ANSI stands for the American National Standards Institute.

Business associate:

(1) Except as provided in paragraph (2) of this definition, *business associate* means, with respect to a covered entity, a person who:

(i) On behalf of such covered entity or of an organized health care arrangement (as defined in § 164.501 of this subchapter) in which the covered entity participates, but other than in the capacity of a member of the workforce of such covered entity or arrangement, performs, or assists in the performance of:

(A) A function or activity involving the use or disclosure of individually identifiable health information, including claims processing or administration, data analysis, processing or administration, utilization review, quality assurance, billing, benefit management, practice management, and repricing; or

(B) Any other function or activity regulated by this subchapter; or

(ii) Provides, other than in the capacity of a member of the workforce of such covered entity, legal, actuarial, accounting, consulting, data aggregation (as defined in § 164.501 of this subchapter), management, administrative, accreditation, or financial services to or for such covered entity, or to or for an organized health care arrangement in which the covered entity participates, where the provision of the service involves the disclosure of individually identifiable health information from such covered entity or arrangement, or from another business associate of such covered entity or arrangement, to the person.

(2) A covered entity participating in an organized health care arrangement that performs a function or activity as described by paragraph (1)(i) of this definition for or on behalf of such organized health care arrangement, or that provides a service as described in paragraph (1)(ii) of this definition to or for such organized health care arrangement, does not, simply through the performance of such function or activity or the provision of such service, become a business associate of other covered entities participating in such organized health care arrangement.

(3) A covered entity may be a business associate of another covered entity.

Compliance date means the date by which a covered entity must comply with a standard, implementation specification, requirement, or modification adopted under this subchapter.

Covered entity means:

(1) A health plan.

(2) A health care clearinghouse.

(3) A health care provider who transmits any health information in electronic form in connection with a transaction covered by this subchapter.

Disclosure means the release, transfer, provision of, access to, or divulging in any other manner of information outside the entity holding the information.

EIN stands for the employer identification number assigned by the Internal Revenue Service, U.S. Department of the Treasury. The EIN is the taxpayer identifying number of an individual or other entity (whether or not an employer) assigned under one or the following:

(1) 26 U.S.C. 6011(b), which is the portion of the Internal Revenue Code dealing with identifying the taxpayer in tax returns and statements, or corresponding provisions of prior law.

(2) 26 U.S.C. 6109, which is the portion of the Internal Revenue Code dealing with identifying numbers in tax returns, statements, and other required documents.

Electronic media means:

(1) Electronic storage media including memory devices in computers (hard drives) and any removable/transportable digital memory medium, such as magnetic tape or disk, optical disk, or digital memory card; or

(2) Transmission media used to exchange information already in electronic storage media. Transmission media include, for example, the internet (wide-open), extranet (using internet technology to link a business with information accessible only to collaborating parties), leased lines, dial-up lines, private networks, and the physical movement of removable/transportable electronic storage media. Certain transmissions, including of paper, via facsimile, and of voice, via telephone, are not considered to be transmissions via electronic media, because the information being exchanged did not exist in electronic form before the transmission.

Electronic protected health care information means information that comes within paragraphs (1)(i) or (1)(ii) of the definition of *protected health information* as specified in this section.

Employer is defined as it is in 26 U.S.C. 3401(d).

Group health plan (also see definition of *health plan* in this section) means an employee welfare benefit plan (as defined in section 3(1) of the Employee Retirement Income and Security Act of 1974 (ERISA), 29 U.S.C. 1002(1)), including insured and self-insured plans, to the extent that the plan provides medical care (as defined in section 2791(a)(2) of the Public Health Service Act (PHS Act), 42 U.S.C. 300gg-91(a)(2)), including items and services paid for as medical care, to employees or their dependents directly or through insurance, reimbursement, or otherwise, that:

(1) Has 50 or more participants (as defined in section 3(7) of ERISA, 29 U.S.C. 1002(7)); or

(2) Is administered by an entity other than the employer that established and maintains the plan.

HCFA stands for Health Care Financing Administration within the Department of Health and Human Services.

HHS stands for the Department of Health and Human Services.

Health care means care, services, or supplies related to the health of an individual.

Health care includes, but is not limited to, the following:

(1) Preventive, diagnostic, therapeutic, rehabilitative, maintenance, or palliative care, and counseling, service, assessment, or procedure with respect to the physical or mental condition, or functional status, of an individual or that affects the structure or function of the body; and

(2) Sale or dispensing of a drug, device, equipment, or other item in accordance with a prescription.

Health care clearinghouse means a public or private entity, including a billing service, repricing company, community health management information system or community health information system, and "value-added" networks and switches, that does either of the following functions:

(1) Processes or facilitates the processing of health information received from another entity in a nonstandard format or containing nonstandard data content into standard data elements or a standard transaction.

(2) Receives a standard transaction from another entity and processes or facilitates the processing of health information into nonstandard format or nonstandard data content for the receiving entity.

Health care provider means a provider of services (as defined in section 1861(u) of the Act, 42 U.S.C. 1395x(u)), a provider of medical or health services (as defined in section 1861(s) of the Act, 42 U.S.C. 1395x(s)), and any other person or organization who furnishes, bills, or is paid for health care in the normal course of business.

Health information means any information, whether oral or recorded in any form or medium, that:

(1) Is created or received by a health care provider, health plan, public health authority, employer, life insurer, school or university, or health care clearinghouse; and

(2) Relates to the past, present, or future physical or mental health or condition of an individual; the provision of health care to an individual; or the past, present, or future payment for the provision of health care to an individual.

Health insurance issuer (as defined in section 2791(b)(2) of the PHS Act, 42 U.S.C. 300gg-91(b)(2) and used in the definition of *health plan* in this section) means an insurance company, insurance service, or insurance organization (including an HMO) that is licensed to engage in the business of insurance in a State and is subject to State law that regulates insurance. Such term does not include a group health plan.

Health maintenance organization (HMO)(as defined in section 2791(b)(3) of the PHS Act, 42 U.S.C. 300gg-91(b)(3) and used in the definition of *health plan* in this section) means a federally qualified HMO, an organization recognized as an HMO under State law, or a similar organization regulated for solvency under State law in the same manner and to the same extent as such an HMO.

Health plan means an individual or group plan that provides, or pays the cost of, medical care (as defined in section 2791(a)(2) of the PHS Act, 42 U.S.C. 300gg-91(a)(2)).

(1) *Health plan* includes the following, singly or in combination:

(i) A group health plan, as defined in this section.

(ii) A health insurance issuer, as defined in this section.

(iii) An HMO, as defined in this section.

(iv) Part A or Part B of the Medicare program under title XVIII of the Act.

(v) The Medicaid program under title XIX of the Act, 42 U.S.C. 1396, et seq.

(vi) An issuer of a Medicare supplemental policy (as defined in section 1882(g)(1) of the Act, 42 U.S.C. 1395ss(g)(1)).

(vii) An issuer of a long-term care policy, excluding a nursing home fixed-indemnity policy.

(viii) An employee welfare benefit plan or any other arrangement that is established or maintained for the purpose of offering or providing health benefits to the employees of two or more employers.

(ix) The health care program for active military personnel under title 10 of the United States Code.

(x) The veterans health care program under 38 U.S.C. chapter 17.

(xi) The Civilian Health and Medical Program of the Uniformed Services (CHAMPUS) (as defined in 10 U.S.C. 1072(4)).

(xii) The Indian Health Service program under the Indian Health Care Improvement Act, 25 U.S.C. 1601, et seq.

(xiii) The Federal Employees Health Benefits Program under 5 U.S.C. 8902, et seq.

(xiv) An approved State child health plan under title XXI of the Act, providing benefits for child health assistance that meet the requirements of section 2103 of the Act, 42 U.S.C. 1397, et seq.

(xv) The Medicare + Choice program under Part C of title XVIII of the Act, 42 U.S.C. 1395w-21 through 1395w-28.

(xvi) A high risk pool that is a mechanism established under State law to provide health insurance coverage or comparable coverage to eligible individuals.

(xvii) Any other individual or group plan, or combination of individual or group plans, that provides or pays for the cost of medical care (as defined in section 2791(a)(2) of the PHS Act, 42 U.S.C. 300gg-91(a)(2)).

(2) *Health plan* excludes:

(i) Any policy, plan, or program to the extent that it provides, or pays for the cost of, excepted benefits that are listed in section 2791(c)(1) of the PHS Act, 42 U.S.C. 300gg-91(c)(1); and

(ii) A government-funded program (other than one listed in paragraph (1)(i)-(xvi) of this definition):

(A) Whose principal purpose is other than providing, or paying the cost of, health care; or

(B) Whose principal activity is:

(*1*) The direct provision of health care to persons; or

(*2*) The making of grants to fund the direct provision of health care to persons.

Implementation specification means specific requirements or instructions for implementing a standard.

Individual means the person who is the subject of protected health information.

Individually identifiable health information is information that is a subset of health information, including demographic information collected from an individual, and:

(1) Is created or received by a health care provider, health plan, employer, or health care clearinghouse; and

(2) Relates to the past, present, or future physical or mental health or condition of an individual; the provision of health care to an individual; or the past, present, or future payment for the provision of health care to an individual; and

(i) That identifies the individual; or

(ii) With respect to which there is a reasonable basis to believe the information can be used to identify the individual.

Modify or *modification* refers to a change adopted by the Secretary, through regulation, to a standard or an implementation specification. *Organized health care arrangement* means:

(1) A clinically integrated care setting in which individuals typically receive health care from more than one health care provider;

(2) An organized system of health care in which more than one covered entity participates and in which the participating covered entities:

(i) Hold themselves out to the public as participating in a joint arrangement; and

(ii) Participate in joint activities that include at least one of the following:

(A) Utilization review, in which health care decisions by participating covered entities are reviewed by other participating covered entities or by a third party on their behalf;

(B) Quality assessment and improvement activities, in which treatment provided by participating covered entities is assessed by other participating covered entities or by a third party on their behalf; or

(C) Payment activities, if the financial risk for delivering health care is shared, in part or in whole, by participating covered entities through the joint arrangement and if protected health information created or received by a covered entity is reviewed by other participating covered entities or by a third party on their behalf for the purpose of administering the sharing of financial risk.

(3) A group health plan and a health insurance issuer or HMO with respect to such group health plan, but only with respect to protected health information created or received by such health insurance issuer or HMO that relates to individuals who are or who have been participants or beneficiaries in such group health plan;

(4) A group health plan and one or more other group health plans each of which are maintained by the same plan sponsor; or

(5) The group health plans described in paragraph (4) of this definition and health insurance issuers or HMOs with respect to such group health plans, but only with respect to protected health information created or received by such health insurance issuers or HMOs that relates to individuals who are or have been participants or beneficiaries in any of such group health plans.

Protected Health information means individually identifiable health information:

(1) Except as provided in paragraph (2) of this definition, that is:

(i) Transmitted by electronic media;

(ii) Maintained in electronic media; or

(iii) Transmitted or maintained in any other form or medium.

(2) Protected health information excludes individually identifiable health information in:

(i) Education records covered by the Family Educational Rights and Privacy Act, as amended, 20 U.S.C. 1232g;

(ii) Records described at 20 U.S.C. 1232g(a)(4)(B)(iv); and

(iii) Employment records held by a covered entity in its role as employer.

Secretary means the Secretary of Health and Human Services or any other officer or employee of HHS to whom the authority involved has been delegated.

Small health plan means a health plan with annual receipts of $5 million or less.

Standard means a rule, condition, or requirement:

(1) Describing the following information for products, systems, services or practices:

(i) Classification of components.

(ii) Specification of materials, performance, or operations; or

(iii) Delineation of procedures; or

(2) With respect to the privacy of individually identifiable health information.

Standard setting organization (SSO) means an organization accredited by the American National Standards Institute that develops and maintains standards for information transactions or data elements, or any other standard that is necessary for, or will facilitate the implementation of, this part.

State refers to one of the following:

(1) For a health plan established or regulated by Federal law, *State* has the meaning set forth in the applicable section of the United States Code for such health plan.

(2) For all other purposes, *State* means any of the several States, the District of Columbia, the Commonwealth of Puerto Rico, the Virgin Islands, and Guam.

Trading partner agreement means an agreement related to the exchange of information in electronic transactions, whether the agreement is distinct or part of a larger agreement, between each party to the agreement. (For example, a trading partner agreement may specify, among other things, the duties and responsibilities of each party to the agreement in conducting a standard transaction.)

Transaction means the transmission of information between two parties to carry out financial or administrative activities related to health care. It includes the following types of information transmissions:

(1) Health care claims or equivalent encounter information.
(2) Health care payment and remittance advice.
(3) Coordination of benefits.
(4) Health care claim status.
(5) Enrollment and disenrollment in a health plan.
(6) Eligibility for a health plan.
(7) Health plan premium payments.
(8) Referral certification and authorization.
(9) First report of injury.
(10) Health claims attachments.
(11) Other transactions that the Secretary may prescribe by regulation.

Use means, with respect to individually identifiable health information, the sharing, employment, application, utilization, examination, or analysis of such information within an entity that maintains such information.

Workforce means employees, volunteers, trainees, and other persons whose conduct, in the performance of work for a covered entity, is under the direct control of such entity, whether or not they are paid by the covered entity.

§ 160.104 Modifications.

(a) Except as provided in paragraph (b) of this section, the Secretary may adopt a modification to a standard or implementation specification adopted under this subchapter no more frequently than once every 12 months.

(b) The Secretary may adopt a modification at any time during the first year after the standard or implementation specification is initially adopted, if the Secretary determines that the modification is necessary to permit compliance with the standard or implementation specification.

(c) The Secretary will establish the compliance date for any standard or implementation specification modified under this section.

(1) The compliance date for a modification is no earlier than 180 days after the effective date of the final rule in which the Secretary adopts the modification.

(2) The Secretary may consider the extent of the modification and the time needed to comply with the modification in determining the compliance date for the modification.

(3) The Secretary may extend the compliance date for small health plans, as the Secretary determines is appropriate.

Subpart B—Preemption of State Law

§ 160.201 Applicability.

The provisions of this subpart implement section 1178 of the Act, as added by section 262 of Public Law 104-191.

§ 160.202 Definitions.

For purposes of this subpart, the following terms have the following meanings:

Contrary, when used to compare a provision of State law to a standard, requirement, or implementation specification adopted under this subchapter, means:

(1) A covered entity would find it impossible to comply with both the State and federal requirements; or

(2) The provision of State law stands as an obstacle to the accomplishment and execution of the full purposes and objectives of part C of title XI of the Act or section 264 of Pub. L. 104-191, as applicable.

More stringent means, in the context of a comparison of a provision of State law and a standard, requirement, or implementation specification adopted under subpart E of part 164 of this subchapter, a State law that meets one or more of the following criteria:

(1) With respect to a use or disclosure, the law prohibits or restricts a use or disclosure in circumstances under which such use or disclosure otherwise would be permitted under this subchapter, except if the disclosure is:

(i) Required by the Secretary in connection with determining whether a covered entity is in compliance with this subchapter; or

(ii) To the individual who is the subject of the individually identifiable health information.

(2) With respect to the rights of an individual, who is the subject of the individually identifiable health information, regarding access to or amendment of individually identifiable health information, permits greater rights of access or amendment, as applicable.

(3) With respect to information to be provided to an individual who is the subject of the individually identifiable health information about a use, a disclosure, rights, and remedies, provides the greater amount of information.

(4) With respect to the form, substance, or the need for express legal permission from an individual, who is the subject of the individually identifiable health information, for use or disclosure of individually identifiable health information, provides requirements that narrow the scope or duration, increase the privacy protections afforded (such as by expanding the criteria for), or reduce the coercive effect of the circumstances surrounding the express legal permission, as applicable.

(5) With respect to recordkeeping or requirements relating to accounting of disclosures, provides for the retention or reporting of more detailed information or for a longer duration.

(6) With respect to any other matter, provides greater privacy protection for the individual who is the subject of the individually identifiable health information.

Relates to the privacy of individually identifiable health information means, with respect to a State law, that the State law has the specific purpose of protecting the privacy of health information or affects the privacy of health information in a direct, clear, and substantial way.

State law means a constitution, statute, regulation, rule, common law, or other State action having the force and effect of law.

§ 160.203 General rule and exceptions.

A standard, requirement, or implementation specification adopted under this subchapter that is contrary to a provision of State law preempts the provision of State law. This general rule applies, except if one or more of the following conditions is met:

(a) A determination is made by the Secretary under § 160.204 that the provision of State law:

(1) Is necessary:

(i) To prevent fraud and abuse related to the provision of or payment for health care;

(ii) To ensure appropriate State regulation of insurance and health plans to the extent expressly authorized by statute or regulation;

(iii) For State reporting on health care delivery or costs; or

(iv) For purposes of serving a compelling need related to public health, safety, or welfare, and, if a standard, requirement, or implementation specification under part 164 of this subchapter is at issue, if the Secretary determines that the intrusion into privacy is warranted when balanced against the need to be served; or

(2) Has as its principal purpose the regulation of the manufacture, registration, distribution, dispensing, or other control of any controlled substances (as defined in 21 U.S.C. 802), or that is deemed a controlled substance by State law.

(b) The provision of State law relates to the privacy of individually identifiable health information and is more stringent than a standard, requirement, or implementation specification adopted under subpart E of part 164 of this subchapter.

(c) The provision of State law, including State procedures established under such law, as applicable, provides for the reporting of disease or injury, child abuse, birth, or death, or for the conduct of public health surveillance, investigation, or intervention.

(d) The provision of State law requires a health plan to report, or to provide access to, information for the purpose of management audits, financial audits, program monitoring and evaluation, or the licensure or certification of facilities or individuals.

§ 160.204 Process for requesting exception determinations.

(a) A request to except a provision of State law from preemption under § 160.203(a) may be submitted to the Secretary. A request by a State must be submitted through its chief elected official, or his or her designee. The request must be in writing and include the following information:

(1) The State law for which the exception is requested;

(2) The particular standard, requirement, or implementation specification for which the exception is requested;

(3) The part of the standard or other provision that will not be implemented based on the exception or the additional data to be collected based on the exception, as appropriate;

(4) How health care providers, health plans, and other entities would be affected by the exception;

(5) The reasons why the State law should not be preempted by the federal standard, requirement, or implementation specification, including how the State law meets one or more of the criteria at § 160.203(a); and

(6) Any other information the Secretary may request in order to make the determination.

(b) Requests for exception under this section must be submitted to the Secretary at an address that will be published in the *Federal Register.* Until the Secretary's determination is made, the standard, requirement, or implementation specification under this subchapter remains in effect.

(c) The Secretary's determination under this section will be made on the basis of the extent to which the information provided and other factors demonstrate that one or more of the criteria at § 160.203(a) has been met.

§ 160.205 Duration of effectiveness of exception determinations.

An exception granted under this subpart remains in effect until:

(a) Either the State law or the federal standard, requirement, or implementation specification that provided the basis for the exception is materially changed such that the ground for the exception no longer exists; or

(b) The Secretary revokes the exception, based on a determination that the ground supporting the need for the exception no longer exists.

Subpart C—Compliance and Enforcement

§ 160.300 Applicability.

This subpart applies to actions by the Secretary, covered entities, and others with respect to ascertaining the compliance by covered entities with and the enforcement of the applicable requirements of this part 160 and the applicable standards, requirements, and implementation specifications of subpart E of part 164 of this subchapter.

§ 160.302 Definitions.

As used in this subpart, terms defined in § 164.501 of this subchapter have the same meanings given to them in that section.

§ 160.304 Principles for achieving compliance.

(a) *Cooperation.* The Secretary will, to the extent practicable, seek the cooperation of covered entities in obtaining compliance with the applicable requirements of this part 160 and the applicable standards, requirements, and implementation specifications of subpart E of part 164 of this subchapter.

(b) *Assistance.* The Secretary may provide technical assistance to covered entities to help them comply voluntarily with the applicable requirements of this part 160 or the applicable standards, requirements, and implementation specifications of subpart E of part 164 of this subchapter.

§ 160.306 Complaints to the Secretary.

(a) *Right to file a complaint.* A person who believes a covered entity is not complying with the applicable requirements of this part 160 or the applicable standards, requirements, and implementation specifications of subpart E of part 164 of this subchapter may file a complaint with the Secretary.

(b) *Requirements for filing complaints.* Complaints under this section must meet the following requirements:

(1) A complaint must be filed in writing, either on paper or electronically.

(2) A complaint must name the entity that is the subject of the complaint and describe the acts or omissions believed to be in violation of the applicable requirements of this part 160 or the applicable standards, requirements, and implementation specifications of subpart E of part 164 of this subchapter.

(3) A complaint must be filed within 180 days of when the complainant knew or should have known that the act or omission complained of occurred, unless this time limit is waived by the Secretary for good cause shown.

(4) The Secretary may prescribe additional procedures for the filing of complaints, as well as the place and manner of filing, by notice in the *Federal Register.*

(c) *Investigation.* The Secretary may investigate complaints filed under this section. Such investigation may include a review of the pertinent policies, procedures,

§ 160.308 Compliance reviews.

The Secretary may conduct compliance reviews to determine whether covered entities are complying with the applicable requirements of this part 160 and the applicable standards, requirements, and implementation specifications of subpart E of part 164 of this subchapter.

§ 160.310 Responsibilities of covered entities.

(a) *Provide records and compliance reports.* A covered entity must keep such records and submit such compliance reports, in such time and manner and containing such information, as the Secretary may determine to be necessary to enable the Secretary to ascertain whether the covered entity has complied or is complying with the applicable requirements of this part 160 and the applicable standards, requirements, and implementation specifications of subpart E of part 164 of this subchapter.

(b) *Cooperate with complaint investigations and compliance reviews.* A covered entity must cooperate with the Secretary, if the Secretary undertakes an investigation or compliance review of the policies, procedures, or practices of a covered entity to determine whether it is complying with the applicable requirements of this part 160 and the standards, requirements, and implementation specifications of subpart E of part 164 of this subchapter.

(c) *Permit access to information.*

(1) A covered entity must permit access by the Secretary during normal business hours to its facilities, books, records, accounts, and other sources of information, including protected health information, that are pertinent to ascertaining compliance with the applicable requirements of this part 160 and the applicable standards, requirements, and implementation specifications of subpart E of part 164 of this subchapter. If the Secretary determines that exigent circumstances exist, such as when documents may be hidden or destroyed, a covered entity must permit access by the Secretary at any time and without notice.

(2) If any information required of a covered entity under this section is in the exclusive possession of any other agency, institution, or person and the other agency, institution, or person fails or refuses to furnish the information, the covered entity must so certify and set forth what efforts it has made to obtain the information.

(3) Protected health information obtained by the Secretary in connection with an investigation or compliance review under this subpart will not be disclosed by the Secretary, except if necessary for ascertaining or enforcing compliance with the applicable requirements of this part 160 and the applicable standards, requirements, and implementation specifications of subpart E of part 164 of this subchapter, or if otherwise required by law.

§ 160.312 Secretarial action regarding complaints and compliance reviews.

(a) *Resolution where noncompliance is indicated.*

(1) If an investigation pursuant to § 160.306 or a compliance review pursuant to § 160.308 indicates a failure to comply, the Secretary will so inform the covered entity and, if the matter arose from a complaint, the complainant, in writing and attempt to resolve the matter by informal means whenever possible.

(2) If the Secretary finds the covered entity is not in compliance and determines that the matter cannot be resolved by informal means, the Secretary may issue to the covered entity and, if the matter arose from a complaint, to the complainant written findings documenting the non-compliance.

(b) *Resolution when no violation is found.* If, after an investigation or compliance review, the Secretary determines that further action is not warranted, the Secretary will so inform the covered entity and, if the matter arose from a complaint, the complainant in writing.

Subpart E—Civil Money Penalties: Procedures for Investigations, Imposition of Penalties, and Hearings

§ 160.500 Applicability.

This subpart applies to investigations conducted, penalties imposed, hearings conducted, and subpoenas issued, under the authority of 42 U.S.C. 1320d-5, relating to the imposition of civil money penalties.

§ 160.502 Definitions.

For the purposes of this subpart:

ALJ means Administrative Law Judge.

Entity means a legal person.

Penalty means the amount calculated under 42 U.S.C. 1320d-5, as determined in accordance with this part, and includes the plural of that term.

Person means a natural or legal person.

Respondent means the person upon whom the Secretary has imposed, or proposes to impose, a penalty.

§ 160.504 Investigational subpoenas and inquiries.

(a) The provisions of this paragraph govern subpoenas issued by the Secretary in accordance with 42 U.S.C. 405(d) and (e), 1320a-7a(j), and 1320d-5 to require the attendance and testimony of witnesses and the production of any other evidence during an investigation pursuant to this part.

(1) A subpoena issued under this paragraph must

(i) State the name of the person to whom the subpoena is addressed;

(ii) State the statutory authority for the subpoena;

(iii) Indicate the date, time, and place that the testimony will take place;

(iv) Include a reasonably specific description of any documents or items required to be produced; and

(v) If the subpoena is addressed to an entity, describe with reasonable particularity the subject matter on which testimony is required. In that event, the named entity must designate one or more natural persons who will testify on its behalf, and must state as to each person so designated that person's name and address and the matters on which he or she will testify. The person so designated must testify as to matters known or reasonably available to the entity.

(2) A subpoena under this section must be served by

(i) Delivering a copy to the natural person named in the subpoena or to the entity named in the subpoena at its last principal place of business; or

(ii) Registered or certified mail addressed to the natural person at his or her last known dwelling place or to the entity at its last known principal place of business.

(3) A verified return by the natural person serving the subpoena setting forth the manner of service or, in the case of service by registered or certified mail, the signed return post office receipt, constitutes proof of service.

(4) Witnesses are entitled to the same fees and mileage as witnesses in the district courts of the United States (28 U.S.C. 1821 and 1825). Fees need not be paid at the time the subpoena is served.

(5) A subpoena under this section is enforceable through the District Court of the United States for the district where the subpoenaed natural person resides or is found or where the entity transacts business.

(b) Investigational inquiries are non-public investigational proceedings conducted by the Secretary.

(1) Testimony at investigational inquiries will be taken under oath or affirmation.

(2) Attendance of non-witnesses is discretionary with the Secretary, except that a witness is entitled to be accompanied, represented, and advised by an attorney.

(3) The proceedings will be recorded and transcribed. The witness is entitled to a copy of the transcript, upon payment of prescribed costs, except that, for good cause, the witness may be limited to inspection of the official transcript of his or her testimony.

§ 160.506 Basis for penalty.

The Secretary shall impose a penalty on a person who is a covered entity and who the Secretary determines in accordance with this subpart has violated a provision of

(a) 42 U.S.C. 1320d-1320d-8, as amended;

(b) Section 264 of Pub. L. 104-191 (42 U.S.C. 1320d-2(note)); or

(c) Parts 160, 162 or 164 of this subchapter.

§ 160.508 Amount of penalty.

The penalty imposed under § 160.506 must be in accordance with 42 U.S.C. 1320d-5 and the applicable provisions of this part.

§ 160.510 Authority to settle.

Nothing in this subpart limits the authority of the Secretary to settle any issue or case or to compromise any penalty.

§ 160.512 [Reserved]

§ 160.514 Notice of proposed determination.

(a) If a penalty is proposed in accordance with this part, the Secretary must deliver, or send by certified mail with return receipt requested, to the respondent written notice of the Secretary's intent to impose a penalty. This notice of proposed determination must include

(1) Reference to the statutory basis for the penalty;

(2) A description of the findings of fact regarding the act(s) or omission(s) with respect to which the penalty is proposed;

(3) The reason(s) why the act(s) or omission(s) subject(s) the respondent to a penalty;

(4) The amount of the proposed penalty;

(5) Instructions for responding to the notice, including a statement of the respondent's right to a hearing, a statement that failure to request a hearing within 60 days permits the imposition of the proposed penalty without the right to a hearing under § 160.554 or a right of appeal under § 160.568, and the address to which the hearing request must be sent.

(b) The respondent may request a hearing before an ALJ on the proposed penalty by filing a request therefor in accordance with § 160.526 of this subpart.

§ 160.516 Failure to request a hearing.

If the respondent does not request a hearing within the time prescribed by § 160.526, the Secretary must impose the proposed penalty or any less severe penalty permitted by 42 U.S.C. 1320d-5. The Secretary must notify the respondent by certified mail, return receipt requested, of any penalty that has been imposed and of the means by which the respondent may satisfy the penalty. The respondent has no right to appeal under § 160.568 with respect to a penalty with respect to which the respondent has not timely requested a hearing.

§ 160.518 Collection of penalty.

(a) Once a determination of the Secretary to impose a penalty has become final, the penalty must be collected by the Secretary.

(b) The penalty may be recovered in a civil action brought in the United States district court for the district where the respondent resides, is found, or is located.

(c) The amount of a penalty, when finally determined, or the amount agreed upon in compromise, may be deducted from any sum then or later owing by the United States, or by a State agency, to the respondent.

(d) Matters that were raised or that could have been raised in a hearing before an ALJ or in an appeal under 42 U.S.C. 1320a-7a(e) may not be raised as a defense in a civil action by the United States to collect a penalty under this part.

§ 160.520 [Reserved]

§ 160.522 Limitations.

No action under this subpart may be entertained unless commenced by the Secretary, in accordance with § 160.514 of this subpart, within 6 years from the date on which the latest act or omission that is the subject of the action occurred.

§ 160.524 [Reserved]

§ 160.526 Hearing before an ALJ.

(a) The respondent may request a hearing before an ALJ. The parties to the hearing proceeding consist of

(1) The respondent; and

(2) The Secretary.

(b) The request for a hearing must be made in writing signed by the respondent or by the respondent's attorney and sent by certified mail, return receipt requested, to the address specified in the notice of proposed determination. The request for a hearing must be mailed within 60 days after notice of the proposed determination is received by the respondent. For purposes of this section, the respondent's date of receipt of the notice of proposed determination is presumed to be 5 days after the date of the notice unless the respondent makes a reasonable showing to the contrary to the ALJ.

(c) The request for a hearing must clearly and directly admit, deny, or explain each of the findings of fact contained in the notice of proposed determination with regard to which the respondent has any knowledge. If the respondent has no knowledge of a particular finding of fact and so states, the finding shall be deemed denied. The request for a hearing must also state the circumstances or arguments that the respondent alleges constitute the grounds for any defense and the factual and legal basis for opposing the penalty.

(d) The ALJ must dismiss a hearing request where

(1) The respondent's hearing request is not filed as required by paragraphs (b) and (c) of this section;

(2) The respondent withdraws the request for a hearing;

(3) The respondent abandons the request for a hearing; or

(4) The respondent's hearing request fails to raise any issue that may properly be addressed in a hearing.

§ 160.528 Rights of parties.

(a) Except as otherwise limited by this part, each party may

(1) Be accompanied, represented, and advised by an attorney;

(2) Participate in any conference held by the ALJ;

(3) Conduct discovery of documents as permitted by this subpart;

(4) Agree to stipulations of fact or law that will be made part of the record;

(5) Present evidence relevant to the issues at the hearing;

(6) Present and cross-examine witnesses;

(7) Present oral arguments at the hearing as permitted by the ALJ; and

(8) Submit written briefs and proposed findings of fact and conclusions of law after the hearing.

(b) A party may appear in person or by a representative. Natural persons who appear as an attorney or other representative must conform to the standards of conduct and ethics required of practitioners before the courts of the United States.

§ 160.530 Authority of the ALJ.

(a) The ALJ must conduct a fair and impartial hearing, avoid delay, maintain order, and ensure that a record of the proceeding is made.

(b) The ALJ may

(1) Set and change the date, time and place of the hearing upon reasonable notice to the parties;

(2) Continue or recess the hearing in whole or in part for a reasonable period of time;

(3) Hold conferences to identify or simplify the issues, or to consider other matters that may aid in the expeditious disposition of the proceeding;

(4) Administer oaths and affirmations;

(5) Issue subpoenas requiring the attendance of witnesses at hearings and the production of documents at or in relation to hearings;

(6) Rule on motions and other procedural matters;

(7) Regulate the scope and timing of documentary discovery as permitted by this subpart;

(8) Regulate the course of the hearing and the conduct of representatives, parties, and witnesses;

(9) Examine witnesses;

(10) Receive, rule on, exclude, or limit evidence;

(11) Upon motion of a party, take official notice of facts;

(12) Conduct any conference, argument or hearing in person or, upon agreement of the parties, by telephone; and

(13) Upon motion of a party, decide cases, in whole or in part, by summary judgment where there is no disputed issue of material fact. A summary judgment decision constitutes a hearing on the record for the purposes of this subpart.

(c) The ALJ may not–

(1) Find invalid or refuse to follow Federal statutes or regulations or delegations of authority by the Secretary;

(2) Enter an order in the nature of a directed verdict;

(3) Compel settlement negotiations; or

(4) Enjoin any act of the Secretary.

§ 160.532 Ex parte contacts.

No party or person (except employees of the ALJ's office) may communicate in any way with the ALJ on any matter at issue in a case, unless on notice and opportunity for both parties to participate. This provision does not prohibit a party or person from inquiring about the status of a case or asking routine questions concerning administrative functions or procedures.

§ 160.534 Prehearing conferences.

(a) The ALJ must schedule at least one prehearing conference, and may schedule additional prehearing conferences as appropriate, upon reasonable notice to the parties.

(b) The ALJ may use prehearing conferences to discuss the following

(1) Simplification of the issues;

(2) The necessity or desirability of amendments to the pleadings, including the need for a more definite statement;

(3) Stipulations and admissions of fact or as to the contents and authenticity of documents;

(4) Whether the parties can agree to submission of the case on a stipulated record;

(5) Whether a party chooses to waive appearance at an oral hearing and to submit only documentary evidence (subject to the objection of the other party) and written argument;

(6) Limitation of the number of witnesses;

(7) Scheduling dates for the exchange of witness lists and of proposed exhibits;

(8) Discovery of documents as permitted by this subpart;

(9) The time and place for the hearing;

(10) The potential for the settlement of the case by the parties; and

(11) Other matters as may tend to encourage the fair, just and expeditious disposition of the proceedings, including the protection of privacy of individually identifiable health information that may be submitted into evidence, if appropriate.

(c) The ALJ must issue an order containing the matters agreed upon by the parties or ordered by the ALJ at a prehearing conference.

§ 160.536 Settlement.

The Secretary has exclusive authority to settle any issue or case without the consent of the ALJ.

§ 160.538 Discovery.

(a) A party may make a request to another party for production of documents for inspection and copying that are relevant and material to the issues before the ALJ.

(b) For the purpose of this section, the term "documents" includes information, reports, answers, records, accounts, papers and other data and documentary evidence. Nothing contained in this section may be interpreted to require the creation of a document, except that requested data stored in an electronic data storage system must be produced in a form accessible to the requesting party.

(c) Requests for documents, requests for admissions, written interrogatories, depositions and any forms of discovery, other than those permitted under paragraph (a) of this section, are not authorized.

(d) This section may not be construed to require the disclosure of interview reports or statements obtained by any party, or on behalf of any party, of persons who will not be called as witnesses by that party, or analyses and summaries prepared in conjunction with the investigation or litigation of the case, or any otherwise privileged documents.

(e)(1) When a request for production of documents has been received, within 30 days the party receiving that request must either fully respond to the request, or state that the request is being objected to and the reasons for that objection. If objection is made to part of an item or category, the part must be specified. Upon receiving any objections, the party seeking production may then, within 30 days or any other time frame set by the ALJ, file a motion for an order compelling discovery. The party receiving a request for production may also file a motion for protective order any time before the date the production is due.

(2) The ALJ may grant a motion for protective order or deny a motion for an order compelling discovery if the ALJ finds that the discovery sought

(i) Is irrelevant;

(ii) Is unduly costly or burdensome;

(iii) Will unduly delay the proceeding; or

(iv) Seeks privileged information.

(3) The ALJ may extend any of the time frames set forth in paragraph (e)(1) of this section.

(4) The burden of showing that discovery should be allowed is on the party seeking discovery.

§ 160.540 Exchange of witness lists, witness statements, and exhibits.

(a) The parties must exchange witness lists, copies of prior written statements of proposed witnesses, and copies of proposed hearing exhibits, including copies of any written statements that the party intends to offer in lieu of live testimony in accordance with § 160.556, at least 15 days before the hearing, unless the ALJ orders an earlier exchange.

(b)(1) If at any time a party objects to the proposed admission of evidence not exchanged in accordance with paragraph (a) of this section, the ALJ must determine whether the failure to comply with paragraph (a) of this section should result in the exclusion of that evidence.

(2) Unless the ALJ finds that extraordinary circumstances justified the failure timely to exchange the information listed under paragraph (a) of this section, the ALJ must exclude from the party's case-in-chief

(i) The testimony of any witness whose name does not appear on the witness list; and

(ii) Any exhibit not provided to the opposing party as specified in paragraph (a) of this section.

(3) If the ALJ finds that extraordinary circumstances existed, the ALJ must then determine whether the admission of that evidence would cause substantial prejudice to the objecting party. If the ALJ finds that there is no substantial prejudice, the evidence may be admitted. If the ALJ finds that there is substantial prejudice, the ALJ may exclude the evidence, or, if he or she does not exclude the evidence, must postpone the hearing for such time as is neces-

sary for the objecting party to prepare and respond to the evidence, unless the objecting party waives postponement.

(c) Unless the other party objects within a reasonable period of time before the hearing, documents exchanged in accordance with paragraph (a) of this section will be deemed to be authentic for the purpose of admissibility at the hearing.

§ 160.542 Subpoenas for attendance at hearing.

(a) A party wishing to procure the appearance and testimony of any person at the hearing may make a motion requesting the ALJ to issue a subpoena if the appearance and testimony are reasonably necessary for the presentation of a party's case.

(b) A subpoena requiring the attendance of a person in accordance with paragraph (a) of this section may also require the person (whether or not the person is a party) to produce relevant and material evidence at or before the hearing.

(c) When a subpoena is served by a respondent on a particular employee or official or particular office of HHS, the Secretary may comply by designating any HHS representative to appear and testify.

(d) A party seeking a subpoena must file a written motion not less than 30 days before the date fixed for the hearing, unless otherwise allowed by the ALJ for good cause shown. That motion must

(1) Specify any evidence to be produced;

(2) Designate the witnesses; and

(3) Describe the address and location with sufficient particularity to permit those witnesses to be found.

(e) The subpoena must specify the time and place at which the witness is to appear and any evidence the witness is to produce.

(f) Within 15 days after the written motion requesting issuance of a subpoena is served, any party may file an opposition or other response.

(g) If the motion requesting issuance of a subpoena is granted, the party seeking the subpoena must serve it by delivery to the person named, or by certified mail addressed to that person at the person's last dwelling place or principal place of business.

(h) The person to whom the subpoena is directed may file with the ALJ a motion to quash the subpoena within 10 days after service.

(i) The exclusive remedy for contumacy by, or refusal to obey a subpoena duly served upon, any person is specified in 42 U.S.C. 405(e).

§ 160.544 Fees.

The party requesting a subpoena must pay the cost of the fees and mileage of any witness subpoenaed in the amounts that would be payable to a witness in a proceeding in United States District Court. A check for witness fees and mileage must accompany the subpoena when served, except that when a subpoena is issued on behalf of the Secretary, a check for witness fees and mileage need not accompany the subpoena.

§ 160.546 Form, filing, and service of papers.

(a) *Forms.* (1) Unless the ALJ directs the parties to do otherwise, documents filed with the ALJ must include an original and two copies.

(2) Every pleading and paper filed in the proceeding must contain a caption setting forth the title of the action, the case number, and a designation of the paper, such as motion to quash subpoena.

(3) Every pleading and paper must be signed by and must contain the address and telephone number of the party or the person on whose behalf the paper was filed, or his or her representative.

(4) Papers are considered filed when they are mailed.

(b) *Service.* A party filing a document with the ALJ or the Secretary must, at the time of filing, serve a copy of the document on the other party. Service upon any party of any document must be made by delivering a copy, or placing a copy of the document in the United States mail, postage prepaid and addressed, or with a private delivery service, to the party's last known address. When a party is represented by an attorney, service must be made upon the attorney in lieu of the party.

(c) *Proof of service.* A certificate of the natural person serving the document by personal delivery or by mail, setting forth the manner of service, constitutes proof of service.

§ 160.548 Computation of time.

(a) In computing any period of time under this part or in an order issued thereunder, the time begins with the day following the act, event or default, and includes the last day of the period unless it is a Saturday, Sunday, or legal holiday observed by the Federal Government, in which event it includes the next business day.

(b) When the period of time allowed is less than 7 days, intermediate Saturdays, Sundays, and legal holidays observed by the Federal Government must be excluded from the computation.

(c) Where a document has been served or issued by placing it in the mail, an additional 5 days must be added to the time permitted for any response. This paragraph does not apply to requests for hearing under § 160.526.

§ 160.550 Motions.

(a) An application to the ALJ for an order or ruling must be by motion. Motions must state the relief sought, the authority relied upon and the facts alleged, and must be filed with the ALJ and served on all other parties.

(b) Except for motions made during a prehearing conference or at the hearing, all motions must be in writing. The ALJ may require that oral motions be reduced to writing.

(c) Within 10 days after a written motion is served, or such other time as may be fixed by the ALJ, any party may file a response to the motion.

(d) The ALJ may not grant a written motion before the time for filing responses has expired, except upon consent of the parties or following a hearing on the motion, but may overrule or deny the motion without awaiting a response.

(e) The ALJ must make a reasonable effort to dispose of all outstanding motions before the beginning of the hearing.

§ 160.552 Sanctions.

The ALJ may sanction a person, including any party or attorney, for failing to comply with an order or procedure, for failing to defend an action or for other misconduct that interferes with the speedy, orderly or fair conduct of the hearing. The sanctions must reasonably relate to the severity and nature of the failure or misconduct. The sanctions may include

(a) In the case of refusal to provide or permit discovery under the terms of this part, drawing negative factual inferences or treating the refusal as an admission by deeming the matter, or certain facts, to be established;

(b) Prohibiting a party from introducing certain evidence or otherwise supporting a particular claim or defense;

(c) Striking pleadings, in whole or in part;

(d) Staying the proceedings;

(e) Dismissal of the action;

(f) Entering a decision by default;

(g) Ordering the party or attorney to pay the attorney's fees and other costs caused by the failure or misconduct; and

(h) Refusing to consider any motion or other action that is not filed in a timely manner.

§ 160.554 The hearing.

(a) The ALJ must conduct a hearing on the record in order to determine whether the respondent should be found liable under this part.

(b) The hearing must be open to the public unless otherwise ordered by the ALJ for good cause shown.

(c) After both parties have presented their cases, evidence may be admitted in rebuttal even if not previously exchanged in accordance with § 160.540.

§ 160.556 Witnesses.

(a) Except as provided in paragraph (b) of this section, testimony at the hearing must be given orally by witnesses under oath or affirmation.

(b) At the discretion of the ALJ, testimony of witnesses other than the testimony of expert witnesses may be admitted in the form of a written statement. Any such written statement must be provided to all other parties along with the last known address of the witness, in a manner that allows sufficient time for the other party to subpoena the witness for cross-examination at the hearing. Prior written statements of witnesses proposed to testify at the hearing must be exchanged as provided in § 160.540. The ALJ may, at his or her discretion, admit prior sworn testimony of experts that has been subject to adverse examination, such as a deposition or trial testimony.

(c) The ALJ must exercise reasonable control over the mode and order of interrogating witnesses and presenting evidence so as to:

(1) Make the interrogation and presentation effective for the ascertainment of the truth;

(2) Avoid repetition or needless consumption of time; and

(3) Protect witnesses from harassment or undue embarrassment.

(d) The ALJ must permit the parties to conduct cross-examination of witnesses as may be required for a full and true disclosure of the facts.

(e) The ALJ may order witnesses excluded so that they cannot hear the testimony of other witnesses. This provision does not authorize the exclusion of

(1) A party who is a natural person;

(2) In the case of a party that is an entity, the officer or employee of the party appearing for the entity pro se or designated as the party's representative; or

(3) A natural person whose presence is shown by a party to be essential to the presentation of its case, including a person engaged in assisting the attorney for the Secretary.

§ 160.558 Evidence.

(a) The ALJ must determine the admissibility of evidence.

(b) Except as provided in this subpart, the ALJ is not bound by the Federal Rules of Evidence. However, the ALJ may apply the Federal Rules of Evidence where appropriate, for example, to exclude unreliable evidence.

(c) The ALJ must exclude irrelevant or immaterial evidence.

(d) Although relevant, evidence may be excluded if its probative value is substantially outweighed by the danger of unfair prejudice, confusion of the issues, or by considerations of undue delay or needless presentation of cumulative evidence.

(e) Although relevant, evidence may be excluded if it is privileged under Federal law.

(f) Evidence concerning offers of compromise or settlement shall be inadmissible to the extent provided in Rule 408 of the Federal Rules of Evidence.

(g) Evidence of crimes, wrongs, or acts other than those at issue in the instant case is admissible in order to show motive, opportunity, intent, knowledge, preparation, identity, lack of mistake, or existence of a scheme. This evidence is admissible regardless of whether the crimes, wrongs, or acts occurred during the statute of limitations period applicable to the acts or omissions that constitute the basis for liability in the case and regardless of whether they were referenced in the Secretary's notice of proposed determination sent in accordance with § 160.514.

(h) The ALJ must permit the parties to introduce rebuttal witnesses and evidence.

(i) All documents and other evidence offered or taken for the record must be open to examination by both parties, unless otherwise ordered by the ALJ for good cause shown.

§ 160.560 The record.

(a) The hearing must be recorded and transcribed. Transcripts may be obtained following the hearing from the ALJ.

(b) The transcript of the testimony, exhibits, and other evidence admitted at the hearing, and all papers and requests filed in the proceeding constitute the record for decision by the ALJ and the Secretary.

(c) The record may be inspected and copied (upon payment of a reasonable fee) by any person, unless otherwise ordered by the ALJ for good cause shown.

(d) For good cause, the ALJ may order appropriate redactions made to the record.

§ 160.562 Post hearing briefs.

The ALJ may require the parties to file posthearing briefs. In any event, any party may file a post-hearing brief. The ALJ must fix the time for filing the briefs. The time for filing may not exceed 60 days from the date the parties receive the transcript of the hearing or, if applicable, the stipulated record. The briefs may be accompanied by proposed findings of fact and conclusions of law. The ALJ may permit the parties to file reply briefs.

§ 160.564 ALJ decision.

(a) The ALJ must issue a decision, based only on the record, which must contain findings of fact and conclusions of law.

(b) The ALJ may affirm, increase, or reduce the penalties imposed by the Secretary.

(c) The ALJ must issue the decision to both parties within 60 days after the time for submission of post-hearing briefs and reply briefs, if permitted, has expired. If the ALJ fails to meet the deadline contained in this paragraph, he or she must notify the parties of the reason for the delay and set a new deadline.

(d) The ALJ's decision is the final decision of the Secretary.

§ 160.566 [Reserved]

§ 160.568 Judicial review.

Judicial review of a penalty that has become final is authorized by 42 U.S.C. 1320a-7a(e).

§ 160.570 Stay of ALJ decision.

(a) Pending judicial review, the respondent may file a request for stay of the effective date of any penalty with the ALJ. The request must be accompanied by a copy of the notice of appeal filed with the Federal court. The filing of the request automatically stays the effective date of the penalty until such time as the ALJ rules upon the request.

(b) The ALJ may not grant a respondent's request for stay of any penalty unless the respondent posts a bond or provides other adequate security.

(c) The ALJ must rule upon a respondent's request for stay within 10 days of receipt.

§ 160.572 [Reserved]

PART 162—ADMINISTRATIVE REQUIREMENTS

Authority: Secs. 1171 through 1179 of the Social Security Act (42 U.S.C. 1320d-1320d- 8), as added by sec. 262 of Pub. L. 104-191, 110 Stat. 2021-2031, and sec. 264 of Pub. L. 104-191, 110 Stat. 2033-2034 (42 U.S.C. 1320d-2 (note))

§ 162.103 [Amended]

2. In § 162.103, the definition of "electronic media" is removed

PART 164—SECURITY AND PRIVACY

Subpart A—General Provisions

164.102 Statutory basis.
164.104 Applicability
164.106 Relationship to other parts.

Subpart B—[Reserved]

Subpart C—Security Standards for the Protection of Electronic Protected Health Information.

164.302 Applicability.
164.304 Definitions.
164.306 Security standards: General rules
164.308 Administrative safeguards.
164.310 Physical safeguards.
164.312 Technical safeguards.
164.314 Organizational requirements.
164.316 Policies and procedures and documentation requirements.
164.318 Compliance dates for the initial implementation of the security standards.

Subpart D—[Reserved]

Subpart E—Privacy of Individually Identifiable Health Information

164.500 Applicability.
164.501 Definitions.
164.502 Uses and disclosures of protected health information: general rules.
164.504 Uses and disclosures: organizational requirements.
164.506 Uses and disclosures to carry out treatment, payment, or health care operations.

164.508 Uses and disclosures for which an authorization is required.
164.510 Uses and disclosures requiring an opportunity for the individual to agree or to object.
164.512 Uses and disclosures for which an authorization or opportunity to agree or object is not required.
164.514 Other requirements relating to uses and disclosures of protected health information.
164.520 Notice of privacy practices for protected health information.
164.522 Rights to request privacy protection for protected health information.
164.524 Access of individuals to protected health information.
164.526 Amendment of protected health information.
164.528 Accounting of disclosures of protected health information.
164.530 Administrative requirements.
164.532 Transition requirements.
164.534 Compliance dates for initial implementation of the privacy standards.

Authority: Secs. 1171 through 1179 of the Social Security Act (42 U.S.C. 1320d-1320d-8), as added by sec. 262 of Pub. L. 104-191, 110 Stat. 2021-2031, and 42 U.S.C. 1320d-2 and 1320d-4, sec. 264 of Pub. L. 104-191, 110 Stat. 2033-2034 (42 U.S.C. 1320d-2(note)).

Subpart A— General Provisions

§ 164.102 Statutory basis.

The provisions of this part are adopted pursuant to the Secretary's authority to prescribe standards, requirements, and implementation specifications under part C of title XI of the Act and section 264 of Public Law 104-191.

§ 164.103 Definitions. As used in this part, the following terms have the following meanings:

Common control exists if an entity has the power, directly or indirectly, significantly to influence or direct the actions or policies of another entity.

Common ownership exists if an entity or entities possess an ownership or equity interest of 5 percent or more in another entity.

Covered functions means those functions of a covered entity the performance of which makes the entity a health plan, health care provider, or health care clearinghouse.

Health care component means a component or combination of components of a hybrid entity designated by the hybrid entity in accordance with § 164.105(a)(2)(iii)(C).

Hybrid entity means a single legal entity:

(1) That is a covered entity;

(2) Whose business activities include both covered and non-covered functions; and

(3) That designates health care components in accordance with paragraph § 164.105(a)(2)(iii)(C).

Plan sponsor is defined as defined at section 3(16)(B) of ERISA, 29 U.S.C. 1002(16)(B).

Required by law means a mandate contained in law that compels an entity to make a use or disclosure of protected health information and that is enforceable in a court of law. *Required by law* includes, but is not limited to, court orders and court-ordered warrants; subpoenas or summons issued by a court, grand jury, a governmental or tribal inspector general, or an administrative body authorized to require the production of information; a civil or an authorized investigative demand; Medicare conditions of participation with respect to health care providers participating in the program; and statutes or regulations that require the production of information, including statutes or regulations that require such information if payment is sought under a government program providing public benefits.

§ 164.104 Applicability.

(a) Except as otherwise provided, the standards, requirements, and implementation specifications adopted under this part apply to the following entities:

(1) A health plan.

(2) A health care clearinghouse.

(3) A health care provider who transmits any health information in electronic form in connection with a transaction covered by this subchapter.

(b) When a health care clearinghouse creates or receives protected health information as a business associate of another covered entity, or other than as a business associate of a covered entity, the clearinghouse must comply with § 164.105 relating to organizational requirements for covered entities, including the designation of health care components of a covered entity.

§ 164.105 Organizational requirements.

(a)(1) *Standard: Health care component.* If a covered entity is a hybrid entity, the requirements of subparts C and E of this part, other than the requirements of this section, § 164.314, and § 164.504, apply only to the health care component(s) of the entity, as specified in this section.

(2) *Implementation specifications:*

(i) *Application of other provisions.* In applying a provision of subparts C and E of this part, other than the requirements of this section, § 164.314, and § 164.504, to a hybrid entity:

(A) A reference in such provision to a "covered entity" refers to a health care component of the covered entity;

(B) A reference in such provision to a "health plan," "covered health care provider," or "health care clearinghouse," refers to a health care component of the covered entity if such health care component performs the functions of a health plan, health care provider, or health care clearinghouse, as applicable;

(C) A reference in such provision to "protected health information" refers to protected health information that is created or received by or on behalf of the health care component of the covered entity; and

(D) A reference in such provision to "electronic protected health information" refers to electronic protected health information that is created, received, maintained, or transmitted by or on behalf of the health care component of the covered entity.

(ii) *Safeguard requirements.* The covered entity that is a hybrid entity must ensure that a health care component of the entity complies with the applicable requirements of this section and subparts C and E of this part. In particular, and without limiting this requirement, such covered entity must ensure that:

(A) Its health care component does not disclose protected health information to another component of the covered entity in circumstances in which subpart E of this part would prohibit such disclosure if the health care component and the other component were separate and distinct legal entities;

(B) Its health care component protects electronic protected health information with respect to another component of the covered entity to the same extent that it would be required under subpart C of this part to protect such information if the health care component and the other component were separate and distinct legal entities;

(C) A component that is described by paragraph (a)(2)(iii)(C)(*2*) of this section does not use or disclose protected health information that it creates or receives from or on behalf of the health care component in a way prohibited by subpart E of this part;

(D) A component that is described by paragraph (a)(2)(iii)(C)(*2*) of this section that creates, receives, maintains, or transmits electronic protected health information on behalf of the health care component is in compliance with subpart C of this part; and

(E) If a person performs duties for both the health care component in the capacity of a member of the workforce of such component and for another component of the entity in the same capacity with respect to that component, such workforce member must not use or disclose protected health information created or received in the course of or incident to the member's work for the health care component in a way prohibited by subpart E of this part.

(iii) *Responsibilities of the covered entity.* A covered entity that is a hybrid entity has the following responsibilities:

(A) For purposes of subpart C of part 160 of this subchapter, pertaining to compliance and enforcement, the covered entity has the responsibility of complying with subpart E of this part.

(B) The covered entity is responsible for complying with § 164.316(a) and § 164.530(i), pertaining to the implementation of policies and procedures to ensure compliance with applicable requirements of this section and subparts C and E of this part, including the safeguard requirements in paragraph (a)(2)(ii) of this section.

(C) The covered entity is responsible for designating the components that are part of one or more health care components of the covered entity and documenting the designation in accordance with paragraph (c) of this section, provided that, if the covered entity designates a health care component or components, it must include any component that would meet the definition of covered entity if it were a separate legal entity. Health care component(s) also may include a component only to the extent that it performs:

(*1*) Covered functions; or

(*2*) Activities that would make such component a business associate of a component that performs covered functions if the two components were separate legal entities.

(b)(1) *Standard: Affiliated covered entities.* Legally separate covered entities that are affiliated may designate themselves as a single covered entity for purposes of subparts C and E of this part.

(2) *Implementation specifications:*

(i) *Requirements for designation of an affiliated covered entity.*

(A) Legally separate covered entities may designate themselves (including any health care component of such covered entity) as a single affiliated covered entity, for purposes of subparts C and E of this part, if all of the covered entities designated are under common ownership or control.

(B) The designation of an affiliated covered entity must be documented and the documentation maintained as required by paragraph (c) of this section.

(ii) *Safeguard requirements.* An affiliated covered entity must ensure that:

(A) The affiliated covered entity's creation, receipt, maintenance, or transmission of electronic protected health information comply with the applicable requirements of subpart C of this part;

(B) The affiliated covered entity's use and disclosure of protected health information comply with the applicable requirements of subpart E of this part; and

(C) If the affiliated covered entity combines the functions of a health plan, health care provider, or health care clearinghouse, the affiliated covered entity complies with § 164.308(a)(4)(ii)(A) and § 164.504(g), as applicable.

(c)(1) *Standard: Documentation.* A covered entity must maintain a written or electronic record of a designation as required by paragraphs (a) or (b) of this section.

(2) *Implementation specification: Retention period.* A covered entity must retain the documentation as required by paragraph (c)(1) of this section for 6 years from the date of its creation or the date when it last was in effect, whichever is later.

§ 164.106 Relationship to other parts.

In complying with the requirements of this part, covered entities are required to comply with the applicable provisions of parts 160 and 162 of this subchapter.

Subpart B—[Reserved]

Subpart C—Security Standards for the Protection of Electronic Protected Health Information.

§ 164.302 Applicability.
A covered entity must comply with the standards, implementation specifications, and requirements of this subpart with respect to electronic protected health information.

§ 164.304 Definitions.
As used in this subpart, the following terms have the following meanings:

Access means the ability or the means necessary to read, write, modify, or communicate data/information or otherwise use any system resource. (This definition applies to "access" as used in this subpart, not as used in subpart E of this part.)

Administrative safeguards are administrative actions, and policies and procedures, to manage the selection, development, implementation, and maintenance of security measures to protect electronic protected health information and to manage the conduct of the covered entity's workforce in relation to the protection of that information.

Authentication means the corroboration that a person is the one claimed.

Availability means the property that data or information is accessible and useable upon demand by an authorized person.

Confidentiality means the property that data or information is not made available or disclosed to unauthorized persons or processes.

Encryption means the use of an algorithmic process to transform data into a form in which there is a low probability of assigning meaning without use of a confidential process or key.

Facility means the physical premises and the interior and exterior of a building(s).

Information system means an interconnected set of information resources under the same direct management control that shares common functionality. A system normally includes hardware, software, information, data, applications, communications, and people.

Integrity means the property that data or information have not been altered or destroyed in an unauthorized manner.

Malicious software means software, for example, a virus, designed to damage or disrupt a system.

Password means confidential authentication information composed of a string of characters.

Physical safeguards are physical measures, policies, and procedures to protect a covered entity's electronic information systems and related buildings and equipment, from natural and environmental hazards, and unauthorized intrusion.

Security or *Security measures* encompass all of the administrative, physical, and technical safeguards in an information system.

Security incident means the attempted or successful unauthorized access, use, disclosure, modification, or destruction of information or interference with system operations in an information system.

Technical safeguards means the technology and the policy and procedures for its use that protect electronic protected health information and control access to it.

User means a person or entity with authorized access.

Workstation means an electronic computing device, for example, a laptop or desktop computer, or any other device that performs similar functions, and electronic media stored in its immediate environment

§ 164.306 Security standards: General rules.

(a) *General requirements.* Covered entities must do the following:

(1) Ensure the confidentiality, integrity, and availability of all electronic protected health information the covered entity creates, receives, maintains, or transmits.

(2) Protect against any reasonably anticipated threats or hazards to the security or integrity of such information.

(3) Protect against any reasonably anticipated uses or disclosures of such information that are not permitted or required under subpart E of this part.

(4) Ensure compliance with this subpart by its workforce.

(b) *Flexibility of approach.*

(1) Covered entities may use any security measures that allow the covered entity to reasonably and appropriately implement the standards and implementation specifications as specified in this subpart.

(2) In deciding which security measures to use, a covered entity must take into account the following factors:

(i) The size, complexity, and capabilities of the covered entity.

(ii) The covered entity's technical infrastructure, hardware, and software security capabilities.

(iii) The costs of security measures.

(iv) The probability and criticality of potential risks to electronic protected health information.

(c) *Standards.* A covered entity must comply with the standards as provided in this section and in § 164.308, § 164.310, § 164.312, § 164.314, and § 164.316 with respect to all electronic protected health information.

(d) *Implementation specifications.* In this subpart:

(1) Implementation specifications are required or addressable. If an implementation specification is required, the word "Required" appears in parentheses after the title of the implementation specification. If an implementation specification is addressable, the word "Addressable" appears in parentheses after the title of the implementation specification.

(2) When a standard adopted in § 164.308, § 164.310, § 164.312, § 164.314, or § 164.316 includes required implementation specifications, a covered entity must implement the implementation specifications.

(3) When a standard adopted is § 164.308, § 164.310, § 164.312, § 164.314, or § 164.316 includes addressable implementation specifications, a covered entity must

(i) Assess whether each implementation specification is a reasonable and appropriate safeguard in its environment, when analyzed with reference to the likely contribution to protecting the entity's electronic protected health information; and

(ii) As applicable to the entity

(A) Implement the implementation specification if reasonable and appropriate; or

(B) If implementing the implementation specification is not reasonable and appropriate

(*1*) Document why it would not be reasonable and appropriate to implement the implementation specification; and

(*2*) Implement an equivalent alternative measure if reasonable and appropriate.

(e) *Maintenance.* Security measures implemented to comply with standards and implementation specifications adopted under § 164.105 and this subpart must be reviewed and modified as needed to continue provision of reasonable and appropriate protection of electronic protected health information as described at § 164.316.

§ 164.308 Administrative safeguards.

(a) A covered entity must, in accordance with § 164.306:

(1)(i) *Standard: Security management process.* Implement policies and procedures to prevent, detect, contain, and correct security violations.

(ii) *Implementation specifications:*

(A) *Risk analysis* (Required). Conduct accurate and thorough assessment of the potential risks and vulnerabilities to the confidentiality, integrity, and availability of electronic protected health information held by the covered entity.

(B) *Risk management* (Required). Implement security measures sufficient to reduce risks and vulnerabilities to a reasonable and appropriate level to comply with § 164.306(a).

(C) *Sanction policy* (Required). Apply appropriate sanctions against workforce members who fail to comply with the security policies and procedures of the covered entity.

(D) *Information system activity review* (Required). Implement procedures to regularly review records of information system activity, such as audit logs, access reports, and security incident tracking reports.

(2) *Standard: Assigned security responsibility.* Identify the security official who is responsible for the development and implementation of the policies and procedures required by this subpart for the entity.

(3)(i) *Standard: Workforce security.* Implement policies and procedures to ensure that all members of its workforce have appropriate access to electronic protected health information, as provided under paragraph (a)(4) of this section, and to prevent those workforce members who do not have access under paragraph (a)(4) of this section from obtaining access to electronic protected health information.

(ii) *Implementation specifications:*

(A) *Authorization and/or supervision* (Addressable). Implement procedures for the authorization and/or supervision of workforce members who work with electronic protected health information or in locations where it might be accessed.

(B) *Workforce clearance procedure* (Addressable). Implement procedures to determine that the access of a workforce member to electronic protected health information is appropriate.

(C) *Termination procedures* (Addressable). Implement procedures for terminating access to electronic protected health information when the employment of a workforce member ends or required by paragraph (a)(3)(ii)(B) of this section.

(4)(i) *Standard: Information access management.* Implement policies and procedures for authorizing access to electronic protected health information that are consistent with the applicable requirements of subpart E of this part.

(ii) Implementation specifications:

(A) *Isolating health care clearinghouse functions* (Required). If a health care clearinghouse is part of a larger organization, the clearinghouse must implement policies and procedures that protect the electronic protected health information of the clearinghouse from unauthorized access by the larger organization.

(B) *Access authorization* (Addressable). Implement policies and procedures for granting access to electronic protected health information, for example, through access to a workstation, transaction, program, process, or other mechanism.

(C) *Access establishment and modification* (Addressable). Implement policies and procedures that, based upon the entity's access authorization policies, establish, document, review, and modify a user's right of access to a workstation, transaction, program, or process.

(5)(i) *Standard: Security awareness and training.* Implement a security awareness and training program for all members of its workforce (including management).

(ii) *Implementation specifications.* Implement:

(A) *Security reminders* (Addressable). Periodic security updates.

(B) *Protection from malicious software* (Addressable). Procedures for guarding against, detecting, and reporting malicious software.

(C) *Log-in monitoring* (Addressable). Procedures for monitoring log-in attempts and reporting discrepancies.

(D) *Password management* (Addressable). Procedures for creating, changing, and safeguarding passwords.

(6)(i) *Standard: Security incident procedures.* Implement policies and procedures to address security incidents.

(ii) *Implementation specification: Response and Reporting* (Required). Identify and respond to suspected or known security incidents; mitigate, to the extent practicable, harmful effects of security incidents that are known to the covered entity; and document security incidents and their outcomes.

(7)(i) *Standard: Contingency plan.* Establish (and implement as needed) policies and procedures for responding to an emergency or other occurrence (for example, fire, vandalism, system failure, and natural disaster) that damages systems that contain electronic protected health information.

(ii) Implementation specifications:

(A) *Data backup plan* (Required). Establish and implement procedures to create and maintain retrievable exact copies of electronic protected health information.

(B) *Disaster recovery plan* (Required). Establish (and implement as needed) procedures to restore any loss of data.

(C) *Emergency mode operation plan* (Required). Establish (and implement as needed) procedures to enable continuation of critical business processes for protection of the security of electronic protected health information while operating in emergency mode.

(D) *Testing and revision procedures* (Addressable). Implement procedures for periodic testing and revision of contingency plans.

(E) *Applications and data criticality analysis* (Addressable). Assess the relative criticality of specific applications and data in support of other contingency plan components.

(8) *Standard: Evaluation.* Perform a periodic technical and nontechnical evaluation, based initially upon the standards implemented under this rule and subsequently, in response to environmental or operational changes affecting the security of the electronic protected health information, that establishes the extent to which an entity's security policies and procedures meet the requirements of this subpart.

(b)(1) *Standard: Business associate contracts and other arrangements.* A covered entity, in accordance with § 164.306, may permit a business associate to create, receive, maintain, or transmit electronic protected health information on the covered entity's behalf only if the covered entity obtains satisfactory assurances, in accordance with § 164.314(a) that the business associate will appropriately safeguard the information.

(2) This standard does not apply with respect to

(i) The transmission by a covered entity of electronic protected health information to a health care provider concerning the treatment of an individual.

(ii) The transmission of electronic protected health information by a group health plan or an HMO or health insurance issuer on behalf of a group health plan to a plan sponsor, to the extent that the requirements of § 164.314(b) and § 164.504(f) apply and are met; or

(iii) The transmission of electronic protected health information from or to other agencies providing the services at § 164.502(e)(1)(ii)(C), when the covered entity is a health plan that is a government program providing public benefits, if the requirements of § 164.502(e)(1)(ii)(C) are met.

(3) A covered entity that violates the satisfactory assurances it provided as a business associate of another covered entity will be in noncompliance with the standards, implementation specifications, and requirements of this paragraph and § 164.314(a).

(4) *Implementation specifications: Written contract or other arrangement* (Required). Document the satisfactory assurances required by paragraph (b)(1) of this section through a written contract or other arrangement with the business associate that meets the applicable requirements of § 164.314(a).

§ 164.310 Physical safeguards.

A covered entity must, in accordance with § 164.306:

(a)(1) *Standard: Facility access controls.* Implement policies and procedures to limit physical access to its electronic information systems and the facility or facilities in which they are housed, while ensuring that properly authorized access is allowed.

(2) *Implementation specifications:*

(i) *Contingency operations* (Addressable). Establish (and implement as needed) procedures that allow facility access in support of restoration of lost data under the disaster recovery plan and emergency mode operations plan in the event of an emergency.

(ii) *Facility security plan* (Addressable). Implement policies and procedures to safeguard the facility and the equipment therein from unauthorized physical access, tampering, and theft.

(iii) *Access control and validation procedures* (Addressable). Implement procedures to control and validate a person's access to facilities based on their role or function, including visitor control, and control of access to software programs for testing and revision.

(iv) *Maintenance records* (Addressable). Implement policies and procedures to document repairs and modifications to the physical components of a facility which are related to security (for example, hardware, walls, doors, and locks).

(b) *Standard: Workstation use.* Implement policies and procedures that specify the proper functions to be performed, the manner in which those functions are to be performed, and the physical attributes of the surroundings of a specific workstation or class of workstation that can access electronic protected health information.

(c) *Standard: Workstation security.* Implement physical safeguards for all workstations that access electronic protected health information, to restrict access to authorized users.

(d)(1) *Standard: Device and media controls.* Implement policies and procedures that govern the receipt and removal of hardware and electronic media that contain electronic protected health information into and out of a facility, and the movement of these items within the facility.

(2) *Implementation specifications:*

(i) *Disposal* (Required). Implement policies and procedures to address the final disposition of electronic protected health information, and/or the hardware or electronic media on which it is stored.

(ii) *Media re-use* (Required). Implement procedures for removal of electronic protected health information from electronic media before the media are made available for reuse.

(iii) *Accountability* (Addressable). Maintain a record of the movements of hardware and electronic media and any person responsible therefore.

(iv) *Data backup and storage* (Addressable). Create a retrievable, exact copy of electronic protected health information, when needed, before movement of equipment.

§ 164.312 Technical safeguards.

A covered entity must, in accordance with § 164.306:

(a)(1) *Standard: Access control.* Implement technical policies and procedures for electronic information systems that maintain electronic protected health information to allow access only to those persons or software programs that have been granted access rights as specified in § 164.308(a)(4).

(2) *Implementation specifications:*

(i) *Unique user identification* (Required). Assign a unique name and/or number for identifying and tracking user identity.

(ii) *Emergency access procedure* (Required). Establish (and implement as needed) procedures for obtaining necessary electronic protected health information during an emergency.

(iii) *Automatic logoff* (Addressable). Implement electronic procedures that terminate an electronic session after a predetermined time of inactivity.

(iv) *Encryption and decryption* (Addressable). Implement a mechanism to encrypt and decrypt electronic protected health information.

(b) *Standard: Audit controls.* Implement hardware, software, and/or procedural mechanisms that record and examine activity in information systems that contain or use electronic protected health information.

(c)(1) *Standard: Integrity.* Implement policies and procedures to protect electronic protected health information from improper alteration or destruction.

(2) *Implementation specification: Mechanism to authenticate electronic protected health information* (Addressable). Implement electronic mechanisms to corroborate that electronic protected health information has not been altered or destroyed in an unauthorized manner.

(d) *Standard: Person or entity authentication.* Implement procedures to verify that a person or entity seeking access to electronic protected health information is the one claimed.

(e)(1) *Standard: Transmission security.* Implement technical security measures to guard against unauthorized access to electronic protected health information that is being transmitted over an electronic communications network.

(2) *Implementation specifications:*

(i) *Integrity controls* (Addressable). Implement security measures to ensure that electronically transmitted electronic protected health information is not improperly modified without detection until disposed of.

(ii) *Encryption* (Addressable). Implement a mechanism to encrypt electronic protected health information whenever deemed appropriate.

§ 164.314 Organizational requirements.

(a)(1) *Standard: Business associate contracts or other arrangements.*

(i) The contract or other arrangement between the covered entity and its business associate required by § 164.308(b) must meet the requirements of paragraph (a)(2)(i) or (a)(2)(ii) of this section, as applicable.

(ii) A covered entity is not in compliance with the standards in § 164.502(e) and paragraph (a) of this section if the covered entity knew of a pattern of an activity or practice of the business associate that constituted a material breach or violation of the business associate's obligation under the contract or other arrangement, unless the covered entity took reasonable steps to cure the breach or end the violation, as applicable, and, if such steps were unsuccessful

(A) Terminated the contract or arrangement, if feasible; or

(B) If termination is not feasible, reported the problem to the Secretary.

(2) *Implementation specifications* (Required).

(i) *Business associate contracts.* The contract between a covered entity and a business associate must provide that the business associate will

(A) Implement administrative, physical, and technical safeguards that reasonably and appropriately protect the confidentiality, integrity, and availability of the electronic protected health information that it creates, receives, maintains, or transmits on behalf of the covered entity as required by this subpart;

(B) Ensure that any agent, including a subcontractor, to whom it provides such information agrees to implement reasonable and appropriate safeguards to protect it;

(C) Report to the covered entity any security incident of which it becomes aware;

(D) Authorize termination of the contract by the covered entity, if the covered entity determines that the business associate has violated a material term of the contract.

(ii) *Other arrangements.*

(A) When a covered entity and its business associate are both governmental entities, the covered entity is in compliance with paragraph (a)(1) of this section, if

(1) It enters into a memorandum of understanding with the business associate that contains terms that accomplish the objectives of paragraph (a)(2)(i) of this section; or

(2) Other law (including regulations adopted by the covered entity or its business associate) contains requirements applicable to the business associate that accomplish the objectives of paragraph (a)(2)(i) of this section.

(B) If a business associate is required by law to perform a function or activity on behalf of a covered entity or to provide a service described in the definition of business associate as specified in § 160.103 of this subchapter to a covered entity, the covered entity may permit the business associate to create, receive, maintain, or transmit electronic protected health information on its behalf to the extent necessary to comply with the legal mandate without meeting the requirements of paragraph (a)(2)(i) of this section, provided that the covered entity attempts in good faith to obtain satisfactory assurances as required by paragraph (a)(2)(ii)(A) of this section, and documents the attempt and the reasons that these assurances cannot be obtained.

(C) The covered entity may omit from its other arrangements authorization of the termination of the contract by the covered entity as required by paragraph (a)(2)(i)(D) of this section, if such authorization is inconsistent with the statutory obligations of the covered entity or its business associate.

(b)(1) *Standard: Requirements for group health plans.* Except when the only electronic protected health information disclosed to a plan sponsor is disclosed pursuant to § 164.504(f)(1)(ii) or (iii), or as authorized under § 164.508, a group health plan must ensure that its plan documents provide that the plan sponsor will reasonably and appropriately safeguard electronic protected health information created, received, maintained, or transmitted to or by the plan sponsor on behalf of the group health plan.

(2) *Implementation specifications* (Required). The plan documents of the group health plan must be amended to incorporate provisions to require the plan sponsor to

(i) Implement administrative, physical, and technical safeguards that reasonably and appropriately protect the confidentiality, integrity, and availability of the electronic protected health information that it creates, receives, maintains, or transmits on behalf of the group health plan;

(ii) Ensure that the adequate separation required by § 164.504(f)(2)(iii) is supported by reasonable and appropriate security measures;

(iii) Ensure that any agent, including a subcontractor, to whom it provides this information agrees to implement reasonable and appropriate security measures to protect the information; and

(iv) Report to the group health plan any security incident of which it becomes aware.

§ 164.316 Policies and procedures and documentation requirements.
A covered entity must, in accordance with § 164.306:

(a) *Standard: Policies and procedures.* Implement reasonable and appropriate policies and procedures to comply with the standards, implementation specifications, or other requirements of this subpart, taking into account those factors specified in § 164.306(b)(2)(i),(ii),(iii), and (iv). This standard is not to be construed to permit or excuse an action that violates any other standard, implementation specification, or other requirements of this subpart. A covered entity may change its policies and procedures at any time, provided that the changes are documented and are implemented in accordance with this subpart.

(b)(1) *Standard: Documentation.*

(i) Maintain the policies and procedures implemented to comply with this subpart in written (which may be electronic) form; and

(ii) If an action, activity or assessment is required by this subpart to be documented, maintain a written (which may be electronic) record of the action, activity, or assessment.

(2) *Implementation specifications:*

(i) *Time limit* (Required). Retain the documentation required by paragraph (b)(1) of this section for 6 years from the date of its creation or the date when it last was in effect, whichever is later.

(ii) *Availability* (Required). Make documentation available to those persons responsible for implementing the procedures to which the documentation pertains.

(iii) *Updates* (Required). Review documentation periodically, and update as needed, in response to environmental or operational changes affecting the security of the electronic protected health information.

§ 164.318 Compliance dates for the initial implementation of the security standards.

(a) *Health plan.*

(1) A health plan that is not a small health plan must comply with the applicable requirements of this subpart no later than April 20, 2005.

(2) A small health plan must comply with the applicable requirements of this subpart no later than April 20, 2006.

(b) *Health care clearinghouse.* A health care clearinghouse must comply with the applicable requirements of this subpart no later than April 20, 2005.

(c) *Health care provider.* A covered health care provider must comply with the applicable requirements of this subpart no later than April 20, 2005.

Subpart D—[Reserved]

Subpart E—Privacy of Individually Identifiable Health Information

§ 164.500 Applicability.

(a) Except as otherwise provided herein, the standards, requirements, and implementation specifications of this subpart apply to covered entities with respect to protected health information.

(b) Health care clearinghouses must comply with the standards, requirements, and implementation specifications as follows:

(1) When a health care clearinghouse creates or receives protected health information as a business associate of another covered entity, the clearinghouse must comply with:

(i) Section 164.500 relating to applicability;

(ii) Section 164.501 relating to definitions;

(iii) Section 164.502 relating to uses and disclosures of protected health information, except that a clearinghouse is prohibited from using or disclosing protected health information other than as permitted in the business associate contract under which it created or received the protected health information;

(iv) Section 164.504 relating to the organizational requirements for covered entities.

(v) Section 164.512 relating to uses and disclosures for which individual authorization or an opportunity to agree or object is not required, except that a clearinghouse is prohibited from using or disclosing protected health information other than as permitted in the business associate contract under which it created or received the protected health information;

(vi) Section 164.532 relating to transition requirements; and

(vii) Section 164.534 relating to compliance dates for initial implementation of the privacy standards.

(2) When a health care clearinghouse creates or receives protected health information other than as a business associate of a covered entity, the clearinghouse must comply with all of the standards, requirements, and implementation specifications of this subpart.

(c) The standards, requirements, and implementation specifications of this subpart do not apply to the Department of Defense or to any other federal agency, or nongovernmental organization acting on its behalf, when providing health care to overseas foreign national beneficiaries.

§ 164.501 Definitions.

As used in this subpart, the following terms have the following meanings:

Correctional institution means any penal or correctional facility, jail, reformatory, detention center, work farm, halfway house, or residential community program center operated by, or under contract to, the United States, a State, a territory, a political subdivision of a State or territory, or an Indian tribe, for the confinement or rehabilitation of persons charged with or convicted of a criminal offense or other persons held in lawful custody. *Other persons held in lawful custody* includes juvenile offenders adjudicated delinquent, aliens detained awaiting deportation, persons committed to mental institutions through the criminal justice system, witnesses, or others awaiting charges or trial.

Data aggregation means, with respect to protected health information created or received by a business associate in its capacity as the business associate of a covered entity, the combining of such protected health information by the business associate with the protected health information received by the business associate in its capacity as a business associate of another covered entity, to permit data analyses that relate to the health care operations of the respective covered entities.

Designated record set means:

(1) A group of records maintained by or for a covered entity that is:

(i) The medical records and billing records about individuals maintained by or for a covered health care provider;

(ii) The enrollment, payment, claims adjudication, and case or medical management record systems maintained by or for a health plan; or

(iii) Used, in whole or in part, by or for the covered entity to make decisions about individuals.

(2) For purposes of this paragraph, the term *record* means any item, collection, or grouping of information that includes protected health information and is maintained, collected, used, or disseminated by or for a covered entity.

Direct treatment relationship means a treatment relationship between an individual and a health care provider that is not an indirect treatment relationship.

Health care operations means any of the following activities of the covered entity to the extent that the activities are related to covered functions:

(1) Conducting quality assessment and improvement activities, including outcomes evaluation and development of clinical guidelines, provided that the obtaining of generalizable knowledge is not the primary purpose of any studies resulting from such activities; population-based activities relating to improving health or reducing health care costs, protocol development, case management and care coordination, contacting of health care providers and patients with information about treatment alternatives; and related functions that do not include treatment;

(2) Reviewing the competence or qualifications of health care professionals, evaluating practitioner and provider performance, health plan performance, conducting training programs in which students, trainees, or practitioners in areas of health care learn under supervision to practice or improve their skills as health care providers, training of non-health care professionals, accreditation, certification, licensing, or credentialing activities;

(3) Underwriting, premium rating, and other activities relating to the creation, renewal or replacement of a contract of health insurance or health benefits, and ceding, securing, or placing a contract for reinsurance of risk relating to claims for health care (including stop-loss insurance and excess of loss insurance), provided that the requirements of § 164.514(g) are met, if applicable;

(4) Conducting or arranging for medical review, legal services, and auditing functions, including fraud and abuse detection and compliance programs;

(5) Business planning and development, such as conducting cost-management and planning-related analyses related to managing and operating

the entity, including formulary development and administration, development or improvement of methods of payment or coverage policies; and

(6) Business management and general administrative activities of the entity, including, but not limited to:

(i) Management activities relating to implementation of and compliance with the requirements of this subchapter;

(ii) Customer service, including the provision of data analyses for policy holders, plan sponsors, or other customers, provided that protected health information is not disclosed to such policy holder, plan sponsor, or customer.

(iii) Resolution of internal grievances;

(iv) The sale, transfer, merger, or consolidation of all or part of the covered entity with another covered entity, or an entity that following such activity will become a covered entity and due diligence related to such activity; and

(v) Consistent with the applicable requirements of § 164.514, creating de-identified health information or a limited data set, and fundraising for the benefit of the covered entity.

Health oversight agency means an agency or authority of the United States, a State, a territory, a political subdivision of a State or territory, or an Indian tribe, or a person or entity acting under a grant of authority from or contract with such public agency, including the employees or agents of such public agency or its contractors or persons or entities to whom it has granted authority, that is authorized by law to oversee the health care system (whether public or private) or government programs in which health information is necessary to determine eligibility or compliance, or to enforce civil rights laws for which health information is relevant.

Indirect treatment relationship means a relationship between an individual and a health care provider in which:

(1) The health care provider delivers health care to the individual based on the orders of another health care provider; and

(2) The health care provider typically provides services or products, or reports the diagnosis or results associated with the health care, directly to another health care provider, who provides the services or products or reports to the individual.

Inmate means a person incarcerated in or otherwise confined to a correctional institution.

Law enforcement official means an officer or employee of any agency or authority of the United States, a State, a territory, a political subdivision of a State or territory, or an Indian tribe, who is empowered by law to:

(1) Investigate or conduct an official inquiry into a potential violation of law; or

(2) Prosecute or otherwise conduct a criminal, civil, or administrative proceeding arising from an alleged violation of law.

Marketing means:

(1) To make a communication about a product or service that encourages recipients of the communication to purchase or use the product or service, unless the communication is made:

(i) To describe a health-related product or service (or payment for such product or service) that is provided by, or included in a plan of benefits of, the covered entity making the communication, including communications about: the entities participating in a health care provider network or health plan network; replacement of, or enhancements to, a health plan; and health-related products or services available only to a health plan enrollee that add value to, but are not part of, a plan of benefits.

(ii) For treatment of the individual; or

(iii) For case management or care coordination for the individual, or to direct or recommend alternative treatments, therapies, health care providers, or settings of care to the individual.

(2) An arrangement between a covered entity and any other entity whereby the covered entity discloses protected health information to the other entity, in exchange for direct or indirect remuneration, for the other entity or its affiliate to make a communication about its own product or service that encourages recipients of the communication to purchase or use that product or service. *Payment* means:

(1) The activities undertaken by:

(i) A health plan to obtain premiums or to determine or fulfill its responsibility for coverage and provision of benefits under the health plan; or

(ii) A health care provider or health plan to obtain or provide reimbursement for the provision of health care; and

(2) The activities in paragraph (1) of this definition relate to the individual to whom health care is provided and include, but are not limited to:

(i) Determinations of eligibility or coverage (including coordination of benefits or the determination of cost sharing amounts), and adjudication or subrogation of health benefit claims;

(ii) Risk adjusting amounts due based on enrollee health status and demographic characteristics;

(iii) Billing, claims management, collection activities, obtaining payment under a contract for reinsurance (including stop-loss insurance and excess of loss insurance), and related health care data processing;

(iv) Review of health care services with respect to medical necessity, coverage under a health plan, appropriateness of care, or justification of charges;

(v) Utilization review activities, including precertification and preauthorization of services, concurrent and retrospective review of services; and

(vi) Disclosure to consumer reporting agencies of any of the following protected health information relating to collection of premiums or reimbursement:

(A) Name and address;

(B) Date of birth;

(C) Social security number;

(D) Payment history;

(E) Account number; and

(F) Name and address of the health care provider and/or health plan.

Psychotherapy notes means notes recorded (in any medium) by a health care provider who is a mental health professional documenting or analyzing the contents of conversation during a private counseling session or a group, joint, or family counseling session and that are separated from the rest of the individual's medical record. *Psychotherapy notes* excludes medication prescription and monitoring, counseling session start and stop times, the modalities and frequencies of treatment furnished, results of clinical tests, and any summary of the following items: diagnosis, functional status, the treatment plan, symptoms, prognosis, and progress to date.

Public health authority means an agency or authority of the United States, a State, a territory, a political subdivision of a State or territory, or an Indian tribe, or a person or entity acting under a grant of authority from or contract with such public agency, including the employees or agents of such public agency or its contractors or persons or entities to whom it has granted authority, that is responsible for public health matters as part of its official mandate.

Research means a systematic investigation, including research development, testing, and evaluation, designed to develop or contribute to generalizable knowledge.

Treatment means the provision, coordination, or management of health care and related services by one or more health care providers, including the coordination or management of health care by a health care provider with a third party; consultation between health care providers relating to a patient; or the referral of a patient for health care from one health care provider to another.

§ 164.502 Uses and disclosures of protected health information: general rules.

(a) *Standard.* A covered entity may not use or disclose protected health information, except as permitted or required by this subpart or by subpart C of part 160 of this subchapter.

(1) *Permitted uses and disclosures.* A covered entity is permitted to use or disclose protected health information as follows:

(i) To the individual;

(ii) For treatment, payment, or health care operations, as permitted by and in compliance with § 164.506;

(iii) Incident to a use or disclosure otherwise permitted or required by this subpart, provided that the covered entity has complied with the applicable requirements of § 164.502(b), § 164.514(d), and § 164.530(c) with respect to such otherwise permitted or required use or disclosure;

(iv) Pursuant to and in compliance with an authorization that complies with § 164.508;

(v) Pursuant to an agreement under, or as otherwise permitted by, § 164.510; and

(vi) As permitted by and in compliance with this section, § 164.512, or § 164.514(e),(f), or (g).

(2) *Required disclosures.* A covered entity is required to disclose protected health information:

(i) To an individual, when requested under, and as required by §§ 164.524 or 164.528; and

(ii) When required by the Secretary under subpart C of part 160 of this subchapter to investigate or determine the covered entity's compliance with this subpart.

(b) *Standard: minimum necessary.*

(1) *Minimum necessary applies.* When using or disclosing protected health information or when requesting protected health information from another covered entity, a covered entity must make reasonable efforts to limit protected health information to the minimum necessary to accomplish the intended purpose of the use, disclosure, or request.

(2) *Minimum necessary does not apply.* This requirement does not apply to:

(i) Disclosures to or requests by a health care provider for treatment;

(ii) Uses or disclosures made to the individual, as permitted under paragraph (a)(1)(i) of this section or as required by paragraph (a)(2)(i) of this section;

(iii) Uses or disclosures made pursuant to an authorization under § 164.508;

(iv) Disclosures made to the Secretary in accordance with subpart C of part 160 of this subchapter;

(v) Uses or disclosures that are required by law, as described by § 164.512(a); and

(vi) Uses or disclosures that are required for compliance with applicable requirements of this subchapter.

(c) *Standard: uses and disclosures of protected health information subject to an agreed upon restriction.* A covered entity that has agreed to a restriction pursuant to § 164.522(a)(1) may not use or disclose the protected health information covered by the restriction in violation of such restriction, except as otherwise provided in § 164.522(a).

(d) *Standard: uses and disclosures of de-identified protected health information.*

(1) *Uses and disclosures to create de-identified information.* A covered entity may use protected health information to create information that is not individually identifiable health information or disclose protected health information only to a business associate for such purpose, whether or not the de-identified information is to be used by the covered entity.

(2) *Uses and disclosures of de-identified information.* Health information that meets the standard and implementation specifications for de-identification under § 164.514(a) and (b) is considered not to be individually identifiable health information, i.e., de-identified. The requirements of this subpart do not

apply to information that has been de-identified in accordance with the applicable requirements of § 164.514, provided that:

(i) Disclosure of a code or other means of record identification designed to enable coded or otherwise de-identified information to be re-identified constitutes disclosure of protected health information; and

(ii) If de-identified information is re-identified, a covered entity may use or disclose such re-identified information only as permitted or required by this subpart.

(e)(1) *Standard: disclosures to business associates.*

(i) A covered entity may disclose protected health information to a business associate and may allow a business associate to create or receive protected health information on its behalf, if the covered entity obtains satisfactory assurance that the business associate will appropriately safeguard the information.

(ii) This standard does not apply:

(A) With respect to disclosures by a covered entity to a health care provider concerning the treatment of the individual;

(B) With respect to disclosures by a group health plan or a health insurance issuer or HMO with respect to a group health plan to the plan sponsor, to the extent that the requirements of § 164.504(f) apply and are met; or

(C) With respect to uses or disclosures by a health plan that is a government program providing public benefits, if eligibility for, or enrollment in, the health plan is determined by an agency other than the agency administering the health plan, or if the protected health information used to determine enrollment or eligibility in the health plan is collected by an agency other than the agency administering the health plan, and such activity is authorized by law, with respect to the collection and sharing of individually identifiable health information for the performance of such functions by the health plan and the agency other than the agency administering the health plan.

(iii) A covered entity that violates the satisfactory assurances it provided as a business associate of another covered entity will be in noncompliance with the standards, implementation specifications, and requirements of this paragraph and § 164.504(e).

(2) *Implementation specification: documentation.* A covered entity must document the satisfactory assurances required by paragraph (e)(1) of this section through a written contract or other written agreement or arrangement with the business associate that meets the applicable requirements of § 164.504(e).

(f) *Standard: deceased individuals.* A covered entity must comply with the requirements of this subpart with respect to the protected health information of a deceased individual.

(g)(1) *Standard: personal representatives.* As specified in this paragraph, a covered entity must, except as provided in paragraphs (g)(3) and (g)(5) of this section, treat a personal representative as the individual for purposes of this subchapter.

(2) *Implementation specification: adults and emancipated minors.* If under applicable law a person has authority to act on behalf of an individual who is an adult or an emancipated minor in making decisions related to health care, a covered entity must treat such person as a personal representative under this subchapter, with respect to protected health information relevant to such personal representation.

(3) *Implementation specification: unemancipated minors.*

(i) If under applicable law a parent, guardian, or other person acting *in loco parentis* has authority to act on behalf of an individual who is an unemancipated minor in making decisions related to health care, a covered entity must treat such person as a personal representative under this subchapter, with respect to protected health information relevant to such personal representation, except that such person may not be a personal representative of an unemancipated minor, and the minor has the authority to act as an individual, with respect to protected health information pertaining to a health care service, if:

(A) The minor consents to such health care service; no other consent to such health care service is required by law, regardless of whether the consent of another person has also been obtained; and the minor has not requested that such person be treated as the personal representative;

(B) The minor may lawfully obtain such health care service without the consent of a parent, guardian, or other person acting *in loco parentis,* and the minor, a court, or another person authorized by law consents to such health care service; or

(C) A parent, guardian, or other person acting *in loco parentis* assents to an agreement of confidentiality between a covered health care provider and the minor with respect to such health care service.

(ii) Notwithstanding the provisions of paragraph (g)(3)(i) of this section:

(A) If, and to the extent, permitted or required by an applicable provision of State or other law, including applicable case law, a covered entity may disclose, or provide access in accordance with § 164.524 to, protected health information about an unemancipated minor to a parent, guardian, or other person acting *in loco parentis;*

(B) If, and to the extent, prohibited by an applicable provision of State or other law, including applicable case law, a covered entity may not disclose, or provide access in accordance with § 164.524 to, protected health information about an unemancipated minor to a parent, guardian, or other person acting *in loco parentis;* and

(C) Where the parent, guardian, or other person acting *in loco parentis,* is not the personal representative under paragraph (g)(3)(i)(A),(B), or (C) of this section and where there is no applicable access provision under State or other law, including case law, a covered entity may provide or deny access under § 164.524 to a parent, guardian, or other person acting *in loco parentis,* if such action is consistent with State or other applicable law, provided that such decision must be made by a licensed health care professional, in the exercise of professional judgment.

(4) *Implementation specification: deceased individuals.* If under applicable law an executor, administrator, or other person has authority to act on behalf of a deceased individual or of the individual's estate, a covered entity must treat such person as a personal representative under this subchapter, with respect to protected health information relevant to such personal representation.

(5) *Implementation specification: abuse, neglect, endangerment situations.* Notwithstanding a State law or any requirement of this paragraph to the contrary, a covered entity may elect not to treat a person as the personal representative of an individual if:

(i) The covered entity has a reasonable belief that:

(A) The individual has been or may be subjected to domestic violence, abuse, or neglect by such person; or

(B) Treating such person as the personal representative could endanger the individual; and

(ii) The covered entity, in the exercise of professional judgment, decides that it is not in the best interest of the individual to treat the person as the individual's personal representative.

(h) *Standard: confidential communications.* A covered health care provider or health plan must comply with the applicable requirements of § 164.522(b) in communicating protected health information.

(i) *Standard: uses and disclosures consistent with notice.* A covered entity that is required by § 164.520 to have a notice may not use or disclose protected health information in a manner inconsistent with such notice. A covered entity that is required by § 164.520(b)(1)(iii) to include a specific statement in its notice if it intends to engage in an activity listed in § 164.520(b)(1)(iii)(A)-(C), may not use or disclose protected health information for such activities, unless the required statement is included in the notice.

(j) *Standard: disclosures by whistleblowers and workforce member crime victims.*

(1) *Disclosures by whistleblowers.* A covered entity is not considered to have violated the requirements of this subpart if a member of its workforce or a business associate discloses protected health information, provided that:

(i) The workforce member or business associate believes in good faith that the covered entity has engaged in conduct that is unlawful or otherwise violates professional or clinical standards, or that the care, services, or conditions provided by the covered entity potentially endangers one or more patients, workers, or the public; and

(ii) The disclosure is to:

(A) A health oversight agency or public health authority authorized by law to investigate or otherwise oversee the relevant conduct or conditions of the covered entity or to an appropriate health care accreditation organization for the purpose of reporting the allegation of failure to meet professional standards or misconduct by the covered entity; or

(B) An attorney retained by or on behalf of the workforce member or business associate for the purpose of determining the legal options of the workforce member or business associate with regard to the conduct described in paragraph (j)(1)(i) of this section.

(2) *Disclosures by workforce members who are victims of a crime.* A covered entity is not considered to have violated the requirements of this subpart if a member of its workforce who is the victim of a criminal act discloses protected health information to a law enforcement official, provided that:

(i) The protected health information disclosed is about the suspected perpetrator of the criminal act; and

(ii) The protected health information disclosed is limited to the information listed in § 164.512(f)(2)(i).

§ 164.504 Uses and disclosures: organizational requirements.

(a) *Definitions.* As used in this section:

Plan administration functions means administration functions performed by the plan sponsor of a group health plan on behalf of the group health plan and excludes functions performed by the plan sponsor in connection with any other benefit or benefit plan of the plan sponsor.

Summary health information means information, that may be individually identifiable health information, and:

(1) That summarizes the claims history, claims expenses, or type of claims experienced by individuals for whom a plan sponsor has provided health benefits under a group health plan; and

(2) From which the information described at § 164.514(b)(2)(i) has been deleted, except that the geographic information described in § 164.514(b)(2)(i)(B) need only be aggregated to the level of a five digit zip code.

Paragraphs (b)-(d)—[Removed and Reserved]

(e)(1) *Standard: business associate contracts.*

(i) The contract or other arrangement between the covered entity and the business associate required by § 164.502(e)(2) must meet the requirements of paragraph (e)(2) or (e)(3) of this section, as applicable.

(ii) A covered entity is not in compliance with the standards in § 164.502(e) and paragraph (e) of this section, if the covered entity knew of a pattern of activity or practice of the business associate that constituted a material breach or violation of the business associate's obligation under the contract or other arrangement, unless the covered entity took reasonable steps to cure the breach or end the violation, as applicable, and, if such steps were unsuccessful:

(A) Terminated the contract or arrangement, if feasible; or

(B) If termination is not feasible, reported the problem to the Secretary.

(2) *Implementation specifications: business associate contracts.* A contract between the covered entity and a business associate must:

(i) Establish the permitted and required uses and disclosures of such information by the business associate. The contract may not authorize the business associate to use or further disclose the information in a manner that would violate the requirements of this subpart, if done by the covered entity, except that:

(A) The contract may permit the business associate to use and disclose protected health information for the proper management and administration of the business associate, as provided in paragraph (e)(4) of this section; and

(B) The contract may permit the business associate to provide data aggregation services relating to the health care operations of the covered entity.

(ii) Provide that the business associate will:

(A) Not use or further disclose the information other than as permitted or required by the contract or as required by law;

(B) Use appropriate safeguards to prevent use or disclosure of the information other than as provided for by its contract;

(C) Report to the covered entity any use or disclosure of the information not provided for by its contract of which it becomes aware;

(D) Ensure that any agents, including a subcontractor, to whom it provides protected health information received from, or created or received by the business associate on behalf of, the covered entity agrees to the same restrictions and conditions that apply to the business associate with respect to such information;

(E) Make available protected health information in accordance with § 164.524;

(F) Make available protected health information for amendment and incorporate any amendments to protected health information in accordance with §164.526;

(G) Make available the information required to provide an accounting of disclosures in accordance with § 164.528;

(H) Make its internal practices, books, and records relating to the use and disclosure of protected health information received from, or created or received by the business associate on behalf of, the covered entity available to the Secretary for purposes of determining the covered entity's compliance with this subpart; and

(I) At termination of the contract, if feasible, return or destroy all protected health information received from, or created or received by the business associate on behalf of, the covered entity that the business associate still maintains in any form and retain no copies of such information or, if such return or destruction is not feasible, extend the protections of the contract to the information and limit further uses and disclosures to those purposes that make the return or destruction of the information infeasible.

(iii) Authorize termination of the contract by the covered entity, if the covered entity determines that the business associate has violated a material term of the contract.

(3) *Implementation specifications: other arrangements.*

(i) If a covered entity and its business associate are both governmental entities:

(A) The covered entity may comply with paragraph (e) of this section by entering into a memorandum of understanding with the business associate that contains terms that accomplish the objectives of paragraph (e)(2) of this section.

(B) The covered entity may comply with paragraph (e) of this section, if other law (including regulations adopted by the covered entity or its business associate) contains requirements applicable to the business associate that accomplish the objectives of paragraph (e)(2) of this section.

(ii) If a business associate is required by law to perform a function or activity on behalf of a covered entity or to provide a service described in the definition of *business associate* in § 160.103 of this subchapter to a covered entity, such covered entity may disclose protected health information to the business associate to the extent necessary to comply with the legal mandate without meeting the requirements of this paragraph (e), provided that the covered entity attempts in good faith to obtain satisfactory assurances as required by paragraph (e)(3)(i) of this section, and, if such attempt fails, documents the attempt and the reasons that such assurances cannot be obtained.

(iii) The covered entity may omit from its other arrangements the termination authorization required by paragraph (e)(2)(iii) of this section, if such authorization is inconsistent with the statutory obligations of the covered entity or its business associate.

(4) *Implementation specifications: other requirements for contracts and other arrangements.*

(i) The contract or other arrangement between the covered entity and the business associate may permit the business associate to use the information received by the business associate in its capacity as a business associate to the covered entity, if necessary:

(A) For the proper management and administration of the business associate; or

(B) To carry out the legal responsibilities of the business associate.

(ii) The contract or other arrangement between the covered entity and the business associate may permit the business associate to disclose the information received by the business associate in its capacity as a business associate for the purposes described in paragraph (e)(4)(i) of this section, if:

(A) The disclosure is required by law; or

(B)(*1*) The business associate obtains reasonable assurances from the person to whom the information is disclosed that it will be held confidentially and used or further disclosed only as required by law or for the purpose for which it was disclosed to the person; and

(2) The person notifies the business associate of any instances of which it is aware in which the confidentiality of the information has been breached.

(f)(1) *Standard: Requirements for group health plans.*

(i) Except as provided under paragraph(f)(1)(ii) or (iii) of this section or as otherwise authorized under § 164.508, a group health plan, in order to disclose protected health information to the plan sponsor or to provide for or permit the disclosure of protected health information to the plan sponsor by a health insurance issuer or HMO with respect to the group health plan, must ensure that the plan documents restrict uses and disclosures of such information by the plan sponsor consistent with the requirements of this subpart.

(ii) The group health plan, or a health insurance issuer or HMO with respect to the group health plan, may disclose summary health information to the plan sponsor, if the plan sponsor requests the summary health information for the purpose of:

(A) Obtaining premium bids from health plans for providing health insurance coverage under the group health plan; or

(B) Modifying, amending, or terminating the group health plan.

(iii) The group health plan, or a health insurance issuer or HMO with respect to the group health plan, may disclose to the plan sponsor information on whether the individual is participating in the group health plan, or is enrolled in or has disenrolled from a health insurance issuer or HMO offered by the plan.

(2) *Implementation specifications: requirements for plan documents.* The plan documents of the group health plan must be amended to incorporate provisions to:

(i) Establish the permitted and required uses and disclosures of such information by the plan sponsor, provided that such permitted and required uses and disclosures may not be inconsistent with this subpart.

(ii) Provide that the group health plan will disclose protected health information to the plan sponsor only upon receipt of a certification by the plan sponsor that the plan documents have been amended to incorporate the following provisions and that the plan sponsor agrees to:

(A) Not use or further disclose the information other than as permitted or required by the plan documents or as required by law;

(B) Ensure that any agents, including a subcontractor, to whom it provides protected health information received from the group health plan agree to the same restrictions and conditions that apply to the plan sponsor with respect to such information;

(C) Not use or disclose the information for employment-related actions and decisions or in connection with any other benefit or employee benefit plan of the plan sponsor;

(D) Report to the group health plan any use or disclosure of the information that is inconsistent with the uses or disclosures provided for of which it becomes aware;

(E) Make available protected health information in accordance with § 164.524;

(F) Make available protected health information for amendment and incorporate any amendments to protected health information in accordance with §164.526;

(G) Make available the information required to provide an accounting of disclosures in accordance with § 164.528;

(H) Make its internal practices, books, and records relating to the use and disclosure of protected health information received from the group health plan available to the Secretary for purposes of determining compliance by the group health plan with this subpart;

(I) If feasible, return or destroy all protected health information received from the group health plan that the sponsor still maintains in any form and retain no copies of such information when no longer needed for the purpose for which disclosure was made, except that, if such return or destruction is not feasible, limit further uses and disclosures to those purposes that make the return or destruction of the information infeasible; and

(J) Ensure that the adequate separation required in paragraph (f)(2)(iii) of this section is established.

(iii) Provide for adequate separation between the group health plan and the plan sponsor. The plan documents must:

(A) Describe those employees or classes of employees or other persons under the control of the plan sponsor to be given access to the protected health information to be disclosed, provided that any employee or person who receives protected health information relating to payment under, health care operations of, or other matters pertaining to the group health plan in the ordinary course of business must be included in such description;

(B) Restrict the access to and use by such employees and other persons described in paragraph (f)(2)(iii)(A) of this section to the plan administration functions that the plan sponsor performs for the group health plan; and

(C) Provide an effective mechanism for resolving any issues of noncompliance by persons described in paragraph (f)(2)(iii)(A) of this section with the plan document provisions required by this paragraph.

(3) *Implementation specifications: uses and disclosures.* A group health plan may:

(i) Disclose protected health information to a plan sponsor to carry out plan administration functions that the plan sponsor performs only consistent with the provisions of paragraph (f)(2) of this section;

(ii) Not permit a health insurance issuer or HMO with respect to the group health plan to disclose protected health information to the plan sponsor except as permitted by this paragraph;

(iii) Not disclose and may not permit a health insurance issuer or HMO to disclose protected health information to a plan sponsor as otherwise permitted by this paragraph unless a statement required by § 164.520(b)(1)(iii)(C) is included in the appropriate notice; and

(iv) Not disclose protected health information to the plan sponsor for the purpose of employment-related actions or decisions or in connection with any other benefit or employee benefit plan of the plan sponsor.

(g) *Standard: requirements for a covered entity with multiple covered functions.*

(1) A covered entity that performs multiple covered functions that would make the entity any combination of a health plan, a covered health care provider, and a health care clearinghouse, must comply with the standards, requirements, and implementation specifications of this subpart, as applicable to the health plan, health care provider, or health care clearinghouse covered functions performed.

(2) A covered entity that performs multiple covered functions may use or disclose the protected health information of individuals who receive the covered entity's health plan or health care provider services, but not both, only for purposes related to the appropriate function being performed.

§ 164.506 Uses and disclosures to carry out treatment, payment, or health care operations.

(a) *Standard: Permitted uses and disclosures.* Except with respect to uses or disclosures that require an authorization under § 164.508(a)(2) and (3), a covered entity may use or disclose protected health information for treatment, payment, or health care operations as set forth in paragraph (c) of this section, provided that such use or disclosure is consistent with other applicable requirements of this subpart.

(b) *Standard: Consent for uses and disclosures permitted.*

(1) A covered entity may obtain consent of the individual to use or disclose protected health information to carry out treatment, payment, or health care operations.

(2) Consent, under paragraph (b) of this section, shall not be effective to permit a use or disclosure of protected health information when an authorization, under § 164.508, is required or when another condition must be met for such use or disclosure to be permissible under this subpart.

(c) *Implementation specifications: Treatment, payment, or health care operations.*

(1) A covered entity may use or disclose protected health information for its own treatment, payment, or health care operations.

(2) A covered entity may disclose protected health information for treatment activities of a health care provider.

(3) A covered entity may disclose protected health information to another covered entity or a health care provider for the payment activities of the entity that receives the information.

(4) A covered entity may disclose protected health information to another covered entity for health care operations activities of the entity that receives the

information, if each entity either has or had a relationship with the individual who is the subject of the protected health information being requested, the protected health information pertains to such relationship, and the disclosure is:

(i) For a purpose listed in paragraph (1) or (2) of the definition of health care operations; or

(ii) For the purpose of health care fraud and abuse detection or compliance.

(5) A covered entity that participates in an organized health care arrangement may disclose protected health information about an individual to another covered entity that participates in the organized health care arrangement for any health care operations activities of the organized health care arrangement.

§ 164.508 Uses and disclosures for which an authorization is required.

(a) *Standard: authorizations for uses and disclosures.*

(1) *Authorization required: general rule.* Except as otherwise permitted or required by this subchapter, a covered entity may not use or disclose protected health information without an authorization that is valid under this section. When a covered entity obtains or receives a valid authorization for its use or disclosure of protected health information, such use or disclosure must be consistent with such authorization.

(2) *Authorization required: psychotherapy notes.* Notwithstanding any provision of this subpart, other than the transition provisions in § 164.532, a covered entity must obtain an authorization for any use or disclosure of psychotherapy notes, except:

(i) To carry out the following treatment, payment, or health care operations:

(A) Use by the originator of the psychotherapy notes for treatment;

(B) Use or disclosure by the covered entity for its own training programs in which students, trainees, or practitioners in mental health learn under supervision to practice or improve their skills in group, joint, family, or individual counseling; or

(C) Use or disclosure by the covered entity to defend itself in a legal action or other proceeding brought by the individual; and

(ii) A use or disclosure that is required by § 164.502(a)(2)(ii) or permitted by § 164.512(a); § 164.512(d) with respect to the oversight of the originator of the psychotherapy notes; § 164.512(g)(1); or § 164.512(j)(1)(i).

(3) *Authorization required: Marketing.*

(i) Notwithstanding any provision of this subpart, other than the transition provisions in § 164.532, a covered entity must obtain an authorization for any use or disclosure of protected health information for marketing, except if the communication is in the form of:

(A) A face-to-face communication made by a covered entity to an individual; or

(B) A promotional gift of nominal value provided by the covered entity.

(ii) If the marketing involves direct or indirect remuneration to the covered entity from a third party, the authorization must state that such remuneration is involved.

(b) *Implementation specifications: general requirements.*

(1) *Valid authorizations.*

(i) A valid authorization is a document that meets the requirements in paragraphs (a)(3)(ii),(c)(1), and (c)(2) of this section, as applicable.

(ii) A valid authorization may contain elements or information in addition to the elements required by this section, provided that such additional elements or information are not inconsistent with the elements required by this section.

(2) *Defective authorizations.* An authorization is not valid, if the document submitted has any of the following defects:

(i) The expiration date has passed or the expiration event is known by the covered entity to have occurred;

(ii) The authorization has not been filled out completely, with respect to an element described by paragraph (c) of this section, if applicable;

(iii) The authorization is known by the covered entity to have been revoked;

(iv) The authorization violates paragraph (b)(3) or (4) of this section, if applicable;

(v) Any material information in the authorization is known by the covered entity to be false.

(3) *Compound authorizations.* An authorization for use or disclosure of protected health information may not be combined with any other document to create a compound authorization, except as follows:

(i) An authorization for the use or disclosure of protected health information for a research study may be combined with any other type of written permission for the same research study, including another authorization for the use or disclosure of protected health information for such research or a consent to participate in such research;

(ii) An authorization for a use or disclosure of psychotherapy notes may only be combined with another authorization for a use or disclosure of psychotherapy notes;

(iii) An authorization under this section, other than an authorization for a use or disclosure of psychotherapy notes, may be combined with any other such authorization under this section, except when a covered entity has conditioned the provision of treatment, payment, enrollment in the health plan, or eligibility for benefits under paragraph (b)(4) of this section on the provision of one of the authorizations.

(4) *Prohibition on conditioning of authorizations.* A covered entity may not condition the provision to an individual of treatment, payment, enrollment in

the health plan, or eligibility for benefits on the provision of an authorization, except:

(i) A covered health care provider may condition the provision of research-related treatment on provision of an authorization for the use or disclosure of protected health information for such research under this section;

(ii) A health plan may condition enrollment in the health plan or eligibility for benefits on provision of an authorization requested by the health plan prior to an individual's enrollment in the health plan, if:

(A) The authorization sought is for the health plan's eligibility or enrollment determinations relating to the individual or for its underwriting or risk rating determinations; and

(B) The authorization is not for a use or disclosure of psychotherapy notes under paragraph (a)(2) of this section; and

(iii) A covered entity may condition the provision of health care that is solely for the purpose of creating protected health information for disclosure to a third party on provision of an authorization for the disclosure of the protected health information to such third party.

(5) *Revocation of authorizations.* An individual may revoke an authorization provided under this section at any time, provided that the revocation is in writing, except to the extent that:

(i) The covered entity has taken action in reliance thereon; or

(ii) If the authorization was obtained as a condition of obtaining insurance coverage, other law provides the insurer with the right to contest a claim under the policy or the policy itself.

(6) *Documentation.* A covered entity must document and retain any signed authorization under this section as required by § 164.530(j).

(c) *Implementation specifications: Core elements and requirements.*

(1) *Core elements.* A valid authorization under this section must contain at least the following elements:

(i) A description of the information to be used or disclosed that identifies the information in a specific and meaningful fashion.

(ii) The name or other specific identification of the person(s), or class of persons, authorized to make the requested use or disclosure.

(iii) The name or other specific identification of the person(s), or class of persons, to whom the covered entity may make the requested use or disclosure.

(iv) A description of each purpose of the requested use or disclosure. The statement "at the request of the individual" is a sufficient description of the purpose when an individual initiates the authorization and does not, or elects not to, provide a statement of the purpose.

(v) An expiration date or an expiration event that relates to the individual or the purpose of the use or disclosure. The statement "end of the research study," "none," or similar language is sufficient if the authorization is for a use or disclosure of protected health information for research, including for the creation and maintenance of a research database or research repository.

(vi) Signature of the individual and date. If the authorization is signed by a personal representative of the individual, a description of such representative's authority to act for the individual must also be provided.

(2) *Required statements.* In addition to the core elements, the authorization must contain statements adequate to place the individual on notice of all of the following:

(i) The individual's right to revoke the authorization in writing, and either:

(A) The exceptions to the right to revoke and a description of how the individual may revoke the authorization; or

(B) To the extent that the information in paragraph (c)(2)(i)(A) of this section is included in the notice required by § 164.520, a reference to the covered entity's notice.

(ii) The ability or inability to condition treatment, payment, enrollment or eligibility for benefits on the authorization, by stating either:

(A) The covered entity may not condition treatment, payment, enrollment or eligibility for benefits on whether the individual signs the authorization when the prohibition on conditioning of authorizations in paragraph (b)(4) of this section applies; or

(B) The consequences to the individual of a refusal to sign the authorization when, in accordance with paragraph (b)(4) of this section, the covered entity can condition treatment, enrollment in the health plan, or eligibility for benefits on failure to obtain such authorization.

(iii) The potential for information disclosed pursuant to the authorization to be subject to redisclosure by the recipient and no longer be protected by this subpart.

(3) *Plain language requirement.* The authorization must be written in plain language.

(4) *Copy to the individual.* If a covered entity seeks an authorization from an individual for a use or disclosure of protected health information, the covered entity must provide the individual with a copy of the signed authorization.

§ 164.510 Uses and disclosures requiring an opportunity for the individual to agree or to object.

A covered entity may use or disclose protected health information, provided that the individual is informed in advance of the use or disclosure and has the opportunity to agree to or prohibit or restrict the use or disclosure, in accordance with the applicable requirements of this section. The covered entity may orally inform the individual of and obtain the individual's oral agreement or objection to a use or disclosure permitted by this section.

(a) *Standard: use and disclosure for facility directories.*

(1) *Permitted uses and disclosure.* Except when an objection is expressed in accordance with paragraphs (a)(2) or (3) of this section, a covered health care provider may:

(i) Use the following protected health information to maintain a directory of individuals in its facility:

(A) The individual's name;

(B) The individual's location in the covered health care provider's facility;

(C) The individual's condition described in general terms that does not communicate specific medical information about the individual; and

(D) The individual's religious affiliation; and

(ii) Disclose for directory purposes such information:

(A) To members of the clergy; or

(B) Except for religious affiliation, to other persons who ask for the individual by name.

(2) *Opportunity to object.* A covered health care provider must inform an individual of the protected health information that it may include in a directory and the persons to whom it may disclose such information (including disclosures to clergy of information regarding religious affiliation) and provide the individual with the opportunity to restrict or prohibit some or all of the uses or disclosures permitted by paragraph (a)(1) of this section.

(3) *Emergency circumstances.*

(i) If the opportunity to object to uses or disclosures required by paragraph (a)(2) of this section cannot practicably be provided because of the individual's incapacity or an emergency treatment circumstance, a covered health care provider may use or disclose some or all of the protected health information permitted by paragraph (a)(1) of this section for the facility's directory, if such disclosure is:

(A) Consistent with a prior expressed preference of the individual, if any, that is known to the covered health care provider; and

(B) In the individual's best interest as determined by the covered health care provider, in the exercise of professional judgment.

(ii) The covered health care provider must inform the individual and provide an opportunity to object to uses or disclosures for directory purposes as required by paragraph (a)(2) of this section when it becomes practicable to do so.

(b) *Standard: uses and disclosures for involvement in the individual's care and notification purposes.*

(1) *Permitted uses and disclosures.*

(i) A covered entity may, in accordance with paragraphs (b)(2) or (3) of this section, disclose to a family member, other relative, or a close personal friend of the individual, or any other person identified by the individual, the protected health information directly relevant to such person's involvement with the individual's care or payment related to the individual's health care.

(ii) A covered entity may use or disclose protected health information to notify, or assist in the notification of (including identifying or locating), a family member, a personal representative of the individual, or another person responsible for the care of the individual of the individual's location, general condition, or death. Any such use or disclosure of protected health information for such notification purposes must be in accordance with paragraphs (b)(2),(3), or (4) of this section, as applicable.

(2) *Uses and disclosures with the individual present.* If the individual is present for, or otherwise available prior to, a use or disclosure permitted by paragraph (b)(1) of this section and has the capacity to make health care decisions, the covered entity may use or disclose the protected health information if it:

(i) Obtains the individual's agreement;

(ii) Provides the individual with the opportunity to object to the disclosure, and the individual does not express an objection; or

(iii) Reasonably infers from the circumstances, based the exercise of professional judgment, that the individual does not object to the disclosure.

(3) *Limited uses and disclosures when the individual is not present.* If the individual is not present, or the opportunity to agree or object to the use or disclosure cannot practicably be provided because of the individual's incapacity or an emergency circumstance, the covered entity may, in the exercise of professional judgment, determine whether the disclosure is in the best interests of the individual and, if so, disclose only the protected health information that is directly relevant to the person's involvement with the individual's health care. A covered entity may use professional judgment and its experience with common practice to make reasonable inferences of the individual's best interest in allowing a person to act on behalf of the individual to pick up filled prescriptions, medical supplies, X-rays, or other similar forms of protected health information.

(4) *Use and disclosures for disaster relief purposes.* A covered entity may use or disclose protected health information to a public or private entity authorized by law or by its charter to assist in disaster relief efforts, for the purpose of coordinating with such entities the uses or disclosures permitted by paragraph (b)(1)(ii) of this section. The requirements in paragraphs (b)(2) and (3) of this section apply to such uses and disclosure to the extent that the covered entity, in the exercise of professional judgment, determines that the requirements do not interfere with the ability to respond to the emergency circumstances.

§ 164.512 Uses and disclosures for which an authorization or opportunity to agree or object is not required.

A covered entity may use or disclose protected health information without the written authorization of the individual, as described in § 164.508, or the opportunity for the individual to agree or object as described in § 164.510, in the situations covered by this section, subject to the applicable requirements of this section. When the covered entity is required by this section to inform the individual of, or when the individual may agree to, a use or disclosure permitted by this section, the covered entity's information and the individual's agreement may be given orally.

(a) *Standard: uses and disclosures required by law.*

(1) A covered entity may use or disclose protected health information to the extent that such use or disclosure is required by law and the use or disclosure complies with and is limited to the relevant requirements of such law.

(2) A covered entity must meet the requirements described in paragraph (c),(e), or (f) of this section for uses or disclosures required by law.

(b) *Standard: uses and disclosures for public health activities.*

(1) *Permitted disclosures.* A covered entity may disclose protected health information for the public health activities and purposes described in this paragraph to:

(i) A public health authority that is authorized by law to collect or receive such information for the purpose of preventing or controlling disease, injury, or disability, including, but not limited to, the reporting of disease, injury, vital events such as birth or death, and the conduct of public health surveillance, public health investigations, and public health interventions; or, at the direction of a public health authority, to an official of a foreign government agency that is acting in collaboration with a public health authority;

(ii) A public health authority or other appropriate government authority authorized by law to receive reports of child abuse or neglect;

(iii) A person subject to the jurisdiction of the Food and Drug Administration (FDA) with respect to an FDA-regulated product or activity for which that person has responsibility, for the purpose of activities related to the quality, safety or effectiveness of such FDA-regulated product or activity. Such purposes include:

(A) To collect or report adverse events (or similar activities with respect to food or dietary supplements), product defects or problems (including problems with the use or labeling of a product), or biological product deviations;

(B) To track FDA-regulated products;

(C) To enable product recalls, repairs, or replacement, or lookback (including locating and notifying individuals who have received products that have been recalled, withdrawn, or are the subject of lookback); or

(D) To conduct post marketing surveillance;

(iv) A person who may have been exposed to a communicable disease or may otherwise be at risk of contracting or spreading a disease or condition, if the covered entity or public health authority is authorized by law to notify such person as necessary in the conduct of a public health intervention or investigation; or

(v) An employer, about an individual who is a member of the workforce of the employer, if:

(A) The covered entity is a covered health care provider who is a member of the workforce of such employer or who provides health care to the individual at the request of the employer:

(*1*) To conduct an evaluation relating to medical surveillance of the workplace; or

(*2*) To evaluate whether the individual has a work-related illness or injury;

(B) The protected health information that is disclosed consists of findings concerning a work-related illness or injury or a workplace-related medical surveillance;

(C) The employer needs such findings in order to comply with its obligations, under 29 CFR parts 1904 through 1928, 30 CFR parts 50 through 90, or under state law having a similar purpose, to record such illness or injury or to carry out responsibilities for workplace medical surveillance; and

(D) The covered health care provider provides written notice to the individual that protected health information relating to the medical surveillance of the workplace and work-related illnesses and injuries is disclosed to the employer:

(*1*) By giving a copy of the notice to the individual at the time the health care is provided; or

(*2*) If the health care is provided on the work site of the employer, by posting the notice in a prominent place at the location where the health care is provided.

(2) *Permitted uses.* If the covered entity also is a public health authority, the covered entity is permitted to use protected health information in all cases in which it is permitted to disclose such information for public health activities under paragraph (b)(1) of this section.

(c) *Standard: disclosures about victims of abuse, neglect or domestic violence.*

(1) *Permitted disclosures.* Except for reports of child abuse or neglect permitted by paragraph (b)(1)(ii) of this section, a covered entity may disclose protected health information about an individual whom the covered entity reasonably believes to be a victim of abuse, neglect, or domestic violence to a government authority, including a social service or protective services agency, authorized by law to receive reports of such abuse, neglect, or domestic violence:

(i) To the extent the disclosure is required by law and the disclosure complies with and is limited to the relevant requirements of such law;

(ii) If the individual agrees to the disclosure; or

(iii) To the extent the disclosure is expressly authorized by statute or regulation and:

(A) The covered entity, in the exercise of professional judgment, believes the disclosure is necessary to prevent serious harm to the individual or other potential victims; or

(B) If the individual is unable to agree because of incapacity, a law enforcement or other public official authorized to receive the report represents that the protected health information for which disclosure is sought is not intended to be used against the individual and that an immediate enforcement activity that depends upon the disclosure would be materially and adversely affected by waiting until the individual is able to agree to the disclosure.

(2) *Informing the individual.* A covered entity that makes a disclosure permitted by paragraph (c)(1) of this section must promptly inform the individual that such a report has been or will be made, except if:

(i) The covered entity, in the exercise of professional judgment, believes informing the individual would place the individual at risk of serious harm; or

(ii) The covered entity would be informing a personal representative, and the covered entity reasonably believes the personal representative is responsible for the abuse, neglect, or other injury, and that informing such person would not be in the best interests of the individual as determined by the covered entity, in the exercise of professional judgment.

(d) *Standard: uses and disclosures for health oversight activities.*

(1) *Permitted disclosures.* A covered entity may disclose protected health information to a health oversight agency for oversight activities authorized by law, including audits; civil, administrative, or criminal investigations; inspections; licensure or disciplinary actions; civil, administrative, or criminal proceedings or actions; or other activities necessary for appropriate oversight of:

(i) The health care system;

(ii) Government benefit programs for which health information is relevant to beneficiary eligibility;

(iii) Entities subject to government regulatory programs for which health information is necessary for determining compliance with program standards; or

(iv) Entities subject to civil rights laws for which health information is necessary for determining compliance.

(2) *Exception to health oversight activities.* For the purpose of the disclosures permitted by paragraph (d)(1) of this section, a health oversight activity does not include an investigation or other activity in which the individual is the subject of the investigation or activity and such investigation or other activity does not arise out of and is not directly related to:

(i) The receipt of health care;

(ii) A claim for public benefits related to health; or

(iii) Qualification for, or receipt of, public benefits or services when a patient's health is integral to the claim for public benefits or services.

(3) *Joint activities or investigations.* Notwithstanding paragraph (d)(2) of this section, if a health oversight activity or investigation is conducted in conjunction with an oversight activity or investigation relating to a claim for public benefits not related to health, the joint activity or investigation is considered a health oversight activity for purposes of paragraph (d) of this section.

(4) *Permitted uses.* If a covered entity also is a health oversight agency, the covered entity may use protected health information for health oversight activities as permitted by paragraph (d) of this section.

(e) *Standard: disclosures for judicial and administrative proceedings.*

(1) *Permitted disclosures.* A covered entity may disclose protected health information in the course of any judicial or administrative proceeding:

(i) In response to an order of a court or administrative tribunal, provided that the covered entity discloses only the protected health information expressly authorized by such order; or

(ii) In response to a subpoena, discovery request, or other lawful process, that is not accompanied by an order of a court or administrative tribunal, if:

(A) The covered entity receives satisfactory assurance, as described in paragraph (e)(1)(iii) of this section, from the party seeking the information that reasonable efforts have been made by such party to ensure that the individual who is the subject of the protected health information that has been requested has been given notice of the request; or

(B) The covered entity receives satisfactory assurance, as described in paragraph (e)(1)(iv) of this section, from the party seeking the information that reasonable efforts have been made by such party to secure a qualified protective order that meets the requirements of paragraph (e)(1)(v) of this section.

(iii) For the purposes of paragraph (e)(1)(ii)(A) of this section, a covered entity receives satisfactory assurances from a party seeking protecting health information if the covered entity receives from such party a written statement and accompanying documentation demonstrating that:

(A) The party requesting such information has made a good faith attempt to provide written notice to the individual (or, if the individual's location is unknown, to mail a notice to the individual's last known address);

(B) The notice included sufficient information about the litigation or proceeding in which the protected health information is requested to permit the individual to raise an objection to the court or administrative tribunal; and

(C) The time for the individual to raise objections to the court or administrative tribunal has elapsed, and:

(*1*) No objections were filed; or

(*2*) All objections filed by the individual have been resolved by the court or the administrative tribunal and the disclosures being sought are consistent with such resolution.

(iv) For the purposes of paragraph (e)(1)(ii)(B) of this section, a covered entity receives satisfactory assurances from a party seeking protected health information, if the covered entity receives from such party a written statement and accompanying documentation demonstrating that:

(A) The parties to the dispute giving rise to the request for information have agreed to a qualified protective order and have presented it to the court or administrative tribunal with jurisdiction over the dispute; or

(B) The party seeking the protected health information has requested a qualified protective order from such court or administrative tribunal.

(v) For purposes of paragraph (e)(1) of this section, a *qualified protective order* means, with respect to protected health information requested under paragraph (e)(1)(ii) of this section, an order of a court or of an administrative tribunal or a stipulation by the parties to the litigation or administrative proceeding that:

(A) Prohibits the parties from using or disclosing the protected health information for any purpose other than the litigation or proceeding for which such information was requested; and

(B) Requires the return to the covered entity or destruction of the protected health information (including all copies made) at the end of the litigation or proceeding.

(vi) Notwithstanding paragraph (e)(1)(ii) of this section, a covered entity may disclose protected health information in response to lawful process described in paragraph (e)(1)(ii) of this section without receiving satisfactory assurance under paragraph (e)(1)(ii)(A) or (B) of this section, if the covered entity makes reasonable efforts to provide notice to the individual sufficient to meet the requirements of paragraph (e)(1)(iii) of this section or to seek a qualified protective order sufficient to meet the requirements of paragraph (e)(1)(iv) of this section.

(2) *Other uses and disclosures under this section.* The provisions of this paragraph do not supersede other provisions of this section that otherwise permit or restrict uses or disclosures of protected health information.

(f) *Standard: disclosures for law enforcement purposes.* A covered entity may disclose protected health information for a law enforcement purpose to a law enforcement official if the conditions in paragraphs (f)(1) through (f)(6) of this section are met, as applicable.

(1) *Permitted disclosures: pursuant to process and as otherwise required by law.* A covered entity may disclose protected health information:

(i) As required by law including laws that require the reporting of certain types of wounds or other physical injuries, except for laws subject to paragraph (b)(1)(ii) or (c)(1)(i) of this section; or

(ii) In compliance with and as limited by the relevant requirements of:

(A) A court order or court-ordered warrant, or a subpoena or summons issued by a judicial officer;

(B) A grand jury subpoena; or

(C) An administrative request, including an administrative subpoena or summons, a civil or an authorized investigative demand, or similar process authorized under law, provided that: (*1*) The information sought is relevant and material to a legitimate law enforcement inquiry, (*2*) The request is specific and limited in scope to the extent reasonably practicable in light of the purpose for which the information is sought; and (*3*) De-identified information could not reasonably be used.

(2) *Permitted disclosures: limited information for identification and location purposes.* Except for disclosures required by law as permitted by paragraph (f)(1) of this section, a covered entity may disclose protected health information in response to a law enforcement official's request for such information for the purpose of identifying or locating a suspect, fugitive, material witness, or missing person, provided that:

(i) The covered entity may disclose only the following information:

(A) Name and address;

(B) Date and place of birth;

(C) Social security number;

(D) ABO blood type and rh factor;

(E) Type of injury;

(F) Date and time of treatment;

(G) Date and time of death, if applicable; and

(H) A description of distinguishing physical characteristics, including height, weight, gender, race, hair and eye color, presence or absence of facial hair (beard or moustache), scars, and tattoos.

(ii) Except as permitted by paragraph (f)(2)(i) of this section, the covered entity may not disclose for the purposes of identification or location under paragraph (f)(2) of this section any protected health information related to the individual's DNA or DNA analysis, dental records, or typing, samples or analysis of body fluids or tissue.

(3) *Permitted disclosure: victims of a crime.* Except for disclosures required by law as permitted by paragraph (f)(1) of this section, a covered entity may disclose protected health information in response to a law enforcement official's request for such information about an individual who is or is suspected to be a victim of a crime, other than disclosures that are subject to paragraph (b) or (c) of this section, if:

(i) The individual agrees to the disclosure; or

(ii) The covered entity is unable to obtain the individual's agreement because of incapacity or other emergency circumstance, provided that:

(A) The law enforcement official represents that such information is needed to determine whether a violation of law by a person other than the victim has occurred, and such information is not intended to be used against the victim;

(B) The law enforcement official represents that immediate law enforcement activity that depends upon the disclosure would be materially and adversely affected by waiting until the individual is able to agree to the disclosure; and

(C) The disclosure is in the best interests of the individual as determined by the covered entity, in the exercise of professional judgment.

(4) *Permitted disclosure: decedents.* A covered entity may disclose protected health information about an individual who has died to a law enforcement offi-

cial for the purpose of alerting law enforcement of the death of the individual if the covered entity has a suspicion that such death may have resulted from criminal conduct.

(5) *Permitted disclosure: crime on premises.* A covered entity may disclose to a law enforcement official protected health information that the covered entity believes in good faith constitutes evidence of criminal conduct that occurred on the premises of the covered entity.

(6) *Permitted disclosure: reporting crime in emergencies.*

(i) A covered health care provider providing emergency health care in response to a medical emergency, other than such emergency on the premises of the covered health care provider, may disclose protected health information to a law enforcement official if such disclosure appears necessary to alert law enforcement to:

(A) The commission and nature of a crime;

(B) The location of such crime or of the victim(s) of such crime; and

(C) The identity, description, and location of the perpetrator of such crime.

(ii) If a covered health care provider believes that the medical emergency described in paragraph (f)(6)(i) of this section is the result of abuse, neglect, or domestic violence of the individual in need of emergency health care, paragraph (f)(6)(i) of this section does not apply and any disclosure to a law enforcement official for law enforcement purposes is subject to paragraph (c) of this section.

(g) *Standard: uses and disclosures about decedents.*

(1) *Coroners and medical examiners.* A covered entity may disclose protected health information to a coroner or medical examiner for the purpose of identifying a deceased person, determining a cause of death, or other duties as authorized by law. A covered entity that also performs the duties of a coroner or medical examiner may use protected health information for the purposes described in this paragraph.

(2) *Funeral directors.* A covered entity may disclose protected health information to funeral directors, consistent with applicable law, as necessary to carry out their duties with respect to the decedent. If necessary for funeral directors to carry out their duties, the covered entity may disclose the protected health information prior to, and in reasonable anticipation of, the individual's death.

(h) *Standard: uses and disclosures for cadaveric organ, eye or tissue donation purposes.* A covered entity may use or disclose protected health information to organ procurement organizations or other entities engaged in the procurement, banking, or transplantation of cadaveric organs, eyes, or tissue for the purpose of facilitating organ, eye or tissue donation and transplantation.

(i) *Standard: uses and disclosures for research purposes.*

(1) *Permitted uses and disclosures.* A covered entity may use or disclose protected health information for research, regardless of the source of funding of the research, provided that:

(i) *Board approval of a waiver of authorization.* The covered entity obtains documentation that an alteration to or waiver, in whole or in part, of the individual authorization required by §164.508 for use or disclosure of protected health information has been approved by either:

(A) An Institutional Review Board (IRB), established in accordance with 7 CFR 1c.107, 10 CFR 745.107, 14 CFR 1230.107, 15 CFR 27.107, 16 CFR 1028.107, 21 CFR 56.107, 22 CFR 225.107, 24 CFR 60.107, 28 CFR 46.107, 32 CFR 219.107, 34 CFR 97.107, 38 CFR 16.107, 40 CFR 26.107, 45 CFR 46.107, 45 CFR 690.107, or 49 CFR 11.107; or

(B) A privacy board that:

(*1*) Has members with varying backgrounds and appropriate professional competency as necessary to review the effect of the research protocol on the individual's privacy rights and related interests;

(*2*) Includes at least one member who is not affiliated with the covered entity, not affiliated with any entity conducting or sponsoring the research, and not related to any person who is affiliated with any of such entities; and

(*3*) Does not have any member participating in a review of any project in which the member has a conflict of interest.

(ii) *Reviews preparatory to research.* The covered entity obtains from the researcher representations that:

(A) Use or disclosure is sought solely to review protected health information as necessary to prepare a research protocol or for similar purposes preparatory to research;

(B) No protected health information is to be removed from the covered entity by the researcher in the course of the review; and

(C) The protected health information for which use or access is sought is necessary for the research purposes.

(iii) *Research on decedent's information.* The covered entity obtains from the researcher:

(A) Representation that the use or disclosure sought is solely for research on the protected health information of decedents;

(B) Documentation, at the request of the covered entity, of the death of such individuals; and

(C) Representation that the protected health information for which use or disclosure is sought is necessary for the research purposes.

(2) *Documentation of waiver approval.* For a use or disclosure to be permitted based on documentation of approval of an alteration or waiver, under paragraph (i)(1)(i) of this section, the documentation must include all of the following:

(i) *Identification and date of action.* A statement identifying the IRB or privacy board and the date on which the alteration or waiver of authorization was approved;

(ii) *Waiver criteria.* A statement that the IRB or privacy board has determined that the alteration or waiver, in whole or in part, of authorization satisfies the following criteria:

(A) The use or disclosure of protected health information involves no more than a minimal risk to the privacy of individuals, based on, at least, the presence of the following elements;

(*1*) An adequate plan to protect the identifiers from improper use and disclosure;

(*2*) An adequate plan to destroy the identifiers at the earliest opportunity consistent with conduct of the research, unless there is a health or research justification for retaining the identifiers or such retention is otherwise required by law; and

(*3*) Adequate written assurances that the protected health information will not be reused or disclosed to any other person or entity, except as required by law, for authorized oversight of the research study, or for other research for which the use or disclosure of protected health information would be permitted by this subpart;

(B) The research could not practicably be conducted without the waiver or alteration; and

(C) The research could not practicably be conducted without access to and use of the protected health information.

(iii) *Protected health information needed.* A brief description of the protected health information for which use or access has been determined to be necessary by the IRB or privacy board has determined, pursuant to paragraph (i)(2)(ii)(C) of this section;

(iv) *Review and approval procedures.* A statement that the alteration or waiver of authorization has been reviewed and approved under either normal or expedited review procedures, as follows:

(A) An IRB must follow the requirements of the Common Rule, including the normal review procedures (7 CFR 1c.108(b), 10 CFR 745.108(b), 14 CFR 1230.108(b), 15 CFR 27.108(b), 16 CFR 1028.108(b), 21 CFR 56.108(b), 22 CFR 225.108(b), 24 CFR 60.108(b), 28 CFR 46.108(b), 32 CFR 219.108(b), 34 CFR 97.108(b), 38 CFR 16.108(b), 40 CFR 26.108(b), 45 CFR 46.108(b), 45 CFR 690.108(b), or 49 CFR 11.108(b)) or the expedited review procedures (7 CFR 1c.110, 10 CFR 745.110, 14 CFR 1230.110, 15 CFR 27.110, 16 CFR 1028.110, 21 CFR 56.110, 22 CFR 225.110, 24 CFR 60.110, 28 CFR 46.110, 32 CFR 219.110, 34 CFR 97.110, 38 CFR 16.110, 40 CFR 26.110, 45 CFR 46.110, 45 CFR 690.110, or 49 CFR 11.110);

(B) A privacy board must review the proposed research at convened meetings at which a majority of the privacy board members are present, including at least one member who satisfies the criterion stated in paragraph (i)(1)(i)(B)(2) of this section, and the alteration or waiver of authorization must be approved by the majority of the privacy board members present at the meeting, unless the privacy board elects to use an expedited review procedure in accordance with paragraph (i)(2)(iv)(C) of this section;

(C) A privacy board may use an expedited review procedure if the research involves no more than minimal risk to the privacy of the individuals who are the subject of the protected health information for which use or disclosure is being sought. If the privacy board elects to use an expedited review procedure, the review and approval of the alteration or waiver of authorization may be carried out by the chair of the privacy board, or by one or more members of the privacy board as designated by the chair; and

(v) *Required signature.* The documentation of the alteration or waiver of authorization must be signed by the chair or other member, as designated by the chair, of the IRB or the privacy board, as applicable.

(j) Standard: uses and disclosures to avert a serious threat to health or safety.

(1) *Permitted disclosures.* A covered entity may, consistent with applicable law and standards of ethical conduct, use or disclose protected health information, if the covered entity, in good faith, believes the use or disclosure:

(i)(A) Is necessary to prevent or lessen a serious and imminent threat to the health or safety of a person or the public; and

(B) Is to a person or persons reasonably able to prevent or lessen the threat, including the target of the threat; or

(ii) Is necessary for law enforcement authorities to identify or apprehend an individual:

(A) Because of a statement by an individual admitting participation in a violent crime that the covered entity reasonably believes may have caused serious physical harm to the victim; or

(B) Where it appears from all the circumstances that the individual has escaped from a correctional institution or from lawful custody, as those terms are defined in § 164.501.

(2) *Use or disclosure not permitted.* A use or disclosure pursuant to paragraph (j)(1)(ii)(A) of this section may not be made if the information described in paragraph (j)(1)(ii)(A) of this section is learned by the covered entity:

(i) In the course of treatment to affect the propensity to commit the criminal conduct that is the basis for the disclosure under paragraph (j)(1)(ii)(A) of this section, or counseling or therapy; or

(ii) Through a request by the individual to initiate or to be referred for the treatment, counseling, or therapy described in paragraph (j)(2)(i) of this section.

(3) *Limit on information that may be disclosed.* A disclosure made pursuant to paragraph (j)(1)(ii)(A) of this section shall contain only the statement described in paragraph (j)(1)(ii)(A) of this section and the protected health information described in paragraph (f)(2)(i) of this section.

(4) *Presumption of good faith belief.* A covered entity that uses or discloses protected health information pursuant to paragraph (j)(1) of this section is presumed to have acted in good faith with regard to a belief described in paragraph (j)(1)(i) or (ii) of this section, if the belief is based upon the covered entity's actual knowledge or in reliance on a credible representation by a person with apparent knowledge or authority.

(k) *Standard: uses and disclosures for specialized government functions.*

(1) *Military and veterans activities.*

(i) *Armed Forces personnel.* A covered entity may use and disclose the protected health information of individuals who are Armed Forces personnel for activities deemed necessary by appropriate military command authorities to assure the proper execution of the military mission, if the appropriate military authority has published by notice in the *Federal Register* the following information:

(A) Appropriate military command authorities; and

(B) The purposes for which the protected health information may be used or disclosed.

(ii) *Separation or discharge from military service.* A covered entity that is a component of the Departments of Defense or Transportation may disclose to the Department of Veterans Affairs (DVA) the protected health information of an individual who is a member of the Armed Forces upon the separation or discharge of the individual from military service for the purpose of a determination by DVA of the individual's eligibility for or entitlement to benefits under laws administered by the Secretary of Veterans Affairs.

(iii) *Veterans.* A covered entity that is a component of the Department of Veterans Affairs may use and disclose protected health information to components of the Department that determine eligibility for or entitlement to, or that provide, benefits under the laws administered by the Secretary of Veterans Affairs.

(iv) *Foreign military personnel.* A covered entity may use and disclose the protected health information of individuals who are foreign military personnel to their appropriate foreign military authority for the same purposes for which uses and disclosures are permitted for Armed Forces personnel under the notice published in the *Federal Register* pursuant to paragraph (k)(1)(i) of this section.

(2) *National security and intelligence activities.* A covered entity may disclose protected health information to authorized federal officials for the conduct of lawful intelligence, counter-intelligence, and other national security activities authorized by the National Security Act (50 U.S.C. 401, *et seq.*) and implementing authority (e.g., Executive Order 12333).

(3) *Protective services for the President and others.* A covered entity may disclose protected health information to authorized federal officials for the provision of protective services to the President or other persons authorized by 18 U.S.C. 3056, or to foreign heads of state or other persons authorized by 22 U.S.C. 2709(a)(3), or to for the conduct of investigations authorized by 18 U.S.C. 871 and 879.

(4) *Medical suitability determinations.* A covered entity that is a component of the Department of State may use protected health information to make medical suitability determinations and may disclose whether or not the individual was determined to be medically suitable to the officials in the Department of State who need access to such information for the following purposes:

(i) For the purpose of a required security clearance conducted pursuant to Executive Orders 10450 and 12698;

(ii) As necessary to determine worldwide availability or availability for mandatory service abroad under sections 101(a)(4) and 504 of the Foreign Service Act; or

(iii) For a family to accompany a Foreign Service member abroad, consistent with section 101(b)(5) and 904 of the Foreign Service Act.

(5) *Correctional institutions and other law enforcement custodial situations.*

(i) *Permitted disclosures.* A covered entity may disclose to a correctional institution or a law enforcement official having lawful custody of an inmate or other individual protected health information about such inmate or individual, if the correctional institution or such law enforcement official represents that such protected health information is necessary for:

(A) The provision of health care to such individuals;

(B) The health and safety of such individual or other inmates;

(C) The health and safety of the officers or employees of or others at the correctional institution;

(D) The health and safety of such individuals and officers or other persons responsible for the transporting of inmates or their transfer from one institution, facility, or setting to another;

(E) Law enforcement on the premises of the correctional institution; and

(F) The administration and maintenance of the safety, security, and good order of the correctional institution.

(ii) *Permitted uses.* A covered entity that is a correctional institution may use protected health information of individuals who are inmates for any purpose for which such protected health information may be disclosed.

(iii) *No application after release.* For the purposes of this provision, an individual is no longer an inmate when released on parole, probation, supervised release, or otherwise is no longer in lawful custody.

(6) *Covered entities that are government programs providing public benefits.*

(i) A health plan that is a government program providing public benefits may disclose protected health information relating to eligibility for or enrollment in the health plan to another agency administering a government program providing public benefits if the sharing of eligibility or enrollment information among such government agencies or the maintenance of such information in a single or combined data system accessible to all such government agencies is required or expressly authorized by statute or regulation.

(ii) A covered entity that is a government agency administering a government program providing public benefits may disclose protected health information relating to the program to another covered entity that is a government agency administering a government program providing public benefits if the programs serve the same or similar populations and the disclosure of protected health information is necessary to coordinate the covered functions of such programs or to improve administration and management relating to the covered functions of such programs.

(l) *Standard: disclosures for workers' compensation.* A covered entity may disclose protected health information as authorized by and to the extent necessary to comply with laws relating to workers' compensation or other similar programs, established by law, that provide benefits for work-related injuries or illness without regard to fault.

§ 164.514 Other requirements relating to uses and disclosures of protected health information.

(a) *Standard: de-identification of protected health information.* Health information that does not identify an individual and with respect to which there is no reasonable basis to believe that the information can be used to identify an individual is not individually identifiable health information.

(b) *Implementation specifications: requirements for de-identification of protected health information.* A covered entity may determine that health information is not individually identifiable health information only if:

(1) A person with appropriate knowledge of and experience with generally accepted statistical and scientific principles and methods for rendering information not individually identifiable:

(i) Applying such principles and methods, determines that the risk is very small that the information could be used, alone or in combination with other reasonably available information, by an anticipated recipient to identify an individual who is a subject of the information; and

(ii) Documents the methods and results of the analysis that justify such determination; or

(2)(i) The following identifiers of the individual or of relatives, employers, or household members of the individual, are removed:

(A) Names;

(B) All geographic subdivisions smaller than a State, including street address, city, county, precinct, zip code, and their equivalent geocodes, except for the initial three digits of a zip code if, according to the current publicly available data from the Bureau of the Census:

(*1*) The geographic unit formed by combining all zip codes with the same three initial digits contains more than 20,000 people; and

(*2*) The initial three digits of a zip code for all such geographic units containing 20,000 or fewer people is changed to 000.

(C) All elements of dates (except year) for dates directly related to an individual, including birth date, admission date, discharge date, date of death; and all ages over 89 and all elements of dates (including year) indicative of such age, except that such ages and elements may be aggregated into a single category of age 90 or older;

(D) Telephone numbers;

(E) Fax numbers;

(F) Electronic mail addresses;

(G) Social security numbers;

(H) Medical record numbers;

(I) Health plan beneficiary numbers;

(J) Account numbers;

(K) Certificate/license numbers;

(L) Vehicle identifiers and serial numbers, including license plate numbers;

(M) Device identifiers and serial numbers;

(N) Web Universal Resource Locators (URLs);

(O) Internet Protocol (IP) address numbers;

(P) Biometric identifiers, including finger and voice prints;

(Q) Full face photographic images and any comparable images; and

(R) Any other unique identifying number, characteristic, or code, except as permitted by paragraph (c) of this section; and

(ii) The covered entity does not have actual knowledge that the information could be used alone or in combination with other information to identify an individual who is a subject of the information.

(c) *Implementation specifications: re-identification.* A covered entity may assign a code or other means of record identification to allow information de-identified under this section to be re-identified by the covered entity, provided that:

(1) *Derivation.* The code or other means of record identification is not derived from or related to information about the individual and is not otherwise capable of being translated so as to identify the individual; and

(2) *Security.* The covered entity does not use or disclose the code or other means of record identification for any other purpose, and does not disclose the mechanism for re-identification.

(d)(1) *Standard: minimum necessary requirements.* In order to comply with § 164.502(b) and this section, a covered entity must meet the requirements of paragraphs (d)(2) through (d)(5) of this section with respect to a request for, or the use and disclosure of, protected health information.

(2) *Implementation specifications: minimum necessary uses of protected health information.*

(i) A covered entity must identify:

(A) Those persons or classes of persons, as appropriate, in its workforce who need access to protected health information to carry out their duties; and

(B) For each such person or class of persons, the category or categories of protected health information to which access is needed and any conditions appropriate to such access.

(ii) A covered entity must make reasonable efforts to limit the access of such persons or classes identified in paragraph (d)(2)(i)(A) of this section to protected health information consistent with paragraph (d)(2)(i)(B) of this section.

(3) *Implementation specification: minimum necessary disclosures of protected health information.*

(i) For any type of disclosure that it makes on a routine and recurring basis, a covered entity must implement policies and procedures (which may be standard protocols) that limit the protected health information disclosed to the amount reasonably necessary to achieve the purpose of the disclosure.

(ii) For all other disclosures, a covered entity must:

(A) Develop criteria designed to limit the protected health information disclosed to the information reasonably necessary to accomplish the purpose for which disclosure is sought; and

(B) Review requests for disclosure on an individual basis in accordance with such criteria.

(iii) A covered entity may rely, if such reliance is reasonable under the circumstances, on a requested disclosure as the minimum necessary for the stated purpose when:

(A) Making disclosures to public officials that are permitted under § 164.512, if the public official represents that the information requested is the minimum necessary for the stated purpose(s);

(B) The information is requested by another covered entity;

(C) The information is requested by a professional who is a member of its workforce or is a business associate of the covered entity for the purpose of providing professional services to the covered entity, if the professional represents that the information requested is the minimum necessary for the stated purpose(s); or

(D) Documentation or representations that comply with the applicable requirements of § 164.512(i) have been provided by a person requesting the information for research purposes.

(4) *Implementation specifications: minimum necessary requests for protected health information.*

(i) A covered entity must limit any request for protected health information to that which is reasonably necessary to accomplish the purpose for which the request is made, when requesting such information from other covered entities.

(ii) For a request that is made on a routine and recurring basis, a covered entity must implement policies and procedures (which may be standard protocols) that limit the protected health information requested to the amount reasonably necessary to accomplish the purpose for which the request is made.

(iii) For all other requests, a covered entity must:

(A) Develop criteria designed to limit the request for protected health information to the information reasonably necessary to accomplish the purpose for which the request is made; and

(B) Review requests for disclosure on an individual basis in accordance with such criteria.

(5) *Implementation specification: other content requirement.* For all uses, disclosures, or requests to which the requirements in paragraph (d) of this section

apply, a covered entity may not use, disclose or request an entire medical record, except when the entire medical record is specifically justified as the amount that is reasonably necessary to accomplish the purpose of the use, disclosure, or request.

(e)(1) *Standard: Limited data set.* A covered entity may use or disclose a limited data set that meets the requirements of paragraphs (e)(2) and (e)(3) of this section, if the covered entity enters into a data use agreement with the limited data set recipient, in accordance with paragraph (e)(4) of this section.

(2) *Implementation specification: Limited data set:* A limited data set is protected health information that excludes the following direct identifiers of the individual or of relatives, employers, or household members of the individual:

(i) Names;

(ii) Postal address information, other than town or city, State, and zip code;

(iii) Telephone numbers;

(iv) Fax numbers;

(v) Electronic mail addresses;

(vi) Social security numbers;

(vii) Medical record numbers;

(viii) Health plan beneficiary numbers;

(ix) Account numbers;

(x) Certificate/license numbers;

(xi) Vehicle identifiers and serial numbers, including license plate numbers;

(xii) Device identifiers and serial numbers;

(xiii) Web Universal Resource Locators (URLs);

(xiv) Internet Protocol (IP) address numbers;

(xv) Biometric identifiers, including finger and voice prints; and

(xvi) Full face photographic images and any comparable images.

(3) *Implementation specification: Permitted purposes for uses and disclosures.*

(i) A covered entity may use or disclose a limited data set under paragraph (e)(1) of this section only for the purposes of research, public health, or health care operations.

(ii) A covered entity may use protected health information to create a limited data set that meets the requirements of paragraph (e)(2) of this section, or disclose protected health information only to a business associate for such purpose, whether or not the limited data set is to be used by the covered entity.

(4) *Implementation specifications: Data use agreement.*

(i) *Agreement required.* A covered entity may use or disclose a limited data set under paragraph (e)(1) of this section only if the covered entity obtains satisfactory assurance, in the form of a data use agreement that meets the requirements of this section, that the limited data set recipient will only use or disclose the protected health information for limited purposes.

(ii) *Contents.* A data use agreement between the covered entity and the limited data set recipient must:

(A) Establish the permitted uses and disclosures of such information by the limited data set recipient, consistent with paragraph (e)(3) of this section. The data use agreement may not authorize the limited data set recipient to use or further disclose the information in a manner that would violate the requirements of this subpart, if done by the covered entity;

(B) Establish who is permitted to use or receive the limited data set; and

(C) Provide that the limited data set recipient will:

(*1*) Not use or further disclose the information other than as permitted by the data use agreement or as otherwise required by law;

(*2*) Use appropriate safeguards to prevent use or disclosure of the information other than as provided for by the data use agreement;

(*3*) Report to the covered entity any use or disclosure of the information not provided for by its data use agreement of which it becomes aware;

(*4*) Ensure that any agents, including a subcontractor, to whom it provides the limited data set agrees to the same restrictions and conditions that apply to the limited data set recipient with respect to such information; and

(*5*) Not identify the information or contact the individuals.

(iii) *Compliance.*

(A) A covered entity is not in compliance with the standards in paragraph(e) of this section if the covered entity knew of a pattern of activity or practice of the limited data set recipient that constituted a material breach or violation of the data use agreement, unless the covered entity took reasonable steps to cure the breach or end the violation, as applicable, and, if such steps were unsuccessful:

(*1*) Discontinued disclosure of protected health information to the recipient; and

(*2*) Reported the problem to the Secretary.

(B) A covered entity that is a limited data set recipient and violates a data use agreement will be in noncompliance with the standards, implementation specifications, and requirements of paragraph (e) of this section.

(f)(1) *Standard: uses and disclosures for fundraising.* A covered entity may use, or disclose to a business associate or to an institutionally related foundation, the following protected health information for the purpose of raising funds for its own benefit, without an authorization meeting the requirements of § 164.508:

(i) Demographic information relating to an individual; and

(ii) Dates of health care provided to an individual.

(2) *Implementation specifications: fundraising requirements.*

(i) The covered entity may not use or disclose protected health information for fundraising purposes as otherwise permitted by paragraph (f)(1) of this section unless a statement required by § 164.520(b)(1)(iii)(B) is included in the covered entity's notice;

(ii) The covered entity must include in any fundraising materials it sends to an individual under this paragraph a description of how the individual may opt out of receiving any further fundraising communications.

(iii) The covered entity must make reasonable efforts to ensure that individuals who decide to opt out of receiving future fundraising communications are not sent such communications.

(g) *Standard: uses and disclosures for underwriting and related purposes.* If a health plan receives protected heath information for the purpose of underwriting, premium rating, or other activities relating to the creation, renewal, or replacement of a contract of health insurance or health benefits, and if such health insurance or health benefits are not placed with the health plan, such health plan may not use or disclose such protected health information for any other purpose, except as may be required by law.

(h)(1) *Standard: verification requirements.* Prior to any disclosure permitted by this subpart, a covered entity must:

(i) Except with respect to disclosures under § 164.510, verify the identity of a person requesting protected health information and the authority of any such person to have access to protected health information under this subpart, if the identity or any such authority of such person is not known to the covered entity; and

(ii) Obtain any documentation, statements, or representations, whether oral or written, from the person requesting the protected health information when such documentation, statement, or representation is a condition of the disclosure under this subpart.

(2) *Implementation specifications: verification.*

(i) *Conditions on disclosures.* If a disclosure is conditioned by this subpart on particular documentation, statements, or representations from the person requesting the protected health information, a covered entity may rely, if such reliance is reasonable under the circumstances, on documentation, statements, or representations that, on their face, meet the applicable requirements.

(A) The conditions in § 164.512(f)(1)(ii)(C) may be satisfied by the administrative subpoena or similar process or by a separate written statement that, on its face, demonstrates that the applicable requirements have been met.

(B) The documentation required by § 164.512(i)(2) may be satisfied by one or more written statements, provided that each is appropriately dated and signed in accordance with § 164.512(i)(2)(i) and (v).

(ii) *Identity of public officials.* A covered entity may rely, if such reliance is reasonable under the circumstances, on any of the following to verify identity when the disclosure of protected health information is to a public official or a person acting on behalf of the public official:

(A) If the request is made in person, presentation of an agency identification badge, other official credentials, or other proof of government status;

(B) If the request is in writing, the request is on the appropriate government letterhead; or

(C) If the disclosure is to a person acting on behalf of a public official, a written statement on appropriate government letterhead that the person is acting under the government's authority or other evidence or documentation of agency, such as a contract for services, memorandum of understanding, or purchase order, that establishes that the person is acting on behalf of the public official.

(iii) *Authority of public officials.* A covered entity may rely, if such reliance is reasonable under the circumstances, on any of the following to verify authority when the disclosure of protected health information is to a public official or a person acting on behalf of the public official:

(A) A written statement of the legal authority under which the information is requested, or, if a written statement would be impracticable, an oral statement of such legal authority;

(B) If a request is made pursuant to legal process, warrant, subpoena, order, or other legal process issued by a grand jury or a judicial or administrative tribunal is presumed to constitute legal authority.

(iv) *Exercise of professional judgment.* The verification requirements of this paragraph are met if the covered entity relies on the exercise of professional judgment in making a use or disclosure in accordance with § 164.510 or acts on a good faith belief in making a disclosure in accordance with § 164.512(j).

§ 164.520 Notice of privacy practices for protected health information.

(a) *Standard: notice of privacy practices.*

(1) *Right to notice.* Except as provided by paragraph (a)(2) or (3) of this section, an individual has a right to adequate notice of the uses and disclosures of protected health information that may be made by the covered entity, and of the individual's rights and the covered entity's legal duties with respect to protected health information.

(2) *Exception for group health plans.*

(i) An individual enrolled in a group health plan has a right to notice:

(A) From the group health plan, if, and to the extent that, such an individual does not receive health benefits under the group health plan through an insurance contract with a health insurance issuer or HMO; or

(B) From the health insurance issuer or HMO with respect to the group health plan though which such individuals receive their health benefits under the group health plan.

(ii) A group health plan that provides health benefits solely through an insurance contract with a health insurance issuer or HMO, and that creates or receives protected health information in addition to summary health information as defined in § 164.504(a) or information on whether the individual is participating in the group health plan, or is enrolled in or has disenrolled from a health insurance issuer or HMO offered by the plan, must:

(A) Maintain a notice under this section; and

(B) Provide such notice upon request to any person. The provisions of paragraph (c)(1) of this section do not apply to such group health plan.

(iii) A group health plan that provides health benefits solely through an insurance contract with a health insurance issuer or HMO, and does not create or receive protected health information other than summary health information as defined in § 164.504(a) or information on whether an individual is participating in the group health plan, or is enrolled in or has disenrolled from a health insurance issuer or HMO offered by the plan, is not required to maintain or provide a notice under this section.

(3) *Exception for inmates.* An inmate does not have a right to notice under this section, and the requirements of this section do not apply to a correctional institution that is a covered entity.

(b) *Implementation specifications: content of notice.*

(1) *Required elements.* The covered entity must provide a notice that is written in plain language and that contains the elements required by this paragraph.

(i) *Header.* The notice must contain the following statement as a header or otherwise prominently displayed: "THIS NOTICE DESCRIBES HOW MEDICAL INFORMATION ABOUT YOU MAY BE USED AND DISCLOSED AND HOW YOU CAN GET ACCESS TO THIS INFORMATION PLEASE REVIEW IT CAREFULLY."

(ii) *Uses and disclosures.* The notice must contain:

(A) A description, including at least one example, of the types of uses and disclosures that the covered entity is permitted by this subpart to make for each of the following purposes: treatment, payment, and health care operations.

(B) A description of each of the other purposes for which the covered entity is permitted or required by this subpart to use or disclose protected health information without the individual's written authorization.

(C) If a use or disclosure for any purpose described in paragraphs (b)(1)(ii)(A) or (B) of this section is prohibited or materially limited by other applicable law, the description of such use or disclosure must reflect the more stringent law as defined in § 160.202.

(D) For each purpose described in paragraph (b)(1)(ii)(A) or (B) of this section, the description must include sufficient detail to place the individual on notice of the uses and disclosures that are permitted or required by this subpart and other applicable law.

(E) A statement that other uses and disclosures will be made only with the individual's written authorization and that the individual may revoke such authorization as provided by § 164.508(b)(5).

(iii) *Separate statements for certain uses or disclosures.* If the covered entity intends to engage in any of the following activities, the description required by paragraph (b)(1)(ii)(A) of this section must include a separate statement, as applicable, that:

(A) The covered entity may contact the individual to provide appointment reminders or information about treatment alternatives or other heath-related benefits and services that may be of interest to the individual;

(B) The covered entity may contact the individual to raise funds for the covered entity; or

(C) A group health plan, or a health insurance issuer or HMO with respect to a group health plan, may disclose protected health information to the sponsor of the plan.

(iv) *Individual rights.* The notice must contain a statement of the individual's rights with respect to protected health information and a brief description of how the individual may exercise these rights, as follows:

(A) The right to request restrictions on certain uses and disclosures of protected health information as provided by § 164.522(a), including a statement that the covered entity is not required to agree to a requested restriction;

(B) The right to receive confidential communications of protected health information as provided by § 164.522(b), as applicable;

(C) The right to inspect and copy protected health information as provided by § 164.524;

(D) The right to amend protected health information as provided by § 164.526;

(E) The right to receive an accounting of disclosures of protected health information as provided by § 164.528; and

(F) The right of an individual, including an individual who has agreed to receive the notice electronically in accordance with paragraph (c)(3) of this section, to obtain a paper copy of the notice from the covered entity upon request.

(v) *Covered entity's duties.* The notice must contain:

(A) A statement that the covered entity is required by law to maintain the privacy of protected health information and to provide individuals with notice of its legal duties and privacy practices with respect to protected health information;

(B) A statement that the covered entity is required to abide by the terms of the notice currently in effect; and

(C) For the covered entity to apply a change in a privacy practice that is described in the notice to protected health information that the covered entity created or received prior to issuing a revised notice, in accordance with § 164.530(i)(2)(ii), a statement that it reserves the right to change the terms of its notice and to make the new notice provisions effective for all protected health information that it maintains. The statement must also describe how it will provide individuals with a revised notice.

(vi) *Complaints.* The notice must contain a statement that individuals may complain to the covered entity and to the Secretary if they believe their privacy rights have been violated, a brief description of how the individual may file a complaint with the covered entity, and a statement that the individual will not be retaliated against for filing a complaint.

(vii) *Contact.* The notice must contain the name, or title, and telephone number of a person or office to contact for further information as required by § 164.530(a)(1)(ii).

(viii) *Effective date.* The notice must contain the date on which the notice is first in effect, which may not be earlier than the date on which the notice is printed or otherwise published.

(2) *Optional elements.*

(i) In addition to the information required by paragraph (b)(1) of this section, if a covered entity elects to limit the uses or disclosures that it is permitted to make under this subpart, the covered entity may describe its more limited uses or disclosures in its notice, provided that the covered entity may not include in its notice a limitation affecting its right to make a use or disclosure that is required by law or permitted by § 164.512(j)(1)(i).

(ii) For the covered entity to apply a change in its more limited uses and disclosures to protected health information created or received prior to issuing a revised notice, in accordance with § 164.530(i)(2)(ii), the notice must include the statements required by paragraph (b)(1)(v)(C) of this section.

(3) *Revisions to the notice.* The covered entity must promptly revise and distribute its notice whenever there is a material change to the uses or disclosures, the individual's rights, the covered entity's legal duties, or other privacy practices stated in the notice. Except when required by law, a material change to any term of the notice may not be implemented prior to the effective date of the notice in which such material change is reflected.

(c) *Implementation specifications: provision of notice.* A covered entity must make the notice required by this section available on request to any person and to individuals as specified in paragraphs (c)(1) through (c)(3) of this section, as applicable.

(1) *Specific requirements for health plans.*

(i) A health plan must provide notice:

(A) No later than the compliance date for the health plan, to individuals then covered by the plan;

(B) Thereafter, at the time of enrollment, to individuals who are new enrollees; and

(C) Within 60 days of a material revision to the notice, to individuals then covered by the plan.

(ii) No less frequently than once every three years, the health plan must notify individuals then covered by the plan of the availability of the notice and how to obtain the notice.

(iii) The health plan satisfies the requirements of paragraph (c)(1) of this section if notice is provided to the named insured of a policy under which coverage is provided to the named insured and one or more dependents.

(iv) If a health plan has more than one notice, it satisfies the requirements of paragraph (c)(1) of this section by providing the notice that is relevant to the individual or other person requesting the notice.

(2) *Specific requirements for certain covered health care providers.* A covered health care provider that has a direct treatment relationship with an individual must:

(i) Provide the notice:

(A) No later than the date of the first service delivery, including service delivered electronically, to such individual after the compliance date for the covered health care provider; or

(B) In an emergency treatment situation, as soon as reasonably practicable after the emergency treatment situation.

(ii) Except in an emergency treatment situation, make a good faith effort to obtain a written acknowledgment of receipt of the notice provided in accordance with paragraph (c)(2)(i) of this section, and if not obtained, document its good faith efforts to obtain such acknowledgment and the reason why the acknowledgment was not obtained;

(iii) If the covered health care provider maintains a physical service delivery site:

(A) Have the notice available at the service delivery site for individuals to request to take with them; and

(B) Post the notice in a clear and prominent location where it is reasonable to expect individuals seeking service from the covered health care provider to be able to read the notice; and

(iv) Whenever the notice is revised, make the notice available upon request on or after the effective date of the revision and promptly comply with the requirements of paragraph (c)(2)(iii) of this section, if applicable.

(3) *Specific requirements for electronic notice.*

(i) A covered entity that maintains a web site that provides information about the covered entity's customer services or benefits must prominently post its notice on the web site and make the notice available electronically through the web site.

(ii) A covered entity may provide the notice required by this section to an individual by e-mail, if the individual agrees to electronic notice and such agreement has not been withdrawn. If the covered entity knows that the e-mail transmission has failed, a paper copy of the notice must be provided to the individual. Provision of electronic notice by the covered entity will satisfy the provision requirements of paragraph (c) of this section when timely made in accordance with paragraph (c)(1) or (2) of this section.

(iii) For purposes of paragraph (c)(2)(i) of this section, if the first service delivery to an individual is delivered electronically, the covered health care provider must provide electronic notice automatically and contemporaneously in response to the individual's first request for service. The requirements in paragraph (c)(2)(ii) of this section apply to electronic notice.

(iv) The individual who is the recipient of electronic notice retains the right to obtain a paper copy of the notice from a covered entity upon request.

(d) *Implementation specifications: joint notice by separate covered entities.* Covered entities that participate in organized health care arrangements may comply with this section by a joint notice, provided that:

(1) The covered entities participating in the organized health care arrangement agree to abide by the terms of the notice with respect to protected health information created or received by the covered entity as part of its participation in the organized health care arrangement;

(2) The joint notice meets the implementation specifications in paragraph (b) of this section, except that the statements required by this section may be altered to reflect the fact that the notice covers more than one covered entity; and

(i) Describes with reasonable specificity the covered entities, or class of entities, to which the joint notice applies;

(ii) Describes with reasonable specificity the service delivery sites, or classes of service delivery sites, to which the joint notice applies; and

(iii) If applicable, states that the covered entities participating in the organized health care arrangement will share protected health information with each other, as necessary to carry out treatment, payment, or health care operations relating to the organized health care arrangement.

(3) The covered entities included in the joint notice must provide the notice to individuals in accordance with the applicable implementation specifications of paragraph (c) of this section. Provision of the joint notice to an individual by any one of the covered entities included in the joint notice will satisfy the provision requirement of paragraph (c) of this section with respect to all others covered by the joint notice.

(e) *Implementation specifications: Documentation.* A covered entity must document compliance with the notice requirements, as required by § 164.530(j), by retaining copies of the notices issued by the covered entity and, if applicable, any written acknowledgments of receipt of the notice or documentation of good faith efforts to obtain such written acknowledgment, in accordance with paragraph (c)(2)(ii) of this section.

§ 164.522 Rights to request privacy protection for protected health information.

(a)(1) *Standard: right of an individual to request restriction of uses and disclosures.*

(i) A covered entity must permit an individual to request that the covered entity restrict:

(A) Uses or disclosures of protected health information about the individual to carry out treatment, payment, or health care operations; and

(B) Disclosures permitted under § 164.510(b).

(ii) A covered entity is not required to agree to a restriction.

(iii) A covered entity that agrees to a restriction under paragraph (a)(1)(i) of this section may not use or disclose protected health information in violation of such restriction, except that, if the individual who requested the restriction is in need of emergency treatment and the restricted protected health information is needed to provide the emergency treatment, the covered entity may use the restricted protected health information, or may disclose such information to a health care provider, to provide such treatment to the individual.

(iv) If restricted protected health information is disclosed to a health care provider for emergency treatment under paragraph (a)(1)(iii) of this section, the covered entity must request that such health care provider not further use or disclose the information.

(v) A restriction agreed to by a covered entity under paragraph (a) of this section, is not effective under this subpart to prevent uses or disclosures permitted or required under §§ 164.502(a)(2)(ii), 164.510(a) or 164.512.

(2) *Implementation specifications: terminating a restriction.* A covered entity may terminate its agreement to a restriction, if:

(i) The individual agrees to or requests the termination in writing;

(ii) The individual orally agrees to the termination and the oral agreement is documented; or

(iii) The covered entity informs the individual that it is terminating its agreement to a restriction, except that such termination is only effective with respect to protected health information created or received after it has so informed the individual.

(3) *Implementation specification: documentation.* A covered entity that agrees to a restriction must document the restriction in accordance with § 164.530(j).

(b)(1) *Standard: confidential communications requirements.*

(i) A covered health care provider must permit individuals to request and must accommodate reasonable requests by individuals to receive communications of protected health information from the covered health care provider by alternative means or at alternative locations.

(ii) A health plan must permit individuals to request and must accommodate reasonable requests by individuals to receive communications of protected health information from the health plan by alternative means or at alternative locations, if the individual clearly states that the disclosure of all or part of that information could endanger the individual.

(2) *Implementation specifications: conditions on providing confidential communications.*

(i) A covered entity may require the individual to make a request for a confidential communication described in paragraph (b)(1) of this section in writing.

(ii) A covered entity may condition the provision of a reasonable accommodation on:

(A) When appropriate, information as to how payment, if any, will be handled; and

(B) Specification of an alternative address or other method of contact.

(iii) A covered health care provider may not require an explanation from the individual as to the basis for the request as a condition of providing communications on a confidential basis.

(iv) A health plan may require that a request contain a statement that disclosure of all or part of the information to which the request pertains could endanger the individual.

§ 164.524 Access of individuals to protected health information.

(a) *Standard: access to protected health information.*

(1) *Right of access.* Except as otherwise provided in paragraph (a)(2) or (a)(3) of this section, an individual has a right of access to inspect and obtain a copy of protected health information about the individual in a designated record set, for as long as the protected health information is maintained in the designated record set, except for:

(i) Psychotherapy notes;

(ii) Information compiled in reasonable anticipation of, or for use in, a civil, criminal, or administrative action or proceeding; and

(iii) Protected health information maintained by a covered entity that is:

(A) Subject to the Clinical Laboratory Improvements Amendments of 1988, 42 U.S.C. 263a, to the extent the provision of access to the individual would be prohibited by law; or

(B) Exempt from the Clinical Laboratory Improvements Amendments of 1988, pursuant to 42 CFR 493.3(a)(2).

(2) *Unreviewable grounds for denial.* A covered entity may deny an individual access without providing the individual an opportunity for review, in the following circumstances.

(i) The protected health information is excepted from the right of access by paragraph (a)(1) of this section.

(ii) A covered entity that is a correctional institution or a covered health care provider acting under the direction of the correctional institution may deny, in whole or in part, an inmate's request to obtain a copy of protected health information, if obtaining such copy would jeopardize the health, safety, security, custody, or rehabilitation of the individual or of other inmates, or the safety of any officer, employee, or other person at the correctional institution or responsible for the transporting of the inmate.

(iii) An individual's access to protected health information created or obtained by a covered health care provider in the course of research that includes treatment may be temporarily suspended for as long as the research is in progress, provided that the individual has agreed to the denial of access when consenting to participate in the research that includes treatment, and the covered health care provider has informed the individual that the right of access will be reinstated upon completion of the research.

(iv) An individual's access to protected health information that is contained in records that are subject to the Privacy Act, 5 U.S.C§ 552a, may be denied, if the denial of access under the Privacy Act would meet the requirements of that law.

(v) An individual's access may be denied if the protected health information was obtained from someone other than a health care provider under a promise of confidentiality and the access requested would be reasonably likely to reveal the source of the information.

(3) *Reviewable grounds for denial.* A covered entity may deny an individual access, provided that the individual is given a right to have such denials reviewed, as required by paragraph (a)(4) of this section, in the following circumstances:

(i) A licensed health care professional has determined, in the exercise of professional judgment, that the access requested is reasonably likely to endanger the life or physical safety of the individual or another person;

(ii) The protected health information makes reference to another person (unless such other person is a health care provider) and a licensed health care professional has determined, in the exercise of professional judgment, that the access requested is reasonably likely to cause substantial harm to such other person; or

(iii) The request for access is made by the individual's personal representative and a licensed health care professional has determined, in the exercise of professional judgment, that the provision of access to such personal -representative is reasonably likely to cause substantial harm to the individual or another person.

(4) *Review of a denial of access.* If access is denied on a ground permitted under paragraph (a)(3) of this section, the individual has the right to have the denial reviewed by a licensed health care professional who is designated by the covered entity to act as a reviewing official and who did not participate in the original decision to deny. The covered entity must provide or deny access in accordance with the determination of the reviewing official under paragraph (d)(4) of this section.

(b) *Implementation specifications: requests for access and timely action.*

(1) *Individual's request for access.* The covered entity must permit an individual to request access to inspect or to obtain a copy of the protected health information about the individual that is maintained in a designated record set. The covered entity may require individuals to make requests for access in writing, provided that it informs individuals of such a requirement.

(2) *Timely action by the covered entity.*

(i) Except as provided in paragraph (b)(2)(ii) of this section, the covered entity must act on a request for access no later than 30 days after receipt of the request as follows.

(A) If the covered entity grants the request, in whole or in part, it must inform the individual of the acceptance of the request and provide the access requested, in accordance with paragraph (c) of this section.

(B) If the covered entity denies the request, in whole or in part, it must provide the individual with a written denial, in accordance with paragraph (d) of this section.

(ii) If the request for access is for protected health information that is not maintained or accessible to the covered entity on-site, the covered entity must take an action required by paragraph (b)(2)(i) of this section by no later than 60 days from the receipt of such a request.

(iii) If the covered entity is unable to take an action required by paragraph (b)(2)(i)(A) or (B) of this section within the time required by paragraph (b)(2)(i) or (ii) of this section, as applicable, the covered entity may extend the time for such actions by no more than 30 days, provided that:

(A) The covered entity, within the time limit set by paragraph (b)(2)(i) or (ii) of this section, as applicable, provides the individual with a written statement of the reasons for the delay and the date by which the covered entity will complete its action on the request; and

(B) The covered entity may have only one such extension of time for action on a request for access.

(c) *Implementation specifications: provision of access.* If the covered entity provides an individual with access, in whole or in part, to protected health information, the covered entity must comply with the following requirements.

(1) *Providing the access requested.* The covered entity must provide the access requested by individuals, including inspection or obtaining a copy, or both, of the protected health information about them in designated record sets. If the same protected health information that is the subject of a request for access is maintained in more than one designated record set or at more than one location, the covered entity need only produce the protected health information once in response to a request for access.

(2) *Form of access requested.*

(i) The covered entity must provide the individual with access to the protected health information in the form or format requested by the individual, if it is readily producible in such form or format; or, if not, in a readable hard copy form or such other form or format as agreed to by the covered entity and the individual.

(ii) The covered entity may provide the individual with a summary of the protected health information requested, in lieu of providing access to the protected health information or may provide an explanation of the protected health information to which access has been provided, if:

(A) The individual agrees in advance to such a summary or explanation; and

(B) The individual agrees in advance to the fees imposed, if any, by the covered entity for such summary or explanation.

(3) *Time and manner of access.* The covered entity must provide the access as requested by the individual in a timely manner as required by paragraph (b)(2) of this section, including arranging with the individual for a convenient time and place to inspect or obtain a copy of the protected health information, or mailing the copy of the protected health information at the individual's request. The covered entity may discuss the scope, format, and other aspects of the request for access with the individual as necessary to facilitate the timely provision of access.

(4) *Fees.* If the individual requests a copy of the protected health information or agrees to a summary or explanation of such information, the covered entity may impose a reasonable, cost-based fee, provided that the fee includes only the cost of:

(i) Copying, including the cost of supplies for and labor of copying, the protected health information requested by the individual;

(ii) Postage, when the individual has requested the copy, or the summary or explanation, be mailed; and

(iii) Preparing an explanation or summary of the protected health information, if agreed to by the individual as required by paragraph (c)(2)(ii) of this section.

(d) *Implementation specifications: denial of access.* If the covered entity denies access, in whole or in part, to protected health information, the covered entity must comply with the following requirements.

(1) *Making other information accessible.* The covered entity must, to the extent possible, give the individual access to any other protected health information requested, after excluding the protected health information as to which the covered entity has a ground to deny access.

(2) *Denial.* The covered entity must provide a timely, written denial to the individual, in accordance with paragraph(b)(2) of this section. The denial must be in plain language and contain:

(i) The basis for the denial;

(ii) If applicable, a statement of the individual's review rights under paragraph (a)(4) of this section, including a description of how the individual may exercise such review rights; and

(iii) A description of how the individual may complain to the covered entity pursuant to the complaint procedures in § 164.530(d) or to the Secretary pursuant to the procedures in § 160.306. The description must include the name, or title, and telephone number of the contact person or office designated in § 164.530(a)(1)(ii).

(3) *Other responsibility.* If the covered entity does not maintain the protected health information that is the subject of the individual's request for access, and the covered entity knows where the requested information is maintained, the covered entity must inform the individual where to direct the request for access.

(4) *Review of denial requested.* If the individual has requested a review of a denial under paragraph (a)(4) of this section, the covered entity must designate

a licensed health care professional, who was not directly involved in the denial to review the decision to deny access. The covered entity must promptly refer a request for review to such designated reviewing official. The designated reviewing official must determine, within a reasonable period of time, whether or not to deny the access requested based on the standards in paragraph (a)(3) of this section. The covered entity must promptly provide written notice to the individual of the determination of the designated reviewing official and take other action as required by this section to carry out the designated reviewing official's determination.

(e) *Implementation specification: documentation.* A covered entity must document the following and retain the documentation as required by § 164.530(j):

(1) The designated record sets that are subject to access by individuals; and

(2) The titles of the persons or offices responsible for receiving and processing requests for access by individuals.

§ 164.526 Amendment of protected health information.

(a) *Standard: right to amend.*

(1) *Right to amend.* An individual has the right to have a covered entity amend protected health information or a record about the individual in a designated record set for as long as the protected health information is maintained in the designated record set.

(2) *Denial of amendment.* A covered entity may deny an individual's request for amendment, if it determines that the protected health information or record that is the subject of the request:

(i) Was not created by the covered entity, unless the individual provides a reasonable basis to believe that the originator of protected health information is no longer available to act on the requested amendment;

(ii) Is not part of the designated record set;

(iii) Would not be available for inspection under § 164.524; or

(iv) Is accurate and complete.

(b) *Implementation specifications: requests for amendment and timely action.*

(1) *Individual's request for amendment.* The covered entity must permit an individual to request that the covered entity amend the protected health information maintained in the designated record set. The covered entity may require individuals to make requests for amendment in writing and to provide a reason to support a requested amendment, provided that it informs individuals in advance of such requirements.

(2) *Timely action by the covered entity.*

(i) The covered entity must act on the individual's request for an amendment no later than 60 days after receipt of such a request, as follows.

(A) If the covered entity grants the requested amendment, in whole or in part, it must take the actions required by paragraphs (c)(1) and (2) of this section.

(B) If the covered entity denies the requested amendment, in whole or in part, it must provide the individual with a written denial, in accordance with paragraph (d)(1) of this section.

(ii) If the covered entity is unable to act on the amendment within the time required by paragraph (b)(2)(i) of this section, the covered entity may extend the time for such action by no more than 30 days, provided that:

(A) The covered entity, within the time limit set by paragraph (b)(2)(i) of this section, provides the individual with a written statement of the reasons for the delay and the date by which the covered entity will complete its action on the request; and

(B) The covered entity may have only one such extension of time for action on a request for an amendment.

(c) *Implementation specifications: accepting the amendment.* If the covered entity accepts the requested amendment, in whole or in part, the covered entity must comply with the following requirements.

(1) *Making the amendment.* The covered entity must make the appropriate amendment to the protected health information or record that is the subject of the request for amendment by, at a minimum, identifying the records in the designated record set that are affected by the amendment and appending or otherwise providing a link to the location of the amendment.

(2) *Informing the individual.* In accordance with paragraph (b) of this section, the covered entity must timely inform the individual that the amendment is accepted and obtain the individual's identification of and agreement to have the covered entity notify the relevant persons with which the amendment needs to be shared in accordance with paragraph (c)(3) of this section.

(3) *Informing others.* The covered entity must make reasonable efforts to inform and provide the amendment within a reasonable time to:

(i) Persons identified by the individual as having received protected health information about the individual and needing the amendment; and

(ii) Persons, including business associates, that the covered entity knows have the protected health information that is the subject of the amendment and that may have relied, or could foreseeably rely, on such information to the detriment of the individual.

(d) *Implementation specifications: denying the amendment.* If the covered entity denies the requested amendment, in whole or in part, the covered entity must comply with the following requirements.

(1) *Denial.* The covered entity must provide the individual with a timely, written denial, in accordance with paragraph (b)(2) of this section. The denial must use plain language and contain:

(i) The basis for the denial, in accordance with paragraph (a)(2) of this section;

(ii) The individual's right to submit a written statement disagreeing with the denial and how the individual may file such a statement;

(iii) A statement that, if the individual does not submit a statement of disagreement, the individual may request that the covered entity provide the individual's request for amendment and the denial with any future disclosures of the protected health information that is the subject of the amendment; and

(iv) A description of how the individual may complain to the covered entity pursuant to the complaint procedures established in § 164.530(d) or to the Secretary pursuant to the procedures established in § 160.306. The description must include the name, or title, and telephone number of the contact person or office designated in § 164.530(a)(1)(ii).

(2) *Statement of disagreement.* The covered entity must permit the individual to submit to the covered entity a written statement disagreeing with the denial of all or part of a requested amendment and the basis of such disagreement. The covered entity may reasonably limit the length of a statement of disagreement.

(3) *Rebuttal statement.* The covered entity may prepare a written rebuttal to the individual's statement of disagreement. Whenever such a rebuttal is prepared, the covered entity must provide a copy to the individual who submitted the statement of disagreement.

(4) *Recordkeeping.* The covered entity must, as appropriate, identify the record or protected health information in the designated record set that is the subject of the disputed amendment and append or otherwise link the individual's request for an amendment, the covered entity's denial of the request, the individual's statement of disagreement, if any, and the covered entity's rebuttal, if any, to the designated record set.

(5) *Future disclosures.*

(i) If a statement of disagreement has been submitted by the individual, the covered entity must include the material appended in accordance with paragraph (d)(4) of this section, or, at the election of the covered entity, an accurate summary of any such information, with any subsequent disclosure of the protected health information to which the disagreement relates.

(ii) If the individual has not submitted a written statement of disagreement, the covered entity must include the individual's request for amendment and its denial, or an accurate summary of such information, with any subsequent disclosure of the protected health information only if the individual has requested such action in accordance with paragraph (d)(1)(iii) of this section.

(iii) When a subsequent disclosure described in paragraph (d)(5)(i) or (ii) of this section is made using a standard transaction under part 162 of this subchapter that does not permit the additional material to be included with the disclosure, the covered entity may separately transmit the material required by paragraph (d)(5)(i) or (ii) of this section, as applicable, to the recipient of the standard transaction.

(e) *Implementation specification: actions on notices of amendment.* A covered entity that is informed by another covered entity of an amendment to an individual's protected health information, in accordance with paragraph (c)(3) of this section, must amend the protected health information in designated record sets as provided by paragraph (c)(1) of this section.

(f) *Implementation specification: documentation.* A covered entity must document the titles of the persons or offices responsible for receiving and processing requests for amendments by individuals and retain the documentation as required by § 164.530(j).

§ 164.528 Accounting of disclosures of protected health information.

(a) *Standard: right to an accounting of disclosures of protected health information.*

(1) An individual has a right to receive an accounting of disclosures of protected health information made by a covered entity in the six years prior to the date on which the accounting is requested, except for disclosures:

(i) To carry out treatment, payment and health care operations as provided in § 164.506;

(ii) To individuals of protected health information about them as provided in § 164.502;

(iii) Incident to a use or disclosure otherwise permitted or required by this subpart, as provided in § 164.502;

(iv) Pursuant to an authorization as provided in § 164.508;

(v) For the facility's directory or to persons involved in the individual's care or other notification purposes as provided in § 164.510;

(vi) For national security or intelligence purposes as provided in § 164.512(k)(2);

(vii) To correctional institutions or law enforcement officials as provided in § 164.512(k)(5);

(viii) As part of a limited data set in accordance with § 164.514(e); or

(ix) That occurred prior to the compliance date for the covered entity.

(2)(i) The covered entity must temporarily suspend an individual's right to receive an accounting of disclosures to a health oversight agency or law enforcement official, as provided in § 164.512(d) or (f), respectively, for the time specified by such agency or official, if such agency or official provides the covered entity with a written statement that such an accounting to the individual would be reasonably likely to impede the agency's activities and specifying the time for which such a suspension is required.

(ii) If the agency or official statement in paragraph (a)(2)(i) of this section is made orally, the covered entity must:

(A) Document the statement, including the identity of the agency or official making the statement;

(B) Temporarily suspend the individual's right to an accounting of disclosures subject to the statement; and

(C) Limit the temporary suspension to no longer than 30 days from the date of the oral statement, unless a written statement pursuant to paragraph (a)(2)(i) of this section is submitted during that time.

(3) An individual may request an accounting of disclosures for a period of time less than six years from the date of the request.

(b) *Implementation specifications: content of the accounting.* The covered entity must provide the individual with a written accounting that meets the following requirements.

(1) Except as otherwise provided by paragraph (a) of this section, the accounting must include disclosures of protected health information that occurred during the six years (or such shorter time period at the request of the individual as provided in paragraph (a)(3) of this section) prior to the date of the request for an accounting, including disclosures to or by business associates of the covered entity.

(2) Except as otherwise provided by paragraphs (b)(3) or (b)(4) of this section, the accounting must include for each disclosure:

(i) The date of the disclosure;

(ii) The name of the entity or person who received the protected health information and, if known, the address of such entity or person;

(iii) A brief description of the protected health information disclosed; and

(iv) A brief statement of the purpose of the disclosure that reasonably informs the individual of the basis for the disclosure or, in lieu of such statement, a copy of a written request for a disclosure under §§ 164.502(a)(2)(ii) or 164.512, if any.

(3) If, during the period covered by the accounting, the covered entity has made multiple disclosures of protected health information to the same person or entity for a single purpose under §§ 164.502(a)(2)(ii) or 164.512, the accounting may, with respect to such multiple disclosures, provide:

(i) The information required by paragraph (b)(2) of this section for the first disclosure during the accounting period;

(ii) The frequency, periodicity, or number of the disclosures made during the accounting period; and

(iii) The date of the last such disclosure during the accounting period.

(4)(i) If, during the period covered by the accounting, the covered entity has made disclosures of protected health information for a particular research purpose in accordance with § 164.512(i) for 50 or more individuals, the accounting may, with respect to such disclosures for which the protected health information about the individual may have been included, provide:

(A) The name of the protocol or other research activity;

(B) A description, in plain language, of the research protocol or other research activity, including the purpose of the research and the criteria for selecting particular records;

(C) A brief description of the type of protected health information that was disclosed;

(D) The date or period of time during which such disclosures occurred, or may have occurred, including the date of the last such disclosure during the accounting period;

(E) The name, address, and telephone number of the entity that sponsored the research and of the researcher to whom the information was disclosed; and

(F) A statement that the protected health information of the individual may or may not have been disclosed for a particular protocol or other research activity.

(ii) If the covered entity provides an accounting for research disclosures, in accordance with paragraph (b)(4) of this section, and if it is reasonably likely that the protected health information of the individual was disclosed for such research protocol or activity, the covered entity shall, at the request of the individual, assist in contacting the entity that sponsored the research and the researcher.

(c) *Implementation specifications: provision of the accounting.*

(1) The covered entity must act on the individual's request for an accounting, no later than 60 days after receipt of such a request, as follows.

(i) The covered entity must provide the individual with the accounting requested; or

(ii) If the covered entity is unable to provide the accounting within the time required by paragraph (c)(1) of this section, the covered entity may extend the time to provide the accounting by no more than 30 days, provided that:

(A) The covered entity, within the time limit set by paragraph (c)(1) of this section, provides the individual with a written statement of the reasons for the delay and the date by which the covered entity will provide the accounting; and

(B) The covered entity may have only one such extension of time for action on a request for an accounting.

(2) The covered entity must provide the first accounting to an individual in any 12 month period without charge. The covered entity may impose a reasonable, cost-based fee for each subsequent request for an accounting by the same individual within the 12 month period, provided that the covered entity informs the individual in advance of the fee and provides the individual with an opportunity to withdraw or modify the request for a subsequent accounting in order to avoid or reduce the fee.

(d) *Implementation specification: documentation.* A covered entity must document the following and retain the documentation as required by § 164.530(j):

(1) The information required to be included in an accounting under paragraph (b) of this section for disclosures of protected health information that are subject to an accounting under paragraph (a) of this section;

(2) The written accounting that is provided to the individual under this section; and

(3) The titles of the persons or offices responsible for receiving and processing requests for an accounting by individuals.

§ 164.530 Administrative requirements.

(a)(1) *Standard: personnel designations.*

(i) A covered entity must designate a privacy official who is responsible for the development and implementation of the policies and procedures of the entity.

(ii) A covered entity must designate a contact person or office who is responsible for receiving complaints under this section and who is able to provide further information about matters covered by the notice required by § 164.520.

(2) *Implementation specification: personnel designations.* A covered entity must document the personnel designations in paragraph (a)(1) of this section as required by paragraph (j) of this section.

(b)(1) *Standard: training.* A covered entity must train all members of its workforce on the policies and procedures with respect to protected health information required by this subpart, as necessary and appropriate for the members of the workforce to carry out their function within the covered entity.

(2) *Implementation specifications: training.*

(i) A covered entity must provide training that meets the requirements of paragraph (b)(1) of this section, as follows:

(A) To each member of the covered entity's workforce by no later than the compliance date for the covered entity;

(B) Thereafter, to each new member of the workforce within a reasonable period of time after the person joins the covered entity's workforce; and

(C) To each member of the covered entity's workforce whose functions are affected by a material change in the policies or procedures required by this subpart, within a reasonable period of time after the material change becomes effective in accordance with paragraph (i) of this section.

(ii) A covered entity must document that the training as described in paragraph (b)(2)(i) of this section has been provided, as required by paragraph (j) of this section.

(c)(1) *Standard: safeguards.* A covered entity must have in place appropriate administrative, technical, and physical safeguards to protect the privacy of protected health information.

(2) *Implementation specification: safeguards.*

(i) A covered entity must reasonably safeguard protected health information from any intentional or unintentional use or disclosure that is in violation of the standards, implementation specifications or other requirements of this subpart.

(ii) A covered entity must reasonably safeguard protected health information to limit incidental uses or disclosures made pursuant to an otherwise permitted or required use or disclosure.

(d)(1) *Standard: complaints to the covered entity.* A covered entity must provide a process for individuals to make complaints concerning the covered entity's policies and procedures required by this subpart or its compliance with such policies and procedures or the requirements of this subpart.

(2) *Implementation specification: documentation of complaints.* As required by paragraph (j) of this section, a covered entity must document all complaints received, and their disposition, if any.

(e)(1) *Standard: sanctions.* A covered entity must have and apply appropriate sanctions against members of its workforce who fail to comply with the privacy policies and procedures of the covered entity or the requirements of this subpart. This standard does not apply to a member of the covered entity's workforce with respect to actions that are covered by and that meet the conditions of § 164.502(j) or paragraph (g)(2) of this section.

(2) *Implementation specification: documentation.* As required by paragraph (j) of this section, a covered entity must document the sanctions that are applied, if any.

(f) *Standard: mitigation.* A covered entity must mitigate, to the extent practicable, any harmful effect that is known to the covered entity of a use or disclosure of protected health information in violation of its policies and procedures or the requirements of this subpart by the covered entity or its business associate.

(g) *Standard: refraining from intimidating or retaliatory acts.* A covered entity may not intimidate, threaten, coerce, discriminate against, or take other retaliatory action against:

(1) *Individuals.* Any individual for the exercise by the individual of any right under, or for participation by the individual in any process established by this subpart, including the filing of a complaint under this section;

(2) *Individuals and others.* Any individual or other person for:

(i) Filing of a complaint with the Secretary under subpart C of part 160 of this subchapter;

(ii) Testifying, assisting, or participating in an investigation, compliance review, proceeding, or hearing under Part C of Title XI; or

(iii) Opposing any act or practice made unlawful by this subpart, provided the individual or person has a good faith belief that the practice opposed is unlawful, and the manner of the opposition is reasonable and does not involve a disclosure of protected health information in violation of this subpart.

(h) *Standard: waiver of rights.* A covered entity may not require individuals to waive their rights under § 160.306 of this subchapter or this subpart as a condition of the provision of treatment, payment, enrollment in a health plan, or eligibility for benefits.

(i)(1) *Standard: policies and procedures.* A covered entity must implement policies and procedures with respect to protected health information that are designed to comply with the standards, implementation specifications, or other requirements of this subpart. The policies and procedures must be reasonably designed, taking into account the size of and the type of activities that relate to protected health information undertaken by the covered entity, to ensure such compliance. This standard is not to be construed to permit or excuse an action that violates any other standard, implementation specification, or other requirement of this subpart.

(2) *Standard: changes to policies or procedures.*

(i) A covered entity must change its policies and procedures as necessary and appropriate to comply with changes in the law, including the standards, requirements, and implementation specifications of this subpart;

(ii) When a covered entity changes a privacy practice that is stated in the notice described in § 164.520, and makes corresponding changes to its policies and procedures, it may make the changes effective for protected health information that it created or received prior to the effective date of the notice revision, if the covered entity has, in accordance with § 164.520(b)(1)(v)(C), included in the notice a statement reserving its right to make such a change in its privacy practices; or

(iii) A covered entity may make any other changes to policies and procedures at any time, provided that the changes are documented and implemented in accordance with paragraph (i)(5) of this section.

(3) *Implementation specification: changes in law.* Whenever there is a change in law that necessitates a change to the covered entity's policies or procedures, the covered entity must promptly document and implement the revised policy or procedure. If the change in law materially affects the content of the notice required by § 164.520, the covered entity must promptly make the appropriate revisions to the notice in accordance with § 164.520(b)(3). Nothing in this paragraph may be used by a covered entity to excuse a failure to comply with the law.

(4) *Implementation specifications: changes to privacy practices stated in the notice.*

(i) To implement a change as provided by paragraph (i)(2)(ii) of this section, a covered entity must:

(A) Ensure that the policy or procedure, as revised to reflect a change in the covered entity's privacy practice as stated in its notice, complies with the standards, requirements, and implementation specifications of this subpart;

(B) Document the policy or procedure, as revised, as required by paragraph (j) of this section; and

(C) Revise the notice as required by § 164.520(b)(3) to state the changed practice and make the revised notice available as required by § 164.520(c). The covered entity may not implement a change to a policy or procedure prior to the effective date of the revised notice.

(ii) If a covered entity has not reserved its right under § 164.520(b)(1)(v)(C) to change a privacy practice that is stated in the notice, the covered entity is bound by the privacy practices as stated in the notice with respect to protected health information created or received while such notice is in effect. A covered entity may change a privacy practice that is stated in the notice, and the related policies and procedures, without having reserved the right to do so, provided that:

(A) Such change meets the implementation specifications in paragraphs (i)(4)(i)(A)-(C) of this section; and

(B) Such change is effective only with respect to protected health information created or received after the effective date of the notice.

(5) *Implementation specification: changes to other policies or procedures.* A covered entity may change, at any time, a policy or procedure that does not materially affect the content of the notice required by § 164.520, provided that:

(i) The policy or procedure, as revised, complies with the standards, requirements, and implementation specifications of this subpart; and

(ii) Prior to the effective date of the change, the policy or procedure, as revised, is documented as required by paragraph (j) of this section.

(j)(1) *Standard: documentation.* A covered entity must:

(i) Maintain the policies and procedures provided for in paragraph (i) of this section in written or electronic form;

(ii) If a communication is required by this subpart to be in writing, maintain such writing, or an electronic copy, as documentation; and (iii) If an action, activity, or designation is required by this subpart to be documented, maintain a written or electronic record of such action, activity, or designation.

(2) *Implementation specification: retention period.* A covered entity must retain the documentation required by paragraph (j)(1) of this section for six years from the date of its creation or the date when it last was in effect, whichever is later.

(k) *Standard: group health plans.*

(1) A group health plan is not subject to the standards or implementation specifications in paragraphs (a) through (f) and (i) of this section, to the extent that:

(i) The group health plan provides health benefits solely through an insurance contract with a health insurance issuer or an HMO; and

(ii) The group health plan does not create or receive protected health information, except for:

(A) Summary health information as defined in § 164.504(a); or

(B) Information on whether the individual is participating in the group health plan, or is enrolled in or has disenrolled from a health insurance issuer or HMO offered by the plan.

(2) A group health plan described in paragraph (k)(1) of this section is subject to the standard and implementation specification in paragraph (j) of this section only with respect to plan documents amended in accordance with § 164.504(f).

§ 164.532 Transition provisions.

(a) *Standard: Effect of prior authorizations.* Notwithstanding §§ 164.508 and 164.512(i), a covered entity may use or disclose protected health information, consistent with paragraphs (b) and (c) of this section, pursuant to an authorization or other express legal permission obtained from an individual permitting the use or disclosure of protected health information, informed consent of the individual to participate in research, or a waiver of informed consent by an IRB.

(b) *Implementation specification: Effect of prior authorization for purposes other than research.* Notwithstanding any provisions in § 164.508, a covered entity may use or disclose protected health information that it created or received prior to the applicable compliance date of this subpart pursuant to an authorization or other express legal permission obtained from an individual prior to the applicable compliance date of this subpart, provided that the authorization or other express legal permission specifically permits such use or disclosure and there is no agreed-to restriction in accordance with § 164.522(a).

(c) *Implementation specification: Effect of prior permission for research.* Notwithstanding any provisions in §§ 164.508 and 164.512(i), a covered entity may, to the extent allowed by one of the following permissions, use or disclose, for research, protected health information that it created or received either before or after the applicable compliance date of this subpart, provided that there is no agreed-to restriction in accordance with § 164.522(a), and the covered entity has obtained, prior to the applicable compliance date, either:

(1) An authorization or other express legal permission from an individual to use or disclose protected health information for the research;

(2) The informed consent of the individual to participate in the research; or

(3) A waiver, by an IRB, of informed consent for the research, in accordance with 7 CFR 1c.116(d), 10 CFR 745.116(d), 14 CFR 1230.116(d), 15 CFR 27.116(d), 16 CFR 1028.116(d), 21 CFR 50.24, 22 CFR 225.116(d), 24 CFR 60.116(d), 28 CFR 46.116(d), 32 CFR 219.116(d), 34 CFR 97.116(d), 38 CFR 16.116(d), 40 CFR 26.116(d), 45 CFR 46.116(d), 45 CFR 690.116(d), or 49 CFR 11.116(d), provided that a covered entity must obtain authorization in accordance with § 164.508 if, after the compliance date, informed consent is sought from an individual participating in the research.

(d) *Standard: Effect of prior contracts or other arrangements with business associates.* Notwithstanding any other provisions of this subpart, a covered entity, other than a small health plan, may disclose protected health information to a business associate and may allow a business associate to create, receive, or use protected health information on its behalf pursuant to a written contract or other written arrangement with such business associate that does not comply with §§ 164.502(e) and 164.504(e) consistent with the requirements, and only for such time, set forth in paragraph (e) of this section.

(e) *Implementation specification: Deemed compliance.*

(1) *Qualification.* Notwithstanding other sections of this subpart, a covered entity, other than a small health plan, is deemed to be in compliance with the documentation and contract requirements of §§ 164.502(e) and 164.504(e),

with respect to a particular business associate relationship, for the time period set forth in paragraph (e)(2) of this section, if:

(i) Prior to October 15, 2002, such covered entity has entered into and is operating pursuant to a written contract or other written arrangement with a business associate for such business associate to perform functions or activities or provide services that make the entity a business associate; and

(ii) The contract or other arrangement is not renewed or modified from October 15, 2002, until the compliance date set forth in § 164.534.

(2) *Limited deemed compliance period.* A prior contract or other arrangement that meets the qualification requirements in paragraph (e) of this section, shall be deemed compliant until the earlier of:

(i) The date such contract or other arrangement is renewed or modified on or after the compliance date set forth in § 164.534; or

(ii) April 14, 2004.

(3) *Covered entity responsibilities.* Nothing in this section shall alter the requirements of a covered entity to comply with Part 160, Subpart C of this subchapter and §§ 164.524, 164.526, 164.528, and 164.530(f) with respect to protected health information held by a business associate.

§ 164.534 Compliance dates for initial implementation of the privacy standards.

(a) *Health care providers.* A covered health care provider must comply with the applicable requirements of this subpart no later than April 14, 2003.

(b) *Health plans.* A health plan must comply with the applicable requirements of this subpart no later than the following date, as applicable:

(1) *Health plans other than small health plans*—April 14, 2003.

(2) *Small health plans*—April 14, 2004.

(c) *Health care clearinghouses.* A health care clearinghouse must comply with the applicable requirements of this subpart no later than April 14, 2003.

Table of Cases

Campos v. Payne, N.Y. City Civ. Ct., 766 N.Y.S.2d 535 (2003), N.Y. slip op. 23810 . . . . . 81–82, 88nn.46, 50

In re Carella, 2004 N.Y. slip op. 50185(u) (N.Y. Sur., 2004), 2 Misc.3d 1007(A), 2004 WL 727094 (N.Y. Sur.) 88n.50

In re PPA Litigation, Superior Court of New Jersey, Law Division Middlesex County, Civil Action Case Code 264, Opinion on HIPAA Preempting *Stempler v. Speidell,* Sept. 23, 2003 . . . . . 80–81, 88nn.39, 44

Lemieux v. Tandem Health Care of Florida, Inc., 2003 WL 22438605 (Fla. App. 2 Dist. 2003) 82, 88n.51

Middlesex County Ethic Committee v. Garden State Bar Ass'n, 457 U.S. 423, 431, 102 S. Ct. 2515, 2521 (1982) 88n.43

National Abortion Federation v. Ashcroft, No. 03 Civ. 8695 (RCC), 2004 WL 555701 (S.D.N.Y. Mar. 19, 2004) 82–83, 88n.53

Stempler v. Speidell, 100 N.J. 368 (1985) 80–81, 88nn.39, 40, 44

U.S. v. Lucien, 347 F.3d 45 (2nd Cir., Oct. 14, 2003) 80, 87n.36

Index

Abortion, 82–83
Abuse victims, 38–39
Accounting of disclosures, 9, 64–70
  business associates and, 69–70
  contents of, 65
  documentation of, 67
  exceptions, 64–65
  fees, 66–67
  public health departments and, 67–68
  requests for, 9
  for research, 66
  response time for requests, 66
  unknown date of service, 68–69
Accreditation organizations, 32
Administrative proceedings, 40–42
Administrative requirements, 51–70
  accounting, 64–70
  notice, 51–58
  policies and procedures, 62–63
  privacy official, 64
  safeguards, 58–62
  training, 63–64
Administrative Simplification Compliance Act, 4
Administrative Simplification provisions, 1, 101–102
  intent and purpose of, 95–96
  state law and, 24
Advisory Commission on Consumer Protection and Quality in the Health Care Industry, 101
Antipreemption provision, 82–83
Authorization for Release of Protected Health Information, 107–108
Authorizations, 13–24
  blanket authorizations, 14
  consent versus authorization, 13–14
  copy to the individual, 20
  core elements of, 14–19
    date of individual's signature, 18–19
    description of disclosure information, 17
    expiration date or event, 18
    identity of party authorizing disclosure, 14–16
    identity of provider of disclosure, 16–17
    identity of recipient of disclosure, 16
    purpose for disclosure, 18
  cover letters, 21–22
  determining need for, 89
  disclosures without, 14, 27–46
  enrollment based on, 20
  example of, 107–108
  exemption from minimum necessary requirement, 22
  format of, 21
  plain language, 20
  prepared by third parties, 21
  required statements in, 19–20
    individual's right of revocation, 19
    redisclosure of PHI, 20
    treatment not conditioned on signing authorization, 19–20
  state law requirements, 22–24
    authorization elements and, 24
    HIPAA preemption of state laws, 22–24
    psychiatric records, 24
  validity of copies, 21

Background information, 93–105
Balanced Budget Act, 101
Blanket authorizations, 14
Blood donation, 5
Brewin, Bob, 88nn.60, 64
Business Associate Agreement, 109–114
Business associates
  accounting and, 69–70
  agents of, 33
  criminal penalties, 80

Business associates (*continued*)
  determining, 91
  disclosure without authorizations, 30–35
  reporting security incidents, 33–34
  safeguards and, 32–33
  sample agreement, 109–114
  termination of contract, 34–35

California Health Care Foundation, 98, 104n.19
Case law, 80–83
  Campos v. Payne, 81–82
  Florida, 82
  Lemieux v. Tandem Health Care of Florida, Inc., 82
  National Abortion Federation v. Ashcroft, 82–83
  New Jersey, 80–81
  New York, 81–82
  In re *PPA Litigation,* 80–81
CHAMPUS (Civilian Health and Medical Program of the Uniformed Services), 3
Child abuse or neglect, 38–39
Child health care plans, 3
Children, parent as personal representative, 15–16
Children's Online Privacy Protection Act, 100, 101
Civil penalties, 78–79
  fines apply to covered entity, 79
  monetary fines, 78
  procedural limitations, 78–79
Civilian Health and Medical Program of the Uniformed Services (CHAMPUS), 3
Clinical Laboratory Improvements Amendments (CLIA), 54
Clinton, Bill, 100
Code of Fair Information Practice Principles, The, 100
Collection agencies, 29
Complaint officers, 8–9, 64
Complaints
  contact person for, 8–9, 64
  enforcement and, 75–76
  filling with OCR, 76–77
  notice and, 56
  policies and procedures for, 62
Compliance reviews and investigations, 77
Compliance with Privacy Rule, 3–4
Consent versus authorization, 13–14
Consumer Bill of Rights and Responsibilities, 101
Consumer influence on privacy protection, 103
Consumer reporting agencies, 29–30
Controlled substances, 23
Court orders, 42
Cover letters, 21–22
Covered entities. *See also* Administrative requirements
  civil penalties, 79
  defined, 3
  determining, 90
  duties and obligations of, 7–9
  notice and, 55, 58
  reporting security incidents to, 33–34
  termination of business associates contract by, 34–35
Criminal penalties, 79–80
  business associates and others, 80
  false pretenses, 79
  intent to sell or use for personal gain or harm, 79–80
  knowingly obtaining or disclosing, 79

Data Privacy Directive, 101
De-identified information, 5
Debt collection agencies, 29
Department of Health, Education, and Welfare, 100
Department of Health and Human Services, 1, 100, 102–103
  administrative requirements and, 56, 60
  disclosures without authorizations and, 29, 34–35
  enforcement/penalties and, 75, 76, 77–78
  state law and, 22–23
Department of Justice, 79, 80, 83
Disclosures. *See also* Disclosures without authorizations
  accounting of, 9, 64–70
  defined, 6
  description of information for, 17
  to family and friends, 5

general rules for, 6–7
identity of authorizing party, 14–16
identity of provider of, 16–17
identity of recipient, 16
incidental, 61
informational and promotional, 42–45
purpose for, 18
redisclosure, 20

Disclosures without authorizations, 27–46
- informational and promotional, 42–45
  - facility directories, 42–43
  - friends and relatives, 43–44
  - fundraising, 45
  - marketing, 44
- judicial and administrative proceedings, 40–42
- law enforcement, 36–38
- lawful oversight activities, 39–40
- public health activities, 38
- research, 45–46
- threat to health or safety, 35–36
- treatment, payment, or health care operations, 27–35
  - business associate agreement, 30–35
  - health care operations, 30–35
  - payment, 29–30
  - reasonable assurances agreement, 35
  - safeguards, 32–33
  - security incidents, 33–34
  - termination of contract, 34–35
  - treatment, 28
- victims of abuse, neglect, or domestic violence, 38–39
- workers' compensation, 46

Discovery requests, 40–42
Documentation
- of accounting, 67
- of notice, 58

Domestic violence, 38–39
Driver's Privacy Protection Act, 101

Electronic Communications Privacy Act, 101
Employee Polygraph Protection Act, 101
Employee welfare benefit plans, 3
Enforcement, 75–78. *See also* Penalties and enforcement
- compliance reviews and investigations, 77
- filing complaints with OCR, 76–77
- resolution by OCR, 77–78

Enrollment based on authorizations, 20
European Union, 101
Ex parte interviews of physicians, 80–81
Expiration date or event, 18

Facility directories, 42–43
Fair Credit Reporting Act, 30, 101
Fair Debt Collection Practices Act, 29
False pretenses, 79
Family Educational Rights and Privacy Act, 101
Family members, disclosures to, 43–44
Federal Employees Health Benefits Program, 3
Federal Register, 76, 103
Federal Rules of Civil Procedure, Rule 4, 78
Fees, 66–67
Fines, 78, 79
Flaherty, Kathleen M., 105n.20
Florida case law, 82
Fraud, 80
Friends, disclosures to, 43–44
Fundraising, 45

Gostin, Lawrence O., 105n.20
Government authorities, 38
Government influence on privacy protection, 100–103
Gramm-Leach-Bliley Act, Title V, 101
Group health plans, 3, 4

Health, Education, and Welfare Department, 100
Health and Human Services Department. *See* Department of Health and Human Services
Health care, defined, 4
Health care clearinghouses, 4
Health care costs, 1
Health care fraud, 80
Health care operations, 30–35
- business associate agreement, 30–35
- defined, 6

Health care privacy, 96–100
impact of Internet, 97–98
need for, 93–96
public disclosures of private information, 99–100
security of confidential information, 96–97
Health care providers
defined, 4
disclosure for its own treatment, payment, or health care operations, 27–35
Health Information Privacy Study, 105n.40
Health insurance issuers, 3
Health insurance portability, 93–95
Health Insurance Portability and Accountability Act of 1996. *See* HIPAA
Health maintenance organizations (HMOs), 3
Health oversight activities, 39–40
Health plans, 3–4
enrollment based on authorization, 20
Hendricks, Evan, 88nn.60, 61, 62, 64
High risk pools, 4
HIPAA (Health Insurance Portability and Accountability Act of 1996), 127–241
Administrative Simplification provisions, 1, 24, 95–96, 101–102
background information, 93–105
enactment of, 93, 101
65 Fed. Reg. 82, 381, 87nn.5, 21
information protected by, 5
introduction, xiii–xv
litigation and, 83–84
overview, 1–10
preemption of state laws, 22–24, 82–83
Privacy Rule, 2–9
§ 160.102, 10n.8, 73n.139
§ 160.103, 11nn.9, 15, 47nn.26, 34, 38
§ 160.201, 10n.6
§ 160.202, 10n.6, 26n.80
§ 160.203, 10n.6, 26nn.66, 79, 48n.76
§ 160.203(a), 26n.78
§ 160.203(a)(1)(i), 26n.69
§ 160.203(a)(1)(ii), 26n.70
§ 160.203(a)(1)(iii), 26n.71
§ 160.203(a)(1)(iv), 26n.72
§ 160.203(a)(2), 26n.73
§ 160.203(b), 26nn.74, 81
§ 160.203(c), 26n.75
§ 160.203(d), 26n.76
§ 160.204, 10n.6, 26n.77
§ 160.205, 10n.6
§ 160.304(a), 87n.1
§ 160.304(b), 87n.2
§ 160.306, 87n.6
§ 160.306(a), 87n.3
§ 160.306(b), 87n.7
§ 160.308, 87n.8
§ 160.310, 87n.9
§ 160.310(a), 87n.10
§ 160.310(b), 87n.11
§ 160.310(c), 87n.12
§ 160.310(c)(1), 87n.13
§ 160.310(c)(2), 87n.15
§ 160.310(c)(3), 87n.16
§ 160.312, 87n.17
§ 160.312(a)(1), 87n.18
§ 160.312(a)(2), 87n.19
§ 160.312(b), 87n.20
§ 160.506, 87n.21
§ 164.104, 11n.13
§ 164.304, 33
§ 164.306(b), 34, 48n.47
§ 164.306(b)(2)(iii), 48n.49
§ 164.308(b)(1), 47nn.41, 42
§ 164.314, 47n.42
§ 164.314(a)(2)(i)(C), 33, 48n.46
§ 164.314(a)(2)(i)(D), 48n.50
§ 164.500, 11nn.13, 36, 70nn.1, 8
§ 164.501, 11nn.15, 16, 19, 26, 27, 24nn.5, 6, 47nn.7, 13, 16, 24, 49nn.96, 97, 100, 73n.128
§ 164.502, 11n.17, 55, 72n.104
§ 164.502(a), 72n.76
§ 164.502(a)(1), 47nn.30, 35
§ 164.502(a)(1)(iii), 72n.77
§ 164.502(a)(1)(iv), 25n.16
§ 164.502(b), 26n.64, 47n.14, 71n.71
§ 164.502(e), 73n.140
§ 164.502(j), 72n.90
§ 164.504(e), 73n.140
§ 164.504(e)(2)(i)(D), 35, 48n.55
§ 164.504(e)(4), 48n.54
§ 164.506, 24n.1, 24n.2, 28, 30, 46n.1, 47nn.11, 22, 72n.103

§ 164.506(c), 47n.13
§ 164.508, 21, 22, 25n.16, 72n.106
§ 164.508(a)(3), 11n.26, 24n.5, 49nn.96, 98
§ 164.508(b)(4)(i), 26n.51
§ 164.508(b)(5), 70n.16
§ 164.508(c)(1)(i), 25n.31
§ 164.508(c)(1)(ii), 25n.27
§ 164.508(c)(1)(iii), 25n.26
§ 164.508(c)(1)(iv), 25n.35
§ 164.508(c)(1)(v), 25n.37
§ 164.508(c)(1)(vi), 25nn.18, 19, 42
§ 164.508(c)(2)(i), 25n.45
§ 164.508(c)(2)(ii), 26nn.50, 53
§ 164.508(c)(2)(iii), 26n.54
§ 164.508(c)(3), 26n.55
§ 164.508(c)(4), 26n.56
§ 164.510, 72n.107
§ 164.510(a), 11n.24, 24n.3, 49n.92, 70n.24
§ 164.510(b), 11n.25, 24n.4, 47n.9, 49n.94
§ 164.510(b)(3), 72n.82
§ 164.512, 54
§ 164.512(a), 11n.32, 25n.12, 48n.77, 49n.105, 70n.26
§ 164.512(b), 11n.31, 25n.11, 48n.67
§ 164.512(b)(1)(ii), 48n.72
§ 164.512(b)(1)(iii), 48n.68
§ 164.512(b)(1)(iv), 48n.69
§ 164.512(b)(1)(v), 48n.70
§ 164.512(b)(2), 48n.71
§ 164.512(c), 11n.34, 25n.14, 39, 48nn.73, 78
§ 164.512(c)(1), 48n.74
§ 164.512(c)(1)(iii), 48n.75
§ 164.512(d), 11n.28, 25n.8, 48nn.81, 82, 72n.112
§ 164.512(d)(4), 48nn.83, 84
§ 164.512(e), 11n.29, 25n.9, 42, 48nn.79, 85
§ 164.512(e)(1)(i), 48n.86
§ 164.512(e)(1)(iii), 49n.88
§ 164.512(e)(1)(iv), 49n.89
§ 164.512(e)(1)(v), 49n.90
§ 164.512(e)(1)(vi), 49n.91
§ 164.512(e)(ii), 49n.87
§ 164.512(f), 11n.30, 25n.10, 48nn.58, 80, 72n.112
§ 164.512(f)(1)(i), 48nn.59, 60
§ 164.512(f)(2)(i), 48n.61
§ 164.512(f)(3), 48n.62
§ 164.512(f)(4), 48n.63
§ 164.512(f)(5), 48n.64
§ 164.512(f)(6), 48nn.65, 66
§ 164.512(i), 11n.33, 25n.13, 46, 49n.101
§ 164.512(j), 11n.22, 24n.7, 48n.56
§ 164.512(k)(2), 72n.108
§ 164.512(k)(5), 72n.109
§ 164.512(l), 11n.35, 25n.15, 46, 49nn.104, 105, 70n.26
§ 164.514(a), 11n.15
§ 164.514(b)(2)(i), 11n.14
§ 164.514(c), 25n.11
§ 164.514(d), 47n.14, 71n.71
§ 164.514(d)(3)(iii)(A), 49n.106
§ 164.514(e), 11nn.15, 31, 33, 25n.13, 46, 47n.39, 48n.67, 49n.101, 55, 71n.36, 72n.110
§ 164.514(f), 11n.27, 24n.6, 49n.100
§ 164.514(h), 25n.21
§ 164.514(i), 49n.102
§ 164.520, 11nn.36, 37, 70nn.1, 2, 8
§ 164.520(a)(2), 70n.4
§ 164.520(a)(3), 70n.7
§ 164.520(b), 70n.9
§ 164.520(b)(1)(i), 70n.10
§ 164.520(b)(1)(ii), 70nn.11, 13, 15, 16
§ 164.520(b)(1)(iii), 70n.17
§ 164.520(b)(1)(iv), 70n.18
§ 164.520(b)(1)(iv)(A), 70n.27
§ 164.520(b)(1)(iv)(E), 71n.36
§ 164.520(b)(1)(iv)(F), 71n.37
§ 164.520(b)(1)(v), 71n.39
§ 164.520(b)(1)(vi), 71n.40
§ 164.520(b)(1)(vii), 71n.43
§ 164.520(b)(1)(viii), 71n.45
§ 164.520(b)(2), 71nn.47, 49
§ 164.520(b)(3), 71n.50
§ 164.520(c)(1), 71n.55
§ 164.520(c)(2), 71n.52
§ 164.520(c)(2)(ii), 71n.54
§ 164.520(c)(3), 71nn.38, 57, 61
§ 164.520(d), 71n.62
§ 164.520(e), 71n.64

HIPAA (*continued*)
§ 164.522, 11nn.25, 27, 24n.6, 47n.14, 49nn.95, 100
§ 164.522(a), 49n.105, 70n.26
§ 164.522(a)(1), 70n.19
§ 164.522(a)(1)(v), 70n.25
§ 164.522(b), 70n.28, 71n.30, 72n.81
§ 164.522(b)(1)(ii), 70n.29
§ 164.524, 55, 69, 71nn.31, 32, 73n.141
§ 164.526, 69, 73n.142
§ 164.526(a)(2), 71n.33
§ 164.528, 11n.42, 35, 69, 71n.34, 73n.143
§ 164.528(a)(1), 72n.111
§ 164.528(a)(2)(i), 72nn.112, 113
§ 164.528(a)(2)(ii), 73n.114
§ 164.528(b), 73n.115
§ 164.528(b)(2), 68, 73n.137
§ 164.528(b)(3), 73n.117
§ 164.528(b)(4)(i), 73n.118
§ 164.528(b)(4)(ii), 73n.119
§ 164.528(c)(1), 73nn.120, 121
§ 164.528(c)(2), 73n.123
§ 164.530(a), 11n.41, 72n.100
§ 164.530(a)(1)(ii), 71n.44
§ 164.530(b), 11n.40, 72n.94
§ 164.530(b)(2), 72n.97
§ 164.530(c), 11n.39
§ 164.530(c)(1), 71n.65
§ 164.530(c)(2), 71nn.66, 67
§ 164.530(c)(2)(i), 71n.70
§ 164.530(d)(1), 72n.87
§ 164.530(e), 72n.89
§ 164.530(e)(2), 72n.93
§ 164.530(g)(2), 72n.92
§ 164.530(i), 72n.83
§ 164.530(j), 73n.127
§ 164.534, 87n.6
§§ 261–264, 101
§ 262, 101–102
§ 264(b), 102
§ 264(c)(1), 102–103
§ 314(a)(2)(i)(B), 48n.45
text of, 127–241
Title I, 1, 9–10, 93–95
Title II, 1, 10, 95–96
HMOs (health maintenance organizations), 3

Identity Theft and Assumption Deterrence Act, 101
Incidental disclosures, 61
Indian Health Care Improvement Act, 3
Indian Health Service, 3
Individual plans, 4
Individually identifiable information, 5
Informational and promotional disclosures, 42–45
Intent to sell or use for personal gain or harm, 79–80
Internet, 97–98, 104n.15

Johnson & Johnson, 99
Joint notice, 58
Judicial proceedings, 40–42
Justice Department, 79, 80, 83

Knowingly obtaining or disclosing PHI, 79

Law enforcement, 36–38
Lawful oversight activities, 39–40
Lazzarini, Zita, 105n.20
Legislative Survey of State Confidentiality Laws, with Specific Emphasis on HIV and Immunization, 105n.20
Litigation, 83–84
Long-term care policies, 3
Louis Harris & Associates, 105n.40

Marketing, 44
Medicaid, 3
Medicare, 3
Medicare + Choice, 4, 101
Medicare supplemental policies, 3
Mental health records, 20, 24, 54
Military personnel, 3
Monetary fines, 78, 79

National Survey of Adults on Technology, 104n.18
Neglect victims, 38–39
Networking Health: Prescriptions for the Internet, 104n.15
New Jersey case law, 80–81
New York case law, 81–82

Notice, 7-8, 51-58
 availability of, 57
 complaints, 56
 contact information, 56
 documentation of, 58
 duties of covered entities, 55
 effective date, 56
 header, 52
 joint notice by separate covered entities, 58
 optional elements, 56
 required elements, 52-56
 revisions to, 56-57
 rights of the individual, 53-55
  right to inspect and copy PHI, 54
  right to receive accounting of disclosures, 55
  right to receive confidential communications, 54
  right to receive paper copy, 55
  right to request amendment, 55
  right to request restrictions on certain uses and disclosures, 53-54
 sample document, 119-126
 separate statements for specific uses or disclosures, 53
 uses and disclosures, 52
Notice of Privacy Practices, 7, 119-126
Nursing home fixed-indemnity policies, 3

Office for Civil Rights (OCR), 75
 civil penalties and, 78-79
 compliance reviews and investigations, 77
 regional addresses, 84-86
 requirements for filing complaints, 76-77
 resolution by, 77-78
Oversight activities, 39-40

Parent, as personal representative of child, 15-16
Patient charts, 60
Patterson, Leigh-Ann M., 88n.61
Payment, 6, 29-30
Penalties and enforcement, 75-86
 case law, 80-83
 civil penalties, 78-79
 criminal penalties, 79-80
 enforcement, 75-78
 litigation, 83-84
 Office for Civil Rights regional addresses, 84-86
Personal representative, 14-16
Pharmacies, 28, 44, 60
PHI (protected health information), defined, 5
Plain language, 20
Policies and procedures, 62-63
Portability, 93-95
Power of attorney, 15
Preexisting condition exclusion, 95
Privacy Act, 100, 101
Privacy officers, 8-9, 64
Privacy protection. *See also* Health care privacy
 consumer influences, 103
 government influences, 100-103
 promotion of, 100-103
Privacy Protection Act, 101
Privacy Rule
 accounting for disclosures, 9
 compliance, 3-4
 duties and obligations of covered entities, 7-9
 general rules for disclosure, 6-7
 information protected by HIPAA, 5
 notice, 7-8
 privacy officer, 8-9
 purpose of, 2, 27
 safeguards, 8
 summary of, 2-9
 training, 8
Procedural limitations on civil penalties, 78-79
Procedures and policies, 62-63
Promotional disclosures, 42-45
Protected health information (PHI), defined, 5
Psychiatric records, 24
Psychotherapy notes, 20, 54
Public disclosures of private information, 99-100

Public health activities, 38
Public health authorities, 38
Public health departments, 67–68
Public Law 104-191. *See* HIPAA
Public Survey of Consumer Attitudes About Health Web Sites, 104n.19

Qualified protective order, 41–42

Reasonable assurances agreement, 35, 115–118
Redisclosure, 20
Relatives, disclosures to, 43–44
Research
  accounting and, 66
  disclosures without authorizations and, 45–46
  treatment conditions and, 19–20
Right to Financial Privacy Act, 101
Rule 4, Federal Rules of Civil Procedure, 78

Safeguards, 8, 58–62
  business associate agreements and, 32–33
Sanctions, 62–63
Satisfactory assurances, 41
Saulny, Susan, 88n.57
Security incidents, 33–34
Security of confidential information, 96–97
Shalala, Donna, 93
Social Security Act
  § 1320a-7(a), 87n.28
  § 1320a-7(a)(c)(1), 87n.29
  § 1320a-7a(c)(2), 87n.31
  § 1320a-7a(c)(4), 87n.32
  § 1320d-5, 87n.23
  § 1320d-5(a), 87n.22
  § 1320d-5(b)(1), 87n.24
  § 1320d-5(b)(2), 87n.25
  § 1320d-5(b)(3), 87n.26
  § 1320d-5(b)(4), 87n.27
  § 1320d-6, 87n.35
  § 1852, 101
  Title XI, 101
Standard of care, 84
State child health plans, 3
State laws, 2
  authorization requirements, 22–24
  preemption of, 22–24, 82–83
  psychiatric records and, 24
State privacy actions, 84
Subpoenas, 40–42, 81–82

Telecommunications Act, 101
Telephone Consumer Protection Act, 101
Termination of business associates contract, 34–35
Threat to health or safety, 35–36
Title I, 1, 9–10, 93–95
Title II, 1, 10, 95–96
Tort laws, 84
Training, 8, 63–64
Transmittal or cover letter, 21–22
Treatment
  defined, 6
  disclosures without authorizations and, 27, 28
  not conditioned on signing authorization, 19–20

Unfair trade practice actions, 84
U.S. Department of Health, Education, and Welfare, 100
U.S. Department of Health and Human Services. *See* Department of Health and Human Services
U.S. Department of Justice, 79, 80, 83
Uses
  accounting for, 9
  notice and, 52, 53–54

Veterans Benefits Section, 101
Veterans health care program, 3
Victims of abuse, neglect, or domestic violence, 38–39
Video Privacy Protection Act, 101

Wall Street Journal/ABC poll, 103
Whistleblowing, 62
Workers' compensation, 46

About the Author

June Sullivan is an associate in the Hartford, Connecticut, office of Halloran & Sage, LLP. Ms. Sullivan practices health law, including medical malpractice defense of health care practitioners. She works with a team of lawyers and paralegals who represent physicians, surgeons, psychiatrists, podiatrists, nursing homes, and psychotherapists.

Prior to becoming a lawyer, Ms. Sullivan worked as a medical technologist in an acute care hospital for several years where she gained experience in clinical chemistry, hematology, microbiology, and immunohematology. She has a master's degree in occupational therapy and over eighteen years of experience in the health care field. She was an assistant professor in occupational therapy at Quinnipiac University in Connecticut. She is a member of the American Bar Association, Health Law Section; Connecticut Health Lawyers Association; Connecticut Bar Association, Health Law Section; and American Society of Clinical Pathology. She is licensed to practice law in New York, Connecticut, and Massachusetts. Along with her juris doctorate degree, Ms. Sullivan also has a certificate in health law from Quinnipiac University.

While in law school, Ms. Sullivan was a member of the Quinnipiac Law Review. She was the first recipient of the Health Law Award at Quinnipiac University for outstanding achievement in the concentration of health law. Ms. Sullivan was also recognized for excellence in the Health Law Clinic. Ms. Sullivan authored articles that were published in the *North Dakota Law Review*, the *Quinnipiac Health Law Journal*, and *The Health Lawyer*.